Classroom Behaviour Management in the Post-School Sector

Mervyn Lebor

Classroom Behaviour Management in the Post-School Sector

Student and Teacher Perspectives on the Battle Against Being Educated

Mervyn Lebor
Leeds City College
Leeds, West Yorkshire, UK

ISBN 978-3-319-86065-7   ISBN 978-3-319-57051-8   (eBook)
DOI 10.1007/978-3-319-57051-8

Cover Design: Tim Macpherson / Getty Images

Printed on acid-free paper

This Palgrave Macmillan imprint is published by Springer Nature
The registered company is Springer International Publishing AG
The registered company address is: Gewerbestrasse 11, 6330 Cham, Switzerland

To my parents, Maisie and Gerald Lebor, who taught me the value of education.

Acknowledgement

I wish to thank the following people and organisations for all their help and involvement in this project. Firstly, I want to thank members of the University of Sunderland (SUNCETT) teacher education department, specifically Prof Maggie Gregson, Dr. Lawrence Nixon and Trish Spedding, but also the ETF for funding some of this research. I also wish to thank the University of Huddersfield (HUDCETT) teacher ed. department for backing research and reading through earlier versions of some chapters; in particular Prof Roy Fisher, Prof Denise Robinson, Dr. David Powell and Dr. Lisa Russell. I am grateful to Sandra Rennie, whose dialogues with me on previous research were really helpful. Of key importance has been the University Centre, Teachers' Training Department, Leeds City College, where I currently work; those involved included Anita Collins, Bally Kaur, Dom Brockway, Susan McGarroch and Dr. Nena Skrbic for their ongoing support, companionship and constant willingness to analyse and debate the meanings of teaching and learning.

I would also like to show gratitude to the many hundreds of heroic teachers, managers and students who have been amazing in giving their time to explore the issue of what happens when learning is resisted. I am very grateful for all contributions. I also want to thank the team at Palgrave Macmillan, particularly Laura Aldridge, for all your help in making this book a reality.

Finally, I want to thank my lovely family, my daughters Sarah and Dani, their husbands Michael and Jonathan, but mostly my wife, Jo, who has assiduously read every version and continually supported me with this highly time-consuming venture. I am very grateful.

CONTENTS

1 The Battle Against Being Educated   1

2 In Theory It All Works...   27

3 Entering the Classroom   49

4 What Do Experienced Tutors Advise?   77

5 Testing Times: What Is the Role of Assessment?   89

6 Could Class Management Be a Management Issue?   107

7 So Why Do Disruptive Students Say They Disrupt Classes?   123

8 A Methodology for Supporting Tutors Who Face Challenging Classes   137

9   What Could Possibly Be Problematic About Digital
    Learning?   151

10 How Do Teacher Educators Prepare Trainees
    for Disruptive Classes?   169

11 And What Did the Trainees Say?   187

12 A Possible Module for Teaching About Disruptive
    Behaviour   203

Bibliography   213

Index   225

CHAPTER 1

The Battle Against Being Educated

THE CURRENT CONTEXT

This is a book analysing how tutors have, could and might deal with difficult, challenging or disruptive students in many different post-school education contexts, currently referred to as the Education and Training sector. It is, overall, a book based on primary research and reflection on experiences, observations, case studies and interviews with teachers and students about challenging experiences in the classroom, particularly showing the differences between what theorists, authorities, trainers and managers say and the reality of what actually happens in classroom practice. It focuses on the 16-plus age group, but many of the ideas and experiences could be translated into other teaching and learning contexts. There are interviews with tutors, teacher educators, trainees and managers who have faced disruptive or difficult students or have worked out strategies for dealing with these situations. It also questions disruptive students and begins the process of hearing the narrative from their point of view. It not only covers what various gurus, theorists, models and textbooks say, but also analyses the complexity and difficulty of the relationship between tutors and learners where disruption takes place in a range of diverse situations and institutions.

This introduction sets the context over several periods of the pressures encountered by teachers coming into what was previously called the Life-long Learning sector where many tutors faced difficult or even violent classes. The pressures are that there is a context of managerialism,

© The Author(s) 2017
M. Lebor, *Classroom Behaviour Management in the Post-School Sector*, DOI 10.1007/978-3-319-57051-8_1

economic survival for institutions based on student numbers, Ofsted (2012) demands, tight controls of curriculum, the raising of the school-leaving age, the infill of 14-year-olds into colleges and a demanding pro-gramme of what teachers have to teach to meet vocational and academic requirements. Typically, many teachers use ground rules and various con-tractual methods for beginning the process of operating in challenging climates. The contracts can be democratically generated, teacher-imposed, signed at enrolment or sometimes placed by the institution on the walls of all classrooms. This sometimes works; but the question is what hap-pens when students do not stick to the rules. What do teachers do? What is their approach? How do they survive these extreme situations? Some teachers have opted for 'one strike and you're out,' 'zero-tolerance' or other punitive methods for dealing with challenging behaviour. Others have, after two or three years, simply left the profession.

The simple meaning of the key part of my title, the battle against being educated, is that students are being offered a gift of education and some are fighting very hard not to accept it. It sometimes feels as if a certain pro-portion of students are heavily resisting a civil right that is being given to them and it is a heroic battle being fought by teachers to prepare these students for their careers, vocational training, academic and personal development. There is sometimes an underlying student culture almost opposed to education and perhaps even operating against the students' own best interests. By way of contrast, we also see cultures where there is a passion to learn. Why is this?

My Own Background

I currently work as a lecturer in teacher education, delivering sessions on teaching, learning and assessment. I am involved with observing Cert Ed and PGCE students. However, the triggers for this book are my own experience of moving from being at a state, grammar school in London in the 1960s and 1970s to being a tutor in the 1980s at technical colleges in the North and working in many institutions of Further and Higher education. I have a deep concern for supporting teaching and learning for individuals in geographic areas of exceptional poverty and deprivation. As a reflexive practitioner (Kennet 2010) it should be said that I am aware that I am from a middle-class background myself and went to a school where in the 1960s there was a corporal punishment regime of teachers beating boys with thick objects. Classes were highly disruptive; students stamped on the floor as the teacher approached or receded from the front of the classroom, passed notes on strings along the (pre-digital) classroom wall and kept competitive accounts of how many times each student was beaten by a teacher. Yet most students achieved their qualifications. Did this show that disruption was not connected with a particular class background or that achievement could happen despite challenging behaviour (Paton 2012)? Am I influenced by my own grammar school experience in understanding aspiration, achievement and what classrooms could or should be like? Although corporal punishment finally disappeared in 1998 (BBC), this school experience may well have instilled in me a sense of self-discipline. On the other hand, ideologically, it gave me a mission to become involved in education and, in opposition to my own experience, take a person-centred, humanist, self-actualising approach as recommended by Rogers (1961) and Maslow (1987).

I was a successful English Language/Literature teacher at GCSE and A level for many years, but also taught communications on many programmes in a wide range of vocational areas from Entry level up to level 6, such as business, health, sports, catering and the arts. I taught what was variously called Literacy, English for Speakers of Other Languages, Special Needs support, Basic, Key and Functional Skills. I have worked in many environments including schools, community centres, Further Education colleges, universities, studios, several mosques and at conferences. I have taught on and managed five different degree programmes in Humanities and Art and Design, and have also been an examiner, external moderator, quality reviewer and senior tutor for Higher Education in an Art college. As the data collector in this book, I am aware of myself as someone who is constantly describing, evolving, analysing and reflecting on strategies for understanding and countering classroom disruptions. I have written about this previously and feel it is still a challenging issue for many trainees and qualified teachers. Does this mean I am always pre-programmed to interpret all learning situations as potentially disruptive?

When Things Go Wrong

This is essentially a book that records what teachers and learners in post-school education believe, do and say, particularly when things go wrong in the teaching process. It could be understood as an attempt to explore situations in classrooms where learning is not happening. There are deep questions about human nature that underpin this investigation. Why do people either conform or not to learning situations? Is conformity good? Can disruption be positive? Why would people with desires, energies, obsessions, addictions or different syndromes wish to listen to a teacher speaking? Is learning merely a question of being socialised, acculturated or schooled into what we institutionally or socially expect? Are there underlying questions here about being 'bad?' This book does not take a moral stance on this issue, but rather explores many situations where the learning process breaks down.

There is an assumption that just because teaching takes place, learning follows. This is continually challenged. It could be argued that it is maybe more surprising that students do mostly sit down in classes and partake in lessons than the many situations where they break the rules. Considering individual passions, quirks, discomforts, idiosyncrasies and school histories, one could ask the question why students do participate in learning as a corporate or communal activity. There are many reasons why this might not be the case.

In the Education and Training sector there are many versions of the classroom from being in a vocational workshop, art-studio, lecture theatre, seminar-room, playing field, gym, out in forests, virtual learning space and college classrooms. There are also arguably many styles of teaching and learning (Honey and Mumford 2000) which have been thoroughly critiqued by Coffield et al. (2004). Learning cannot be understood as a simple activity.

Then What Is Learning?

Disruption is normally defined as activities that are 'perceived' to stop learning from taking place (Ofsted 2015; Dfes 2012). But then this assumes definitions of what 'learning' is, and also raises the question of whose 'perception' of learning is being privileged. Contexts might be critical. Screaming in a maths lesson might be totally unacceptable; screaming in a sports class could be part of the accepted norms of behaviour on a football pitch. Learning is a highly disputed process and different definitions have implications for what it would mean to 'disrupt' this activity. How we define learning might have implications for whether it is more or less difficult to disrupt. Thus, for Dewey, learning was the 'severe discipline' of positioning experience 'to the tests of intelligent development and direction,' so that students keep developing 'intellectually and morally' (1938, p. 114). If this high-minded definition was generally accepted, most activities in the classroom would be seen as never reaching that level of consciousness to be classified as learning. It would be easy to disrupt this version of learning. By this definition how do we know whether learning is taking place? Do teachers, observers or students all have access to Dewey's level of consciousness? The higher the bar by which learning is defined, the easier it is to disrupt the learning process.

Wenger differentiated learning from other activities in that it is supposed to change 'who we are by changing our ability to participate, to belong, to negotiate meaning' (1998, p. 226). This is again a highly sophisticated understanding of learning that assumes some psychological process of change happening to all individuals in every class if learning is to have taken place. It assumes that a session on chemistry formulae or basic numeracy must in some way be emotionally transformative. If this was truly the criteria of what learning was, few sessions would be characterised as having contained any learning whatsoever. All sessions where this process did not take place might be considered as having been disrupted.

Illeris defined learning as 'any process that in living organisms leads to permanent capacity to change' (2007, p. 3). This definition is also problematic because it assumes that the students' minds fundamentally change in every session. Does this happen to all students? How do we know? Who assesses this? This definition also assumes that the ability to change is more important than the content of lessons. Students may have engaged with the processes, skills and information of sessions, but this long-term change might just have not taken place or if it has, it might be for the worse. It assumes that change always means improvement.

Many definitions of learning are deeply ideological or based within a particular outlook. Hence, if Behaviourist, then it is a form of conditioning, whilst if Gestalt, learning is a type of perception. In cognitive terms, learning might be viewed as mental process, whereas learning from a humanistic perspective could involve development of values, student potential and overcoming personal barriers (Curzon and Tummons 2013). However, these definitions might discount any thought process or activity that takes place not adhering to these particular ideologies or perspectives.

In 2000, Coffield said that learning referred only to significant changes in capability, understanding, knowledge or values by individuals or groups etc. The problem with this definition is that the arbitration of what is 'significant' is open to subjective judgement. How do we know when and who decides what significant change in students' knowledge or values actually are? Are there assessments to determine this? Can observers see inside students' heads to determine whether significant change has taken place? In Special Education (LDD), students often have to repeat the same information. They may not 'change significantly.' Are we going to say they never learn (Lebor 2011)? Again, the higher the standard demanded of what is defined as learning, the less likely it is that learning can be said to have taken place. Thus, if activities in a class are not bringing about significant changes to students, then most classes will not involve learning. However, it is very difficult for even the keenest observer to judge from external behaviour as to whether internal change is taking place in students' minds.

The issue is that we can only know whether these features of learning are happening through examining the internal life of students which is not feasibly possible. Other than through the norms of assessment, what sorts of mechanisms could be used for delving into students' consciousnesses? If learning is not taking place in the ways previously defined, then disruption could be said to be continually happening in many classrooms. A definition has to set the bar, so that what is generally understood as learning can be empirically observed or proven to be happening. A more workable definition also suggested by Coffield is the transmission and assimilation of knowledge and skills (2008). The OED says learning is 'the acquisition of knowledge or skills through study, experience, or being taught.' For the purposes of this book, maybe a combination of these two definitions might offer a practicable way of understanding what we mean by learning.

So the working definition of learning for our context will be the acquisition, transmission or assimilation of skills and knowledge through study, experience and/or being taught. At least this definition tries to use language that will be understood by most teachers in the UK Education and Training sector.

EXTREME BEHAVIOUR

However, this book explores some of the extreme behaviours that I have encountered in many different locations through direct observation or interviewing teachers. The rationale for focussing specifically on dramatic or particularly challenging behaviour that stops learning taking place in this sector is that there are few books which are willing to even acknowledge that such behaviour is a staple part of many tutors' experience. There is a paucity of advice or even discourse on how teachers might deal with these fraught, human relationships in this sector. On speaking to one particular trainee teacher working in a northern city, Keith reported on violent incidents at the college where he worked, but said there was little in text books written on these events or even opening a debate that scrutinised these incidents from any perspectives. This is the gap which this book is attempting to fill.

THE METHODOLOGIES

My methodologies range from auto-ethnographic, critical self-reflective practice to qualitative methods where teachers, managers, trainers and students are questioned via interviews, dialogues, questionnaires and focus groups. Accessing experience is a highly complex process; making use of narrative is problematic. Evoking storied accounts of what happened in classrooms in many different situations could verge on the anecdotal or construction of reality, perhaps ill-remembered (Shacklock and Thorp 2005). Why should we believe what is said?

Narratives of what happened in classrooms have to be verified for authenticity. Where I have inserted personal narratives, they have been based on detailed self-reflective notes from the period. Generally, I have tried to avoid unsubstantiated narrative and rather put in place a structure of self-criticism where events in classrooms are mediated through the prism of academic discourse, offering a critical framework that listens and heeds the voices of others. The questions raised are whether accounts are reliable. There may be many agendas as to why teachers, managers, unions or students might either fabricate narratives about the problematic nature of their situations, upgrading or downgrading the nature of an event in order to make a political or institutional point.

There could also be very good reasons why teachers may wish to suppress data about the negative activities that go on in their classrooms. Unions may wish to focus on negative student behaviours as a way of justifying pay claims or proffer a critique of college management. This is a highly sensitive area mainly because of commercial concerns with respect to colleges, the professional standing and esteem of individual reputations. It might impact on receiving qualifications, passing observations or even admitting that there are problems in classrooms which can lead to a threat of credibility for individuals, institutions or even the sector itself. Admissions of incompetence could easily lead to dismissal. It is an issue of professionalism.

In order to balance narratives, I have tried to offer analysis of what is purported to have happened. Classroom events are complex, open to interpretation and because many people are involved, they are subject to multi-faceted perspectives. Each moment could be spliced into many other moments possibly only explicable in terms of complex micro-histories and interactions. There is also a socio-economic, historical, political and cultural context. Many other books on this topic do not refer to these dimensions outside the confines of the teaching environment. However, classrooms do not stand in a vacuum. They are, arguably, not only reflections or products of the societies in which they operate, but also places of potential transformation of the wider community.

The book represents an analysis, description, narrative, dialogues and reflection on so many different styles of what goes on under the name of pedagogy. It mainly operates as a conversation, listening to the voices of hundreds of different teachers, managers, trainers and students, exploring their feelings, attitudes and perspectives on effective teaching and learning.

A Brief History of Violence in the Classroom

Corporal Punishment in the 1970s

There is a long history of conflict in the classroom, going back at least to the Medieval period in this country (Holton, 1995). In the 1970s up to the 1990s when it was finally banned, there was corporal punishment. Teachers used the cane, sticks, slaps, kicks, punches and deadly sarcasm in order to control and often degrade students. In my own sixth form one teacher said: 'If your brain was filled with gunpowder, there wouldn't be enough to blow your stupid head off'; another teacher said: 'as a present I will slap your face for you!' And then he proceeded to slap the student's face until the student screamed in pain. Another teacher beat a student on the head with a stick until blood poured out of his forehead. Being a teacher was almost a licence to be sadistic or at least carry out abuse with impunity. Safeguarding of students was a little understood concept. These events were episodic, not every day, but sometimes every week; always memorable. Disruption was kept to a minimum, by methods which would be considered highly unacceptable by contemporary standards. Teachers often wanted to humiliate and downgrade students in the class, to assert their own power and authority, supposedly to create space so that their version of teaching if not learning could be dominant. Corporal punishment was banned in England in state-funded schools in 1986 and in all private schools in 1998.

The violence came from teachers towards students.

Confronting Racism in the 1980s

It was a dark, cold November night in 1980. In a northern, industrial city there was a Further Education Technical College, now anonymised as Elsino Tower. I travelled by lift up to the 11th floor. The lift door opened. Someone threw a firework. The explosion reverberated against the bleak, concrete walls. The lift doors closed and I carried on up to the 13th floor. I opened the classroom door T.13X. A flurry of empty tin cans was thrown like grenades on top of the spiked haircuts and skinned white heads of hostile groups in the class. A scream was heard as a leather-jacketed young man hit back at an enemy. I opened the classroom door again with a flourish of authority and approached the nerve-wracked teacher who was standing at the front supposedly informing his students about engineering. My job was harder. I had the late shift teaching 'Communications' to students who despised this subject. 'What's the point; it's meaningless...' said Brian.

'I wish you all the best, mate!' croaked my colleague, anonymised as Ray, as he scuttled from the room, backwards with papers flapping. A dark face appeared at the classroom door-window. A white, male student immediately stood up and karate kicked the classroom-door. I said, 'This is unacceptable.' The racism in the room was now palpable. Claude was spitting on pictures of black people in a magazine. I said:

'Why are you doing that?'
'We hate them...'
'Why do you hate, so much?'

All 20 white male students in the class were suddenly alert to tension. They were bristling. This was the only 'Communications' subject that absorbed them. They also wanted to see me humiliated or beaten by their National Front indoctrination, the insignia of which several wore on their leather jackets. It was 'one-on-one,' as such. It was a drama of conflict and differences in ideology. I repeated 'Why do you hate so much?' The red-faced young man said: 'they take our jobs...''But why do you hate?' I persisted. 'They take our women...' he asserted. He was getting upset. He thought his arguments would somehow convince me.

'But hatred?' I questioned. He was almost crying with frustration at my lack of collusion with his outlook. 'Would you like to be spat on?' I said. The class laughed. There was no point sending this student to be disciplined to the department head or college authorities as many of the other teachers shared the students' attitudes and often (this was the 1980s) displayed pornographic calendars on the walls of the staff room. The Commission for Racial Equality was only starting to impact on institutional racism that was still openly prevalent at this period. Sexist attitudes in this all-male environment were the normative culture. This was a different context to one of authoritarian power for teachers that I had experienced myself at age 18.

I started to explore the Equal Opportunities arguments of that time. But this more nuanced stance had most students slumped in their seats. They did not want to know arguments. At that time there were no computers or white boards, few films, except to be shown in a large lecture theatre to be booked a month in advance. All we had were some role play games that could misfire or overhead projector slides that students found generally unconvincing. Boredom was all engrossing. Even the anger had gone limp. Some students were still gripped by hatred, but I now began the class. There were tasks, handouts replicated from the Banda machine, pens and paper. The lesson had begun in earnest. There was a strong smell of masculine sweat, motorbike helmets were ranged on the desks; one student was listlessly sticking a knife into the side of his chair. NF for National Front was carved into the desks. The violence was emotional, political and physical. The boredom had sunk in for the evening. The class now reluctantly started their tasks.

The violence was from students towards other students.

SOME STRATEGIES FOR DEALING WITH RACISM

There was also an implicit threat towards the teacher. If this situation would arise in a current classroom, teachers would hopefully have already set ground rules to ensure that it was not permissible to express these views. If these views were still being expressed, the teacher might use what is called a blocking device: holding up the hand and saying 'Stop,' or insist, 'This is racism; this is unacceptable' and maybe repeat this several times until the offending student's perspective was totally closed down, so as to make the atmosphere of the class safe for other students particularly from ethnic or different backgrounds. The offending student might be asked to leave the class and be spoken to individually later. However, the whole class might hold these views, in which case questioning of students' assumptions could be highly effective.

Depending on how comfortable the teacher felt, s/he might wish to open the conversation so that the racism was challenged at a deeper level, relevant films could be presented, discussion extended, racism shown to be deeply damaging to the self, others and community. Many students have grown up in an environment where they mix with students from other ethnicities or see equality and diversity enacted on their TV screens or computers. However, many communities are self-contained and foster suspicion and hatred of the other. Racism is unfortunately endemic on the Internet. To counter these influences maybe role plays where students took on the persona of those from different cultures to their own might be productive.

Cutting short the conversation might be viewed as a missed opportunity by observers, Ofsted or management. This might have been a chance where students could be deeply educated or challenged on race/ethnic/sexism awareness. In order to have the confidence to confront these views, the teacher needs to feel that giving space for racists to work through their negative views is not going to be counter-productive or hurtful for other students in the class. These discussions can have the effect of giving expression to fascism in an educative environment where such views should theoretically have no place.

The reason I mention these alternative perspectives in this context is to evolve an ongoing culturally critical, self-reflective pedagogy as the multiplicity of perspectives on different classroom situations are explored. Although these situations could be described as narrative, they are partly self-reflection, but also ways of characterising the sorts of problems tutors faced during an earlier era and often face in today's return to a more xenophobic environment.

Nevertheless, this was the 1980s. It was an era before the formal introduction of equality and diversity, pre-The Equality Act (2010) before there were notions of safeguarding explicitly identified as an issue of national concern. Brutal attitudes as illustrated above could be normative within classrooms and even staff-rooms.

The Violence from Outside...

A second example I will begin to explore from the 1980s was when I team-taught a class as an English literacy outreach worker for Bengali adult factory workers who wanted English classes on a Sunday afternoon. This class was located in a large, Victorian school anonymised as the Britannia Institute. The two-hour sessions were well-attended and consisted of drills and conversation, forming simple sentences and questions, filling out forms and dealing with practical language situations from everyday life. There were often role plays of, for example, going to shops, the bank or the hospital. The atmosphere was amicable. The students and teachers enjoyed these classes. However, there was a sense of threat, this time from outside the class. A fascist group made it clear that they did not want these classes to take place in 'their' community. Large swastikas appeared on the building. Threats were made to members of the management of the school, citing these classes as a provocation for violence. We were locked in the school during sessions. As classes took place, members of the fascist group hid behind walls waiting to attack teachers and/or students when they arrived or emerged from classes. It was a chilling atmosphere. In fact, no one from the class was actually hurt, but this was because the school caretaker had two Alsatians, which blunted the enthusiasm of the attackers. There were no mobile phones; the police were not called. After a few months the head teacher was physically assaulted ostensibly because he had allowed this class to take place.

The violence came from outside the classroom towards the class.

The reason I mention this episode is to show that disruption in class is a highly complex phenomenon, not merely confined to following rules or teachers' ability to sustain class control. There are sometimes issues outside the classroom impacting what is taught within. Pre-incorporation, when colleges were still within local authority control, before they became self-financing businesses, there were open access policies of allowing anyone into college buildings. This was justified on the grounds of widening participation and that education should be 'open to all.' However, this meant that drug-dealers, prostitutes and petty criminals could prey on students during breaks in college canteens. This sort of intrusion, violence and illegal activity in certain colleges was deeply threatening for students and staff. After incorporation in 1993, methods of surveillance became more sophisticated in many colleges. Security officers checked the identity of students coming into college buildings. More formal methods were installed for controlling the student body, such as electronic gates, name tags, security cameras, barbed fences and security guards patrolling corridors. Paul Mackney, chief executive of the lecturers' union Natfhe in 2000, accepted there were problems at the time. 'Most colleges have door stewards to contain the possibility of violence,' yet 'racism and sexism do go on.' In that year, I wrote in *The Guardian* about how I had to stand between two students who were attacking each other. The aggressor thanked me because I had actually stopped him from 'getting into trouble' (Crace and Lebor 2000).

Again, the violence was from student to student.

Teachers Attacked

A teacher being attacked by students is a relatively rare occurrence. Nevertheless, I spoke recently to one female teacher in a Pupil Referral Unit (PRU) who had been head-butted by a student. Another male teacher had been physically attacked twice and had given up teaching (Cf. Parry and Taubman 2013). In 2017, I was told about two technology students coming into a university lecture, drunk and abusing the lecturer. Violence can be verbal. Another university teacher reported on students falling asleep during a lecture. This could be interpreted as over-work, tiredness, boredom or passive aggression.

Higher Education is not immune.

However, a complex case of bullying by students of a teacher in the post-school sector came to light when I interviewed two 'ex-students' from the 1990s who claimed they had lugged an 'under-sized' Maths teacher to the centre of the room and for the whole 45-minute period, forced him to sit petrified in the middle of a circle, whilst other students flicked pellets at him. He was known as a competent teacher who achieved good results in GCSEs in other contexts. The 'ex-students' regretted what they had done, especially because one of them was now a teacher himself.

The violence was coming from the students towards the teacher.

There are at least three issues here. Firstly, protection of staff needs to be given the utmost priority. Teaching staff are the main resource in education. Management must make it clear that they are ready to support and protect their staff under all circumstances. Secondly, if this situation had been allowed to happen, quality infrastructure and support could not have been in place. Thirdly, with incorporation in 1993, there was more institutional concern for the individual needs of learners and arguably teachers. Nowadays, the process of walk-in observations would hopefully have stopped this sort of extreme behaviour from taking place. Nevertheless, teachers need to feel that they can share their problems with colleagues and management with impunity.

In the 1980–1990s, Further Education classrooms had cultures more like fiefdoms where teachers were left to their own devices. Teachers' resources were kept in their own locked cupboards. There was a sense of competition, but also isolation, very little checking or quality assurance. The emphasis was more on teaching than learning. The policy at this stage known informally as 'bums on seats' meant that as many students as possible were crammed into classes with little regard as to whether there was a need for these vocational courses in a commercial or industrial context or if they were relevant for that specific student (Wallace 2007).

The brief case study above shows that teachers can perform well in one environment, but be vulnerable, incompetent or ineffective in another. Even Chris Hughes, Chief Executive of The Further Education Development Agency (FEDA) in the year 2000, referred to an apprentice pulling a knife on him to ensure that the class took place in the pub (Crace and Lebor 2000). There were many challenging incidents reported at this time. The violence seemed perennial. It was almost independent of the relations teachers built with specific groups. Much evidence for this happening on a wider scale in contemporary classrooms can be gained from the ATL report (2016); however, this report is focussed on schools. The assumption is that this behaviour should stop as students grow up or move into the more adult environment of colleges. In fact, when questioned, in some current research I carried out in 2016, 30 level-1 18-year-old students, from mixed ethnic identities, said they found the environment in a large city college very threatening and frightening and were worried about being attacked when they walked into the building.

Violence Against the Self

I interviewed a trainee teacher at Strath College. He gave an extraordinary account of a student's behaviour which I will quote in full.

> Although not quite as problematic in our college as some of the other situations we have heard about, we had a student who tied himself by the waist to a 60 foot rope and lowered himself down over a stairwell and was just hanging there with the rope attached to his middle. No one realised that the student was hanging there until the caretaker found him in the stairwell. The management wanted to punish him. It wasn't clear whether this was a cry for help or was he trying to draw attention to himself? It turned out he wanted to make a self-expressive statement. This was a safeguarding issue, but when the management punished him, he started to do more dramatic things like asking another student to keep punching him on the jaw until he was knocked unconscious. The violence was collusive or masochistic, but I feel we are not given any training on how to approach these dramatic sorts of incidents…they are not discussed in any of the text books and don't appear under any of the theories we have talked about in class.

The violence had been from teachers to students, students to teachers, students to students and from outside the classroom towards those inside the class. It was now as if the violence was moving against the self. This was almost a symbolic shift. One trainee teacher, Heller reported on two female students in her degree classroom, both highly affluent, finished their work and then started to 'happy-slap' one another round the face which they filmed and sent out by cell phones to an interested audience outside their university.

The violence was moving from inside the class to outside the classroom.

The question still remains as to how teachers should be trained to deal with these multifarious situations. I would suggest by at least beginning to acknowledge that these things happen.

Is It Getting Worse?

There is an argument that disruption and violence are getting worse. This could be countered with many examples in reports and newspaper accounts of challenging, violent and disruptive behaviours mentioned in earlier periods.

The problem with trying to ascertain any objective measure of whether the number or intensity of incidents has risen is that the information is simply not there. Some systematic quantitative data is available as a small sample through Parry and Taubman's report for UCU (2013), but there were and are vested interests to ensure that descriptions of disruptive classes are or are not publicised. Too much is at stake for individual teachers, managers, the reputation of departments, colleges and other institutions. It cannot be shown that learning is not taking place. Why would one voluntarily go, as a student, to a college where it is known that there are difficulties of class management? On the other hand there has also been an attempt by unions to publicise the difficulties faced by school teachers and their assistants (ATL 2016; NASUWT 2016; Unison 2016; UCU 2013). Again, this information could have ideological undertones or be part of an argument for better pay and conditions. Nevertheless, despite contrary claims (OECD 2011, p. 4), it could be argued that disruptive classes are actually getting worse (Sellgren 2013; ATL 2013, 2016; Townend 2013).

The Historical Context

As in the present, it depended on which course students were taking at which college, the culture and attitude of the departments, managers, the principal and the Local Education Authority politicians who had considerable power over the ethos of pre-1993 incorporation colleges.

Disruptive behaviour in the 1980s could be characterised by Paul Willis' ethnographic account of training as being part of the patriarchal factory culture through which boys' fathers offered models of masculine camaraderie and potential aggression towards anything that presented a threat to their understanding of the classroom (1977). Willis argued that male students became disillusioned with education, forming counter-cultures that emulated the factory work environment of their fathers, making academic failure desirable if not inevitable. Sub-cultures were formed and teachers tended to stereotype these students as disruptive. Teachers would try to 'manage' these groups by using draconian measures. The group's alienation from education culture led to these students being categorised as 'low ability.'

Education as a preparation for factory culture is now a phenomenon of the past. Youth Opportunities Programme (Y.O.Ps) in the 1990s and then numbers of students Not in Education Employment or Training (NEETS) in the 2000s presented a new culture of dislocation between being trained and getting jobs as more fractured. The raising of the school-leaving age to 18 in 2016 has meant that unwilling students have been forced to stay within the confines of education in which environment they have failed for many years and now be made to continue with a process which they have rejected (Simmons and Thompson 2011). Sometimes cohorts of 14–16-year-olds are sent from schools on 'links' to colleges in the hope that this 'adult environment' will have an effect on their behaviour. University and College Union (UCU's) report explained that information about individual student needs was rarely passed on to the college (Parry and Taubman 2013). This was confirmed at a UCU day school in Leeds in March 2017, but also through my personal experience of this in a previous post and on discussions with three current lecturers at different colleges involved in this process. Despite growing relationships between schools and colleges, school students merely continued their previous 'disruptive' behaviour in the new environment.

It should be said that, we find in this book many instances of 'disruptive behaviour' at different economic, social, age, gender and intellectual levels. The problems also occur in a variety of different vocational and academic contexts. This challenges the stereotype that disruption is associated with class issues or is fundamentally related to not having wealth or students' belief that they have no investment in their future career.

It could also be argued that the causes of disruptive behaviour are conjecture because the same features, for example, poverty, might lead to disruption, whereas economically deprived backgrounds might lead to high levels of achievement in order for students to escape these conditions. The sense of entitlement associated with wealth could be attributed as a reason for disruption as we find in one of the later case studies. However, causes could include the raising of the school-leaving age, students mandated to do courses they do not want to do (Wallace 2007), but also more vulnerable students are now coming into our colleges with biological and medical conditions such as ADHD (Wolf 2011). Disruptive behaviours could be explained as the negative side in people's character or merely students' limited social skills. Other causes might be physiological: drug dependency or psychosis, personality or character disorders. It could be extremes of extroversion, introversion or dominance. Other explanations could involve emotional states, prejudices or self-esteem issues, the quality of the environment or being placed in a powerless or difficult situation. Taubman and Parry in their UCU report see it as management's responsibility (2013). Managers, in a later chapter, see the reasons mostly in terms of poor teaching. In one chapter, I ask students who have been categorised as 'disruptive' why they were disruptive. Their answers seemed quite individual. However, there are a plethora of explanations that could be attributed to this phenomenon. Throughout the book this is open to debate.

THE WHOLE COLLEGE APPROACH

The beginnings of a whole-college approach (Parry and Taubman 2013) with clear policies implemented can be seen in Ross Rospigliosi's account of running Plymouth College in a more structured way, whereby he claimed to have 'very little disruptive behaviour in his college.' He reported: 'On average we expel about three students out of a total body of 20,000 each year. Our rules are made clear at induction: one strike and you're out. We ask for similar standards to those expected in the workplace.' When Ruth Silver took over as principal of Lewisham College, she was appalled by the grills on the windows and the security turnstiles on the doors. Her first reaction was to dispose of these draconian attitudes to education. A student challenged her view and said: 'This is the safest place in south London.' (Crace and Lebor 2000).

Incorporation brought in new attitudes, a sense that students were clients who had to be protected. They were now consumers. However, the question remained for teachers how they would deal with disruptive students. What was acceptable or unacceptable behaviour? Initially, behaviour policies were either nonexistent, non-effective or at a very basic level, but later became so complex that no student could possibly remember even a fraction of what they were supposed to do and, therefore, the rules became unenforceable in practice (Dix 2015). There were accounts of students continually swearing, creating high levels of noise, fighting, punching and intimidating other students, acting in insulting or sometimes threatening ways to members of staff. But how should individual teachers respond to this behaviour?

Why Be at College?

Up until 2015, post-school education could be described as voluntary, except that there were often few alternatives in terms of work, particularly in 'working class' areas. Post 16, students were present in colleges, subject to financial controls via grants, attendance money and in some cases social security. There were some financial and physical controls over students, but students could theoretically walk out of college if they did not like what was happening in their lessons. This in turn could have disastrous implications for college finances. There was a growing culture in many institutions of post-school, and therefore voluntary, education where much negative behaviour was not abnormal at GNVQ Foundation to Intermediate level. The problems were focussed on delivering what has been called a deficit model of the curriculum. Students were coming into colleges at level 1 or just achieving level 2 skills, yet expecting training to help them gain vocational qualifications often highly gendered choices of hairdressing for girls and construction for boys at least at GCSE or in level 2 vocational areas (Wallace 2007).

However, when the class contained more than 20 students who often needed basic, remedial, literacy work; it was difficult for teachers to concentrate on the personal or academic weaknesses of individuals. Successful or effective teachers began reverting to tougher disciplinary measures in the hope of establishing a creative working environment within which students could concentrate for slightly longer on finishing curriculum tasks. Support workers were introduced to help students with a range of special needs, yet achieve qualifications. The class layout of desks in a horseshoe, or even tables for group work, were now seen as recipes for casual chatting and socialising rather than focussing on tasks, and were being rejected in favour of a more formal pre-1970s style of control by desks in rows. Lecturers and tutors were under greater pressure to retain students in the class in order to meet targets and gain the full share of government funding as student numbers represented financial survival for each college.

The problem was that as more was demanded of students, academically, in order to meet the requirements of employment that was no longer factory based, so students felt more deeply challenged. They might need to disrupt classes to put off the humiliating moment when it would be revealed that at 18 they still could only read or write at a basic primary school level. Basic, Key and eventually Functional Skills became critical in preparing students for the work-force. However, these were the subjects at which students were most vulnerable. They had failed so often before in the school environment. This was the greatest threat to students' self-esteem and, therefore these were the classes where behaviour was worst. The aim of raising standards was taking place as a backcloth to a culture of occasional racist and sexist tensions, acts of violence, open and under-cover hate campaigns. Anger, frustration and aggression flared to the sur-face, or equally problematic, the bored malaise of stultified classes were offered where students had to do the same work they had done under different guises for the last five years at school.

Extra teachers and resources for Further Education, or payment related to the sheer stress of bringing the disruptive energies of young people into some sort of creative order, were all highly desirable aims. However, much of the work with respect to lower level students in the 16+ sector was often poorly paid on limited part-time contracts (Simmons 2009). Possibly the most productive use of time in classes would have been building rela-tionships with individuals, listening to embittered or resentful voices, as a means of trying to break the cyclic pattern of chronic underachievement. In order to counter these tendencies, Blair's government of 1997 intro-duced several initiatives to support education for marginalised groups, such as Sure Start. Underpinning the thinking behind these schemes was the idea of mentors who would help support individuals' progress (Colley 2003). However, due to financial considerations under the Coalition and subsequent Conservative Government, many of these initiatives were cut in the name of austerity.

It has been argued that violence has increased and that problems faced by tutors are getting worse (e.g. Spiers 2011; Townend 2013). There is a con-text of teachers giving up the profession within the five years of qualifying (Weale 2016). The Association of Teachers and Lecturers (ATL) reported that 40% of teachers within schools have said they had been physically attacked. Has this behaviour continued into the Education and Training sector? Once the more authoritarian, systematised controlling atmosphere of schools is released, do students feel that they can unleash the violence that was previously repressed? Or do they feel they have a licence to behave 'badly' because, as Wallace says, the Cinderella status of the sector means that students do not feel the same respect for the Further Education environment that they might have had for previous institutions they attended (2007)? The 'Behaviour Tsar,' Tom Bennett has explained the need for more training in schools (2017), but in this book I make the case for this in the post-school sector. The problems have possibly just continued.

The methodology here offers primary research into many classrooms. Experiences critique theory and theory critiques experience. It is a dialectical process whereby the particularities of each individual case in a classroom are a critique of generalised models; the meta-language of theory describes and subjects to analysis what happens in classrooms. It is a continually evolving dialectical process.

Chapters are based on empirical research, observations, interviews, questionnaires and narratives. This is an academic book, deploying a range of sampling methods to argue the case that there needs to be far greater engagement in understanding the complex sphere of disruptive classroom relationships. This will hopefully begin to address the sorts of relationship problems tutors face in Further Education and Training.

SUBSEQUENT CHAPTERS EXPLAINED

Chapter 2 puts theories of class management under scrutiny. In most books on this topic, theory is based in the school sector and usually presents one set of strategies or tactics. Books on this topic tend to offer a specific philosophy with little regard to what other writers have said or different contexts. Writers speak with authority that, if their procedures are followed, then problems will not occur. The assumption is that all teachers are the same and have the same personality, emotional range, equanimity of mood and capabilities, but also that they are involved in classes of the same emotional intensity and social complexity. This chapter will analyse the strengths and weaknesses of a range of models, analysing what is said by various theoreticians of classroom practice, including Kounin, Kohn, Cowley and Wallace. I will also examine some differences between schools and colleges.

Chapter 3 explores the problems of entering classrooms and strategies that teachers deploy in these opening moments. There is analysis of situations where teachers entered classrooms and their presence was immediately rejected. How did they deal with these unnerving challenges? There is little written on this key moment of teaching other than benign platitudes of being pleasant or greeting students at the door, setting up learner contracts, but sometimes these initial moments have their own complexities. What do educational writers recommend? The problems faced by teachers often go beyond what is said in textbooks about class management and lesson preparation. How could tutors improve their teaching under more difficult pressures?

Chapter 4 questions experienced teachers on the interventions they made in order to overcome challenging classes. What were some of the worst situations that experienced teachers faced in the Education and Training sector during their careers and what strategies did they use in order to overcome these difficulties? This research investigates how a sample of experienced teachers of more than 10 years standing dealt with disruptive students in their careers. I wanted to listen to what teachers said about extreme experiences where they interfaced with negative student behaviour. The conclusion analyses the findings and questions the problematics of this research, its meaning, validity and possible application in other teaching contexts.

Chapter 5 involves case studies exploring the problematics of assessment and how this can alienate students, cause disruption and ultimately undermine learning. Several case studies are covered in this chapter, the first of which is an auto-ethnographic study based on a one-to-one encounter with a very challenging individual. The assumption is that those who carry out violence are at a low level academically or are from deprived backgrounds. This is a counter-example case study where the student was high-achieving and affluent. It outlines strategies used in a range of circumstances. The research is based on observation, interviews and a narrative of the researcher's involvement in different teaching situations. In this and subsequent chapters there is a subtext of questioning the use of counselling and therapy models in teaching disaffected students. Is education quite separate from psychological interventions?

Chapter 6 questions managers on how they might support tutors in dealing with stressful situations where staff are attacked, little learning takes place and students are constantly involved in activities that have nothing to do with the ostensible subject of sessions. The methodology is to offer qualitative practitioner research which suggests recommendations to improve practice on how managers might support teachers in their institutions. Research methods aimed to determine managers' perspectives. Findings showed that there were widespread problems in many classes where this research took place. Managers offered a range of localised and wider strategies for supporting teachers. Offering whole institution approaches, training on interventions and opening spaces for tutors and managers to explore these issues in a blame-free environment were all possible recommendations.

Chapter 7 deploys data from over 100 students to explore how students, categorised as 'disruptive,' view challenging or difficult classes. Classes were identified as 'disruptive' by their institution, department or individual tutors, but this opened up questions about how we determine or identify students as disruptive. What are the criteria for being disruptive? Would students be prepared to identify themselves or answer questions about being 'badly' behaved in sessions? This chapter's scope is to report on the findings of what students said about their classes. The students' concerns and feelings might be critical. Should these students be merely referred for professional counselling? Could the system ever cope? Interviewing students on their expectations about sessions gave some clues as to the other side of the teacher/learner relationship.

Chapter 8 outlines a strategy for supporting teachers in developing their ability to deal with disruptive student behaviour in classes. This chapter outlines a methodology for offering joint-practitioner practice, buddying systems and support outside the classroom context. I describe peer-reflective/support practice and demonstrate how this has been effective in impacting on trainees dealing with disruptive groups and how this helps improve teaching. Some epistemological questions are raised as to the problematics of how teachers know whether improvements take place when an intervention is made. The idea of improvement rather than mere change is highly loaded and open to interpretation. The beginnings of a discussion on the nature of improvement is fraught with ideological, vested-interest and value-laden overtones. Exploring these complexities is part of this book's process.

The triggers for research in Chap. 9 are the problematic aspects of Information and Communication Technology (ICT) learning. Despite notes of caution, there is an assumption that we are all part of a culture where ICT is so deeply embedded into every activity that supports learning that we are almost unable to see beyond the parameters of all ICT learning as being positive. Yet, there are many pedagogic concerns, such as the assumption that time online is necessarily spent learning, that all students' work can be authenticated as their own, but also that abuse is not taking place within social media supposedly devoted to learning contexts. The assumption is that blended learning will dissipate the whole problem of students' 'mis-behaviour' in classrooms. I argue that problems may have been merely relocated to the virtual world.

Chapter 10 examines the issue of how teacher educators approach training teachers to prepare them for working within the Education and Training sector in terms of disruptive classes. This chapter focuses on empirical research into what teacher educators say about the training they offer to trainees. Do they recommend specific theorists? Do they teach particular strategies? Is there a module devoted to behaviour management on their training courses? In fact, most courses embed behaviour management into other areas of teachers' training. There is a question as to which approach is the most effective. This research questions lecturers and managers of training courses at various universities, colleges and other training centres.

The final research-based chapter asks trainees about their experiences of disruptive student behaviour on teaching practice in a wide variety of teaching and training contexts. The questions are how were they trained for these situations, how effective was this training, how did PGCE/Cert Ed courses support their trainees and what was recommended? Were there specific theorists or strategies that were useful? Furthermore, how did trainees make use of the advice given in observations and training sessions? The key question for this chapter is, considering the situations they have to face, 'What do trainees need from training?'

Conclusions are multifarious. It is difficult to argue causality on issues of why disruptive behaviour happens as causes are not easily determined. There might be socio-economic, biological, gender and ethnicity aspects or specific contexts to the situations discussed. Any reductionism to simplistic causes attributed to challenging behaviour is avoided. Although practical solutions are analysed in this book, the central perspective is to examine the complex nature of these challenging situations, view different sets of recommendations and sum up the key elements of research undertaken. However, ultimately I believe that trainees need to be taught behaviour management as a separate module and a possible version of this programme is outlined in this chapter.

Suggested Strategies Based on Points Covered in This Chapter

1. Management to ensure that safeguarding policies for staff and students are in place and fully implemented.
2. Ground rules are democratically worked out between each teacher and student.
3. If students express racist/sexist attitudes, these are to be subject to rigorous questioning. Ultimately, these attitudes cannot be tolerated in the classroom.
4. If students display deep psychological problems, they may need to be referred for specialist counselling.
5. Open up supportive discussions with teachers in staff rooms or training events about the difficulties they are facing with disruptive classes. This must be the first step towards resolving problems.
6. If students express anger, it might be important to ask them why they are angry. It can be part of the process of calming and re-engaging them in a dialogue about their feelings.
7. In situations of extreme violence, the pirority is to protect the most vulnerable students in the class.

Bibliography

Association of Teachers and Lecturers (ATL). (2013). Disruptive behaviour in schools and colleges rises alongside increase in children with behavioural and mental health problems. *Annual Conference Press Release*, 24 March.

ATL. (2016). Education staff facing physical violence from pupils. https://www.atl.org.uk/media-office/2016/education-staff-facing-physical-violence-from-pupils.asp

Coffield, F. (2008). *Just suppose teaching and learning became the first priority*. London: Learning and Skills Network.

Coffield, F., Moseley, D., Hall, E., & Ecclestone, K. (2004). *Learning styles and pedagogy in post-16 learning: A systematic and critical review*. London: Learning & Skills Research Centre.

Colley, H. (2003). *Mentoring for social inclusion: A critical approach to nurturing mentor relationships*. London: RoutledgeFalmer.

Crace, J., & Lebor, M. (2000). One strike and you're out. *The Guardian*. https://www.theguardian.com/education/2000/feb/08/furthereducation.theguardian1

Curzon, L., & Tummons, J. (2013). *Teaching in further education: An outline of principles and practice* (7th ed.). London: Bloomsbury.

Dewey, J. (1938). *Experience and education Kappa Delta PI.* New York: Free Press.

DFE. (2012). Pupil behaviour in schools in England. *DFE-RR218.* https://www.education.gov.uk/publications/

Dix, P. (2015). Three secrets to a successful FE behaviour policy. *TES.* https://www.tes.com/news/further-education/breaking-views/three-secrets-a-successful-fe-behaviour-policy

Holton, S. (1995). It's nothing new! A history of conflict in higher education. *New Directions for Higher Education, 92,* 11–18.

Honey, P., & Mumford, A. (2000). *The learning styles helpers guide.* Maidenhead: Peter Honey Publications.

Illeris, K. (2007). *How we learn: Learning and non-learning in school and beyond.* Oxon: Routledge.

Kennet, K. (2010). Professionalism and reflective practice. In S. Wallace (Ed.), *The lifelong learning sector reflective reader* (pp. 66–79). Exeter: Learning Matters.

Lebor, M. (2011). Licence to teach. *Every Child Matters,* Vol. 2.4.

Maslow, A. (1987). *Motivation and personality.* New York: Harper and Row.

NASUWT. (2016). *Behaviour management.* https://www.nasuwt.org.uk/advice/in-the-classroom/behaviour-management.html

Ofsted. (2012). *Ofsted changes inspections of schools, further education and skills, and initial teacher education.* HM Government UK. http://www.ofsted.gov.uk/news/ofsted-announces-changes-inspections-of-schools-further-education-and-skills-and-initial-teacher-edu

Ofsted. (2015). *Initial teacher education inspection handbook.* https://www.gov.uk/government/uploads/system/uploads/attachment_data/file/459282/Initial_Teacher_Eduction_handbook_from_September_2015.pdf

Organisation for Economic Co-operation and Development. (2011). *Has discipline in school deteriorated?* PISA in Focus 2011/4 May. Paris: OECD Publishing. http://wwwoecd/dataoecd/18/63/47944912

Parry, D., & Taubman, D. (2013). *UCU whole college behaviour management: Final report.* UCU, funded by LSIS.

Paton, G. (2012). Bad behaviour in schools 'fuelled by over-indulgent parents'. http://www.telegraph.co.uk/education/educationnews/9173533/Bad-behaviour-in-schools-fuelled-by-over-indulgent-parents.html

Rogers, C. (1961). *On becoming a person: A therapist's view of psychotherapy.* London: Constable.

Sellgren, K. (2013). Disruptive behaviour rising, teachers say. *BBC.* http://www.bbc.co.uk/news/education-21895705.

Shacklock, G., & Thorp, L. (2005). Life history and narrative approaches. In B. Somekh & C. Lewin (Eds.), *Research methods in the social sciences* (pp. 156–163). London: Sage.

Simmons, R. (2009). An overview of the lifelong learning sector and its 'condition. In J. Avis, R. Fisher, & R. Simmons (Eds.), *Issues in post-compulsory education and training: Critical perspectives.* Huddersfield: University of Huddersfield Press.

Simmons, R., & Thompson, R. (2011). *Education and training for young people at risk of becoming NEET: Findings from an ethnographic study of work-based learning programmes.* London: Routledge.

Spiers, E. (2011). Bad behaviour in the classroom is not the problem. http://www.guardian.co.uk/teacher-network/2011/nov/03/bad-behaviour-classroom

Townend, M. (2013). Massive rise in disruptive behaviour, warn teachers. http://www.guardian.co.uk/education/2013/mar/24/schools-disruptive-behaviour

UCU. (2013). *Classroom management: UCU continuing professional development.* http://cpd.web.ucu.org.uk/files/2013/07/CPD-factsheet-6.pdf

UNISON. (2016). School support staff facing high levels of violence and abuse, says UNISON. https://www.unison.org.uk/news/press-release/2016/06/school-support-staff-facing-high-levels-of-violence-and-abuse-says-unison/

Wallace, S. (2007). *Managing behaviour in the lifelong learning sector.* Exeter: Learning Matters.

Wallace, S. (2017). *Behaviour management: Getting it right in a week.* St. Albans: Critical Publishing.

Weale, S. (2016). Almost a third of teachers quit state sector within five years of qualifying. https://www.theguardian.com/education/2016/oct/24/almost-third-of-teachers-quit-within-five-years-of-qualifying-figures

Wenger, E. (1998). *Communities of practice: Learning, meaning and identity.* Cambridge: Cambridge University Press.

Willis, P. (1977). *Learning to labour: How working class kids get working class jobs.* Aldershot: Ashgate.

Wolf, A. (2011, March). *Wolf review of 14–19 vocational education.* London: DfE.

CHAPTER 2

In Theory It All Works...

In this chapter a range of classic theories and models of class management are critically explained. Then some key differences are outlined between school and college education. This is relevant because so much of the current behaviour management theory is school based. Some theorists are critiqued in terms of their practical application in the Education and Training sector. The majority of texts in this area are focussed on younger students in the school sector rather than colleges (Parry and Taubman 2013), but often there are differences in approach and understanding within these contexts. Thus, statements of advice assume that teachers work within the school sector; for example, the Behaviour Czar Tom Bennett, in his top tips (2015), advises teaching staff to contact parents where there are problems in the classroom. However, this is irrelevant to students in the post-school sector as often students are not living with their parents, are adults or are parents themselves, but assumes that the classroom is sufficiently ordered that the teacher **can** create a positive atmosphere.

THE GURUS

Do the models or strategies outlined in this chapter work in all circumstances or only specific contexts? The question is whether the strategy needs modifying in different environments. Does it always work? What is the empirical evidence? Typically, Fred Jones (2007), for example, recommends that teachers create a positive classroom atmosphere which

© The Author(s) 2017
M. Lebor, *Classroom Behaviour Management in the Post-School Sector*, DOI 10.1007/978-3-319-57051-8_2

will prevent problems from occurring in the first place. This is a standard approach used by many writers on this topic, such as Geoff Petty (2014).

Fred Jones

But what are Jones' specific methods for creating this ideal situation? He believed in eliminating wasted time and teaching students responsibility, independence and co-operation. He promoted helping students to gain self-control and felt that the structure of the classroom should discourage misbehaviour. This all seems very good practice.

In order to achieve this, he suggested that the teacher should move amongst the students and that there should be physical closeness with an inner loop defining the space where the teacher moves in the classroom. Proxemics are actually often culturally determined. Jones' view is that students should be working on tasks, rules, 'chores' and rituals from the beginning of the session, placing much emphasis on body language, proximity, correct breathing and posture. He invented a repeated 'say, see, do cycle' by which students could be told what to do and would repeat what was required in class through practice several times throughout the session. Students could earn or lose Positive Activity Time which would motivate students to learn during their lessons.

This approach is obviously very constructive and could be a model for well-taught classes. However, there are some problematic aspects. As proposed in the chapter title, in theory it works, but physical proximity to students could be viewed as intruding on students' space. It assumes that teachers can intimidate students through their physicality, but say if the students are far bigger physically than the teacher. This strategy becomes even more questionable if a male teacher moves closer to female students or female teachers are asked to move physically close to male students. If sexuality and gender are not experienced or understood as binary by students or lecturers, this advice becomes yet more fraught with complexity. There seems to be no awareness of sexual dynamics and assumptions. In fact, when questioned, as part of research into 40 trainee teachers' views as to the most significant challenges in being a new teacher, female trainees said that unwanted sexist remarks or references to their sexuality were some of the most negative aspects of being within a classroom environment with male students. Once this is said, advising teachers to become physically closer to students just seems naive.

Furthermore, there is an assumption that teachers can have control over their physical space in the teaching environment. Often classrooms have already been set out for previous lessons or have preset furniture. In the Education and Training sector, classrooms are often set up in a fixed geography, with chairs and tables in predetermined positions. The students are often already seated in their places and it would cause considerable effort and possibly be a waste of time to move them. There is also an implication that classrooms should be potentially boring places where students are ritualised into the conformity of 'chores' and 'rules,' whilst motivation is extrinsic to the actual work being done and that students are in need of rewards beyond or outside the work that has been set. The repeated cycles might be counter-productive in terms of developing creativity, questioning or deeper-level cognitive skills. It should be said that Positive Activity Time implies that all the work not being done during that period is negative. Doesn't this compromise the idea of wanting students to view what they are studying as attractive, new or interesting?

Finally, Jones speaks of conserving time, showing that the teacher means 'business,' using incentives, offering rules and routines, but also engaging students. This is a highly controlled version of the classroom and again implies acculturation, behaviour control and an authoritarian version of the teacher's role. The question with respect to the engagement of students remains 'how?'

Maslow

Maslow's hierarchy of needs is often cited as addressing the underlying psychological reality of students in classrooms, whereby there are levels of need in students that must be addressed in order for learning to take place effectively (1987). The highest level of supposed need is enlightenment or self-actualisation that will only be reached once all other levels have been overcome. Again, this could be a very useful way of understanding student behaviour in terms of motivation and the basic physical and psychological requirements of students before teaching can take place. It is true that there are often issues for poorer students not being able to concentrate because their physiological needs for food and warmth have not been met. This is critical.

Support and understanding for students in these circumstances must be a priority in any civilised education system. However, there are many problematic aspects of Maslow's system that have been rehearsed before in other contexts. The rigidity of the hierarchy is open to question. For example, students might have higher-level needs met before lower ones are addressed. It could be argued that students might deprive themselves of basic physiological needs, such as sleep and food, in order to prepare for an exam, so lower levels of need not being fulfilled could be purpose-fully determined by the students themselves. Other critiques might view the hierarchy of needs as an inadequate picture of the classroom because individuals and groups could have spiky profiles, characterised by a range of needs, some of which have been and/or have not been met. It is pos-sible that students could be highly enlightened, religious, aesthetes or Buddhists who view bodily needs as quite irrelevant. Maslow and his suc-cessors' focus might be useful as a frame for understanding the physi-cal and psychological situation before students are taught and this might be part of an ongoing dialogue between teacher and student which can-not be ignored. Although Maslow was not originally writing specifically about classrooms, his work has been consistently applied in this context. Nevertheless, for the purposes of this book, his work might help to under-stand students' predicaments, but does not directly address the issue of teaching challenging, disruptive or difficult students per se.

Harry Wong

Harry Wong's view is less rigid and possibly more realistic and applicable to a range of contexts (2009) than, for example, Jones. Wong understands behaviour problems as an issue of a lack of class facilitation rather than dis-cipline. His outlook claims to offer methodologies for structuring lessons through organisation, creating a safe and positive environment for stu-dents of all ages, presumably including the Education and Training sector. Nevertheless, his book is really about the 'first days of school' rather than college. He explains a series of procedures that can supposedly be applied, changed, adapted and incorporated into any classroom management plan. The main idea is that teachers need to be flexible, but the key is lesson preparation. It is a perspective that focusses on the teacher as manager in the learning context, creating an environment that is supposedly produc-tive for students.

The fact that every class, teacher and teaching environment is different means that his approach is not a model or theory of teaching, but rather a series of suggestions. Although this perspective offers a view of classroom relationships between teacher and students as open to adaptation, it is based on experience rather than research. There is a feeling that it has been developed as a response to classroom behaviour in Wong's own sphere of expertise. These are tips from an experienced teacher. This is problem-atic because it assumes that what works in one context will be applicable elsewhere. However, he does not claim to base this on research, but rather on a series of pieces of advice on practical strategies that are connected to schools in America rather than colleges in the UK. The dynamics are totally different.

Harry Wong proposes that teachers work collaboratively with students. This is good advice. Nevertheless, he tells teachers to explain, rehearse and then reinforce work. He discusses the notion of teachers managing classrooms, but also discusses how effective teachers establish classroom procedures to create achievement. The idea of the teacher as a manager constructs education in the image of the world of work. It is an understanding that classrooms are a preparation for working practice. Training is constructed as a kind of behaviour modification for allowing students to enter employment. But doesn't the academic world also have its own culture of research, curiosity and an interest in knowledge for its own sake? More seriously his methods assume that all students will co-operate and act in a mutually civil and fundamentally civilised way. Unfortunately, as we find out in this book, that is not always the case.

Jean Gibbs

Jean Gibbs initially offered a two-stage strategy to prevent substance abuse, but this methodology had implications for developing inclusion and valuing community for all students as a way of stopping isolation and negative behaviours in classrooms. It is also a method of training staff and parents to evolve small group engagement and co-operative learning. Again this was a school-based initiative leading to increased student self-esteem and significant decreases in student behaviour problems. The main strategies are to teach students in small groups thereby engaging all students in the classroom. The second stage of the strategy is to build long-term, small membership groups, referred to as 'tribes' in order to develop peer support, democratic group skills, but also co-operative learning strategies to help students with their personal development and their understanding of academic concepts (2001).

The 'key skills' students have to evolve are attentive listening and mutual respect. The main ideas in this system are offering a whole-school model, which has been replicated in much literature concerning schools and colleges. However, Gibbs' focus is on the development of individual young people as active citizens, contributing to society, educated to fulfil themselves in the social, intellectual and emotional realms. This is a student-centred model, positing specific training, the build-up of tribe identities, developing caring communities, partnerships and a culture of responsive education. Responsibility in assessment is passed onto students as part of their personal development.

Although admirable in terms of ticking many of the key ideas of inclusive learning in potentially fraught situations, the problematic aspects of this model are that there is a resource issue as it relies on sufficient teachers to lead small groups. There is also a concern that once students are identified into tribes, this could lead to rivalry, competition and hatred. Can pride in the tribe extend to other tribes? Again it is centred within the American school sector, but, nevertheless, offers a possible model for breaking larger groups down into smaller sections so as to develop individuals and their ability to operate within a positive social framework, which could be highly useful for preparing students for the working world and adult life.

Jere Brophy

Brophy (2010) puts the emphasis on goal orientation, intrinsic motivation in learning and students' engagement in cognitive skills so that they can gain rewards without being pressurised, which he claims is counter-productive. For him the key is offering strategies for repairing the damage that has accumulated for students who have become disaffected through the education system. He wants to re-socialise committed low-achievers, thus weaning damaged students away from performance-related targets towards building self-esteem. All this again sounds extremely positive.

He covers a range of possible strategies for stimulating student motivation, such as self-regulated learning and scaffolding students' efforts. He believes in offering incentives for those disengaged in classroom sessions, but also developing a close relationship with individual students and discovering their areas of interest. This describes a deeply positive relationship. However, underpinning his understanding of the relationship between extrinsic and intrinsic motivation, there is a belief in learning styles (Honey, Mumford ibid.), multiple intelligences (Gardner 2011) and psychological differentiation in classrooms. However, learning styles have been heavily critiqued as being a counter-productive way of understanding student motivation because this construction of intelligence categorises students so that they resist working in any style other than the one to which they have been designated. The tests for determining each student's propensities are also flawed because they assume every student answers in a totally honest way. The other problem is that learning styles theory views each mode of intelligence as an entirely distinctive entity that can be objectively measured. This seems quite unrealistic (Coffield 2004).

Brophy also talks about the effects of teacher's expectations and self-fulfilling prophecies that are created in the minds and later behaviours of students. He believed that the learning context was critical and thought that lessons needed to be made meaningful. These are all useful concepts. However, the meaning of being meaningful can be highly subjective, can be different for each individual in the class and can be problematic where one teacher is required to work with 30 or more students. The question then becomes 'how can that teacher deploy resources so that each individual learner is motivated to learn?' Sometimes these questions are difficult to answer within the resource framework of each context where they are applied. Although teachers' knowledge of what is meaningful to each student in their classes is highly desirable, sometimes teachers in this sector may only see their students for an hour or two per week. Exploring what is meaningful might need extensive conversations with students beyond a one-hour time-tabled slot with 30 other students present.

Mendler and Curwin

Mendler and Curwin's 'discipline with dignity' approach (2008) covers many of the same ideas as previously expounded, including co-operation, mutual respect, developing responsibility and shared decision-making. This is a supposedly soft-styled, preventative and reactive strategy for gaining control over classrooms. Their view speaks of three dimensions, identified as prevention, action and resolution. They recommend consequences, which are intended to teach proactive lessons to students, rather than punishments, which merely discomfort the learner, promoting obedience, but are also more likely to lead to the student's resentment and disaffection. Nevertheless, they say that there must always be consequences for disruptive behaviour. They advise using a soft voice; however, this raises the issue that sometimes teachers cannot make themselves heard in noisy classrooms. They also say that students should not be humiliated or disciplined in such a way as to compromise students' motivation to learn. Again this is focussed on teachers being as 'tough as is necessary' whereby there are different gradations of disruptive behaviour each with its own consequence that must be consistently applied to students who 'misbehave.' They propose physical proximity and direct eye contact again with all the problematic implications of intrusion into students' space, mentioned earlier.

There is a wide cross-over between many of these models; most are related to school behaviour which might be either condescending or infantilising for adult students who either have been failed by the school system or are often trying to re-engage with education and training in a more mature environment.

William Glasser

Glasser's (1986) control theory, a variation on Maslow's hierarchy, contended that behaviour is inspired by basic human needs, but this time characterised as love, freedom and power. He claims that, if students are not motivated to carry out tasks or do work, it is because they view the work as irrelevant to their needs. Instead of using rewards and punishment which merely force students to comply with institutional power and carry out low-level meaningless tasks, teachers should avoid coercion completely and focus on the intrinsic needs of their students, correlating the importance of assignments to students' interests. Work set should be of use to students either in their personal development or as part of the vocational career to which they aspire. Good teachers fight to protect engaged, highly motivated students who are doing quality work, shielding them from having to fulfil meaningless chores. His view depends on the ability of students to be involved with the shaping of the curriculum, but this is not always possible as the curriculum is set by vocational, academic or government authorities. Teachers are asked to develop their loyalty to the learning process rather than boring activities, but, unfortunately, in many realms of vocational work, some tasks may need to be repeated until perfected. It would, for example, be unsafe to teach students to drive or carry out potentially dangerous activities unless these were internalised until faultless through constant repetition (Dreyfus 1986).

Kounin Versus Kohn

There is often a dichotomy between theorists who espouse either intrinsic or extrinsic motivation as a factor in determining classroom management. This polarisation can be seen by contrasting the work of Kounin (1997) and Kohn (2006) both of whom write from within the American compulsory education system. Both theorists are used by many teacher educators in post-compulsory education in the UK, offering different theoretical models as paradigms of how teachers should operate within classroom contexts.

Kounin accepts the notion of behaviour being managed in classrooms, whereas Kohn believes in intrinsic motivation and that behaviour management is not a problem if students are sufficiently engaged in their learning. Kounin (1997) is a key figure in formulating techniques and strategies of classroom management. He believed in six main principles of class control, for the first of which he invented the term 'with-it-ness.' This meant that the teacher has to not only know each student on a personal basis, be focussed on the well-being of each individual in the class and be aware of everyone's strengths, weaknesses and interests, but also be involved in each student's progress. This is again patently ideal, but often teachers in post-compulsory education might only see a class once a week, every month or only on one occasion. Many students are on quick turn-over classes lasting three weeks. Thus, it can become difficult to build a complex understanding of individuals in this short time. It also makes assumptions as to the type of person a teacher must be in order to be successful. There is an awareness and dynamism that is implicit in this description. Again, whilst this may be an ideal, many teachers might be very effective, but have a quieter, introverted style, or have a view that students are adults and can be trusted as self-directed learners (Knowles 1975).

Teachers might facilitate learning through offering leadership or even power to students. It is also problematic that this 'with-it-ness' is, as an inner state, almost non-observable. Being 'with-it' was a phrase associated with the 1960s and implied being up to date or even 'trendy.' Here it takes on a meaning of high-level social consciousness: an understanding of 'everything' that is happening in an environment. But it might be difficult for an observer to tell whether a teacher is or is not focussed on the 'well-being' of each individual student. In other words, lessons are complex events: the level of caring not easily determined.

Kounin also believed in a process of overlapping where the teacher has sufficient control to be able to allow individuals or groups of students to be able to carry out different tasks at the same time. Classrooms offer opportunities for breaking conformity and allowing students to work at their own pace on possibly different topics concomitantly. It seems to mean differentiated learning where new work is available for students to start, whilst other students are completing earlier set tasks. It also implies that the teacher might be involved with one student, making eye contact with another individual, whilst giving instructions to a third. Again, the implication is that the teacher has to be able to communicate at multiple levels at once. There seems to be this double relationship of teacher as controller and omniscient being of communication.

Kounin believed in what he called 'momentum,' which meant that lecturers' talk should be limited, and tasks and exercises should also remain short, so that students do not get bored and are engaged in purposeful activity throughout. He believed in using 'timers,' so that tasks in class are completed within deadlines and best use is made of each moment of the session. This is ideal for a highly controlled session. It can be problematic because it assumes that students might not be sufficiently interested or self-motivated to be curious about ideas that are being generated or that they may wish to explore the subject or its implications in more detail. They may be doing creative subjects where time is not necessarily linear. Paintings cannot be done by rote! Again, his concept of 'smoothness' involves moving from one topic to another, facilitating and changing the direction of class or group discussions, so as to sustain a lively interest. This is again all good practice to which many teachers aspire.

He encouraged accountability, grading students for their participation in discussion and offering rewards at random so as to keep students concentrating throughout the session. There is a strong behaviourist undertone to elements of his strategies. Many teacher educators and trainees, as we find later, subscribe to his outlook.

However, these ideas also assume that students will not be intrinsically motivated. His views also imply that the outward behaviours of students accurately represent what is happening in their inner lives or that the rate, mind set or 'learning' of students can be regulated or understood purely by visual clues, tasks carried out with or without a deeper comprehension. He is not necessarily writing about art school.

In contrast to Kounin is Kohn whose key theme is his criticality towards competition and external or extrinsic motivation. Kohn is a significant figure in compulsory education and became a key exponent of developing the idea that education should be enjoyable. He offers an oppositional ideology to Kounin and other theorists who believe in 'classroom management' as a method of class control and posits instead a model devoted to the intrinsic interests of learners. He radically critiques hierarchical social structures on the basis that only the elite will feel temporarily secure in their superiority and this state of affairs will ultimately only satisfy the few learners at the top of the class. He rejects the concept of classroom management and instead suggests a notion of co-operation and curiosity in the classroom, believing that these intrinsic values are the rewards of education (1993). Classroom management, he argues, fosters extrinsic motivation as opposed to developing the personal growth of individuals. He believed that if classrooms are set up to foster learning, then management issues will take care of themselves. Furthermore, he thought that the concern of teachers is to create an atmosphere where students are deeply immersed in the subjects they are studying (Kohn 2006). This is the ideal state of students not conscious of their own level in competition with others in the class, but being intrinsically motivated. His critical pedagogy perspective is very much rooted in the work of Freire and Illich, in opposition to the performativity culture as has been outlined by, for example, Steven Ball (2003).

The problem with Kohn's view is that it assumes all academic or vocational subjects are intrinsically interesting to all students or that all subjects can be made interesting. What is 'interesting' is subjective. The other issue is that teachers could be faced with students who are highly competitive, are games-orientated and are only motivated by the sense of wanting to achieve at an elite level or to be rewarded for ambition and success. They may find Kohn's student-centred, humanistic approach quite alien, boring or counter-productive to their view of the purpose of education. They might also feel that this view of the classroom does not reflect the reality of what happens in the capitalist world of jobs, employment or the more competitive worlds of academe to which they may be aspiring.

The problem is that much theory, even that taught within the Education and Training sector, is written in the context of schools. There are clear differences.

What's the Difference Between School and College?

The question is whether these philosophies can be applied to the practical realms and policies of teaching in the Education and Training sector. There is much writing on the need for colleges and schools to take what is referred to as a 'whole institution' policy. Thus, Clarke and Murray (1996) suggested that behaviour management could be planned as a systematic approach in a similar way to evolving the curriculum within one institution. Again, Powell and Tod (2004) found that dealing with disruptive behaviour was the main concern for tutors and suggested a wider outlook in managing behaviour. This meant offering a positive policy across the whole institution where learners worked. Massey (2011) expressed the need for a consistent whole-school behaviour policy as the answer to improving class management. He promoted the idea that, without training within the cultural norms of the specific institution, teachers were left vulnerable and lacked the tools needed to manage student behaviour effectively. Parry and Taubman (2013) agree that a whole-institution approach as conceived within the school sector should be applied to colleges.

However, it must be said that there are some significant differences between colleges and schools in this respect. Firstly, colleges can be on many sites across cities or even operate under one managerial aegis, but in separate towns (e.g. Kirklees College), whereas schools are usually geographically on one site, possibly following a Panopticon model (Foucault 1991) where students can always be viewed by staff. This makes a considerable difference in implementing whole-college policies as each part of a college venue can be quite different in design, atmosphere, culture, mood and tone to other buildings in the same institution.

Secondly, there is a question of numbers. Even large schools usually have not more than 1500 pupils, but often several hundred, whilst colleges can have 10,000 or 20,000 students, studying a wide range of subjects. The large numbers in colleges make them far less personal, corporate or community-like places. The loyalty, if it exists, is to the course, department, fellow students or teachers. In schools there is a limited curriculum, appropriate for each age, level or cohort. In colleges, students are often covering a wide range of vocational or academic subjects. Schools usually have a uniform which is a method of control and conformity. Sometimes certain departments, such as catering, beauty or mechanics, have a uniform within colleges, but generally clothing is left to individual choice. In schools there can be bells to control students, whereas in colleges there is generally a more adult atmosphere. There are also issues of power and how this is established and held. In schools it tends to be more centralised, in colleges more diffuse.

Schools often have whole- or part-school assemblies where an institutional message can be delivered authoritatively from the front. Colleges do not usually have the facilities for an equivalent meeting of all students. The larger population of colleges means that, whereas schools are often subject to assemblies, the whole population of a college (unless it is very small) is virtually never brought together in the same room or venue. Students at schools are always younger than the teachers; in colleges, tutors can be the same age or younger than the students. School children often address teachers as Mr or Mrs X, Miss or sir. Students and teachers in colleges are usually on first name terms. Strict or more 'discipline-minded' teachers can be well-known throughout a school, whilst such figures in colleges would probably only be known within their department or local vicinity. Although a photograph of a college principal might be on walls and literature at different sites, it is more likely that at a school the head will be known to pupils through assemblies, interviews, personal meetings or the head coming round classrooms. Normally, pupils spend five to seven years at school, so school pupils are more likely to build up a relationship with teachers and other students, developing reactions and understanding of the school for better or worse. Students at college might stay for a course lasting one day, one month or often at most a couple of years. There is not the same commitment of time or build up of relationship within the institution.

These differences are not absolute. There are smaller colleges and large schools, friendlier principals and distant heads, schools with liberal outlooks and few rules as opposed to highly conformist colleges. However, in general, the above-mentioned differences hold and this means that the advice given in a school context often is not relevant to students in a college. Some of these points become relevant when discussing school-based models and advice in college classroom practice.

It might also be said that the power or authority of the school teacher can derive from differentiating adults as in control over younger, possibly smaller people, that is, teachers being in loco parentis. The school system can emphasise these differences between teachers and pupils through clothing, areas forbidden to students, stance and attitudes. The teachers are on the stage, at the front of the class, standing whilst pupils can be sitting at a lower level more passively on chairs, sitting on the floor, lining up or being ordered to carry out instructions in many situations. In colleges it is assumed that andragogy (Knowles 1975) is in place and that there are different models for teaching older rather than younger students.

These differences are not always apparent or structured within all college environments. If Knowles' view of the differences between teaching adults as andragogy and children as pedagogy is accepted, there can still be overlaps, ambiguities and a complex understanding of how adults are taught differently from 'children.' The differences between older and younger students are usually assumed to be that adults have more 'experience' unavailable to children, which they bring to class discussion. Adults are supposed to be more independent, self-motivated and self-directed learners who are in education on a voluntary basis, whilst younger students currently up to aged 18 are there on a compulsory basis; that is, they are possibly reluctantly forced to attend classes.

However, many counter-examples can be found to these assumptions. Thus, even in primary schools, we find children are encouraged to use the Internet regularly to research and discuss complex areas of study by themselves (Mitra 2010). In school environments there might be highly complex discussions of say ethical or philosophical issues within literature, religious studies or personal development tutorials. On the other hand, adults' personal experience might be quite irrelevant in subjects, such as chemistry or maths, whilst children have sometimes been subject to vast learning experiences through their family lives, which give them great intellectual, emotional and/or psychological understanding beyond the range of many adults. We now have refugee children in our classes who have travelled many hundreds of miles and experienced horrific scenes of violence, whilst adults might have spent 70 years of a peaceful life in one village. Through work or because of social security systems adults can quite often be forced to attend classes against their will, thus making them compulsory students, whilst children, in positive environments, can, of course, be highly self-motivated learners. These are arguments to show that there are many complexities in comparing adult and children's learning.

The overall point to be taken from this discussion is that the theories that are applied to schools are not necessarily appropriate to Education and Training environments as a range of different circumstances are embedded into each context, and therefore, it is hard to legislate for all situations. By being mainly focussed on school education, the key ideas of behaviour management outlined above, which are often used and taught on PGCE and Cert Ed courses, have been transplanted into colleges and adult education where they may seem either condescending or irrelevant.

Some Post-school Theorists

Approaches in texts used within the Education and Training sector, discussed below, tend to be highly pragmatic, which is good, but do not refer to research in a systemic or coherent way. For example, they seldom look at the strengths and weaknesses of each other's theories or compare and contrast different methodologies or even teacher behaviours, with some exceptions, when confronted by extreme situations. The belief is that, if good teaching happens, then problems will not occur. The assumption is that all teachers have the same personality, emotional range and capabilities. The other assumption is that classes will behave in the same way, will conform or have the same cultures and dynamics no matter the subject matter, academic level, economic/social context, geographical area or the institutional ethos. The theoreticians tend not to show how their theories work in practice or say what happens when students do not conform to what they expect.

The Further Education and Development Agency publication *Ain't Misbehavin'* defines disruptive behaviour as 'patterns of repeated behaviour which significantly interrupt the learning of others or threaten their personal security or well being' (Mitchell et al. 1998). Their examples of disruptive behaviour, repeated by UCU (2013, p. 2.), include:

> not finishing work or avoiding the task set; teasing or bullying other people; calling out and interrupting; coming in noisily/late; constant talking; refusal to comply with reasonable instruction; mobile phone use and texting; poor attendance or persistent lateness; putting on make-up, combing hair; rude, cheeky or inappropriate comments; eating and drinking in lessons; not respecting other people's property; substance abuse. These behaviours are problematic because of their frequency, severity, or duration. They undermine teaching and learning and are a significant cause of stress for all concerned.

It is notable that putting on make-up and combing hair are normative in college hair and beauty classes. Context is here critical.

Context Is All

My interest is to explore those instances when models of behaviour management are problematic or cannot be applied to all circumstances. Thus, Geoff Petty offers several pieces of homely advice based across all sectors of education in two chapters of *Teaching Today: A Practical Guide* (2014). However, behaviour management is not the main focus of his perspective which assumes that, if teaching is well-prepared and normative strategies of learning well-deployed, then disruption will not happen. It is part of a more general introductory book on the skills, practice and theory of being a novice teacher. He claims his book is 'procedural' (p. 5) explaining how teaching is done, rather than declarative, that is, saying what should happen. He speaks in a familiar tone addressing trainee teachers directly in the second person, 'You are there to teach and you cannot teach without order' (p. 98).

This advice is punctuated with cartoons; lists of 'don'ts'; dialogues; a series of bullet points; a mnemonic; exercises; problems and answers; adages, such as 'don't smile till Easter'; plus a smattering of academic references. It is very engaging; however, there are concerns with some of the advice put forward in these sections, thus telling teachers to 'appear confident' and 'business-like' (p. 104) might not be an easily followed instruction. It is not problematic for those who are already confident, but potentially counter-productive for those who suffer from nerves. It is left open to the 'novice's' own interpretation as to what this state of confidence or being 'business-like' might actually involve. Again telling teachers to clap hands (p. 105) for silence can have an infantilising effect on older students who might feel they are back in primary school, a culture which they came into adult education to escape. In the instruction to 'arrive before your class' (p. 104) and greet students at the door, there is an assumption that teachers can always be in the classroom before their students. Often in Further Education colleges, teachers have to take over from other teachers with students already in place or deal with classes that have their own departments, classrooms or environment into which the teacher has to enter, sometimes at their peril.

According to Petty the solution to difficult classes is a 'well-conceived curriculum,' 'good organisational skills,' 'good teacher-student relations' and 'effective discipline' (p. 109). This is all true. But the problem with a well-conceived curriculum is that most teachers have limited control over the curriculum as it is usually constructed prior to their involvement. The meaning of 'discipline' might also be outdated or inappropriate for contemporary teachers as facilitators in the Education and Training sector.

It is true that organisational skills and relationships between teachers and students are crucial, but again the meaning of what 'good' might mean in these contexts is a value judgement, open to interpretation. One teacher's creative, dynamic atmosphere might be another's disordered nightmare. Finally, it has to be said that it is unclear as to the basis of much of the research within these two chapters. At times it is based on Petty's own experience; for example, with a 13-year-old student, outside the Education and Training sector, but also draws on secondary sources of social psychologists, such as Hargreaves (p. 98). There is a short bibliography at the end of each chapter, but it is not clear which pieces of advice come from which sources. We do not know who says what. What is the research for each statement? Are the dialogues actual conversations that took place in classrooms or are they fictitious constructions, advising teachers what they could, should or might say in these particular circumstances? Petty does not clarify these matters.

Whilst two chapters are devoted to this topic in Petty's book, many key texts on teacher education do not focus on this problem at all (Reece and Walker 2003) or offer less than a single chapter (Gravells 2014). The assumption is often that if teaching is carried out effectively in the prescribed manner, problems will not occur.

However, a very useful intervention in this discussion is by Sue Cowley where she outlines what to do in cases of extreme violence, explaining that the teacher should use 'reasonable force', blocking or restricting the violent student's movement if possible without causing damage or any form of perceived indecency (Cowley 2007, 168–169). Another key book for many tutors and trainees is her *Getting the Buggers to Behave* (2014). Although highly regarded in terms of the practical advice on offer, the problem with Cowley from the point of view of this study is that her experience is self-reflectively based within the school sector. She conflates schools and colleges as being the same with respect to behaviour management, but the contexts are often quite different. The strong aspects of her work are that it is grounded in and educationally effective on case studies and practical situations of growing intensity. In her essay on tips for the post-school sector in *Readings for Reflective Learning* (Gregson et al. 2015) there are some useful ideas, edited from her previous book, based in schools.

It is problematic that there is a diminution or demonization of students through the use of the word 'buggers' in her title which possibly aligns itself with teachers' anger and frustration rather than building relationships or focussing on the intrinsic motivation associated with the work of Kohn and Dweck (2000). This is referred to as a provocative title (Gregson et al. 2015), but more deeply problematic is its lack of respect for learners. There is also little mention of the problems associated with urban, inner city, multi-cultural pedagogy. There is notably an index, but no bibliography in her work. The implication is that her work is a practical guide, centred, as she says, on her own experience, without reference to the theories or experiences of others.

Sue Wallace offers a more academic approach in that her work is based on research carried out through interviewing and listening to the voices of trainees, teachers and students, but also offering many practical strategies (2007, 2013b, 2017). In the opening chapters of *Managing Behaviour and Motivating Students in Further Education* (2002), there are accounts of disengaged, un-co-operative student behaviour. This is explained in the context of students' lack of choice with respect to job prospects and careers. She also posits Further Education as having lower social standing than universities which have always been privileged over vocational education. Unacceptable behaviour is tolerated in Further Education because there are no consequences, such as expulsion or exclusion, which would lead to financial costs for the college. She argues that we can only understand what students feel and what motivates them by questioning their experiences. This is a process which is also followed by my book.

Wallace's outlook is very useful because it establishes the widespread and problematic nature of student behaviours within the Education and Training sector. This is generally not acknowledged in many books on teacher education. It also researches the feelings and attitudes of trainees and students, recommending practical solutions in terms of relationships, rules, changing the ways students feel about learning, emphasising intrinsic motivation and focussing on students' strengths and abilities. She writes practical books, based on research, offering questions for discussion, extracts from reflective journals, dialogues, tasks and exercises for opening up the complexity of a range of classroom situations.

The problem in Wallace's explanation as to why disruptive behaviour happens in Further Education could be questioned. Her perspective seems to be that the reason for disruption is that the sector has low status. The lower status of FE or the Cinderella syndrome has been heavily debated. It is not necessarily a good explanation because there have been substantial changes, such as the new builds which make Further Education colleges look like shopping malls or airports, possibly enhancing the view that education and training are part of a consumer culture; products to be sold. The point is that some of these buildings offer an environment that might be said to equal the modernity and high-tech image of many universities and schools.

She also suggests that students' lack of choice or being on the wrong course can be a key feature as to why students disrupt sessions to which they are not really committed. This is true. But there are many other possible explanations. It could be the student's discomfort at being in the wrong intellectual/vocational environment for their personal needs; psychological phobias, fears and aggressions; social reasons of students not being integrated; economic deprivation or as we see later the entitlement of wealth; emotional: feelings of being excluded and/or biological factors, for example, ADHD or Pathological Demand Avoidance syndrome, where students could scream if asked to do something. It is a vastly complex area, possibly edging into sociological constructions of deviance. But does categorising students help? In each learning context, the explanations could be different.

Student disruption could be merely a continuation of behaviour that has been previously taking place in the school sector. There are now many more complex tensions concerned with multi-ethnic environments, young people without the prospect of meaningful work, psychological problems, older students mandated to come to colleges and deep resentments to be expressed when individuals encounter representatives of the state via education. A further explanation might be that the regimentation and discipline of schooling systems have been unshackled in a less authoritarian regime, and therefore, students feel they have a licence to do as they wish in this new 'adult' environment.

For more direct practical advice on how teachers might react to challenging students in this sector, it would be good to look at Wallace (2017) and Vizard (2012). However, as we progress through this book we see many instances of the tensions or contrasts between what is said by theorists and the actual realities of what happens in lessons. In the next chapter we begin to explore what happened when individual teachers entered their classrooms. But was there a theory that could predict, encapsulate or even advise teachers on what to do if this situation went radically wrong?

Some Suggested Strategies

1. Prepare sessions thoroughly, offering differentiated relevant and meaningful tasks for individual levels within the group.
2. Engage in dialogue and questioning students about what is important to them. This humanises the learning situation.
3. Co-operate with students, involving them in collaborative or negotiated decisions as to the management of classroom processes.
4. Develop social understanding of what is happening in classrooms and offer a series of ploys for interacting with what students say and do. This can be as simple as asking students what they are doing and why.
5. Treat all students as adult learners who are self-directed, curious and want to develop themselves and an understanding of the skills and knowledge of 'the world.'
6. In case of extreme violence, teachers can use reasonable force to block or restrict the movement of violent students, without inflicting damage or possible perceived indecency.

BIBLIOGRAPHY

Ball, S. (2003). The teacher's soul and the terrors of performativity. *Journal of Education Policy, 18*(2), 215–228.

Bennett, T. (2015). New behaviour tsar Tom Bennett's top ten tips for maintaining classroom discipline. *TES*. https://www.tes.com/news/school-news/breaking-views/new-behaviour-tsar-tom-bennetts-top-ten-tips-maintaining-classroom

Brophy, J. (2010). *Motivating students to learn* (2nd ed.). New York: Routledge.

Clarke, D., & Murray, A. (1996). *Developing and implementing a whole-school behaviour policy*. London: David Fulton Publishers.

Coffield, F., Moseley, D., Hall, E., & Ecclestone, K. (2004). *Learning styles and pedagogy in post-16 learning: A systematic and critical review*. London: Learning & Skills Research Centre.

Cowley, S. (2007). *Guerilla guide to teaching*. London: Continuum.

Cowley, S. (2014). *Getting the buggers to behave* (5th ed.). London: Bloomsbury Education.

Dreyfus, H., Dreyfus, S., & Athanasiou, T. (1986). *Mind over machine: The power of human intuition and expertise in the era of the computer*. New York: Free Press.

Dweck, C. (2000). *Self-theories: Their role in motivation, personality and development*. Philadelphia: Taylor & Francis.

Foucault, M. (1991). *Discipline and punish*. Harmondsworth: Penguin.

Gardner, H. (2011). *Frames of mind: The theory of multiple intelligences*. New York: Basic Books.

Gibbs, J. (2001). *A new way of learning and being together*. Windsor: Centresource Systems.

Glasser, W. (1986). *Control theory in the classroom*. New York: Perennial Library.

Gravells, A., & Simpson, S. (2014). *The certificate in education and training*. London: Sage.

Gregson, M., Nixon, L., Pollard, A., & Spedding, P. (Eds.). (2015). *Readings for reflective teaching*. London: Bloomsbury.

Jones, F., Jones, P., & Jones, J. (2007). *Tools for teaching: discipline, instruction, motivation*. Santa Cruz: F.H. Jones & Associates.

Knowles, M. (1975). *Self-directed learning. A guide for learners and teachers*. Cambridge/Englewood Cliffs: Prentice Hall.

Kohn, A. (1993). *Punished by rewards*. Boston/New York: Houghton Mifflin.

Kohn, A. (2006). *Beyond discipline: From compliance to community* (2nd ed.). Alexandria: ASCD Books.

Kounin, J. (1997). *Discipline and group management in classrooms*. New York: Holt, Rhinehart and Winston.

Maslow, A. (1987). *Motivation and personality*. New York: Harper and Row.

Massey, A. (2011). *Best behaviour school discipline, intervention and exclusion*. London: Policy Exchange.

Mendler, A., & Curwin, R. (2008). *Discipline with dignity.* Virginia: ASCD.

Mitchell, C., Pride, D., Howard, L., & Pride, B. (1998). *Ain't misbehavin'. Managing disruptive behavior.* London: Further Education Development Agency.

Mitra, S. (2010). The hole in the wall. http://www.ted.com/talks/sugata_mitra_the_child_driven_education.html

Parry, D., & Taubman, D. (2013). *UCU whole college behaviour management: Finalreport.* https://www.ucu.org.uk/media/5693/UCU-whole-college-behaviour-policy-project-report/pdf/UCU_Whole_College_Behaviour_Management_Final_Report_June_2013.pdf

Petty, G. (2014). *Teaching today: A practical guide* (5th ed.). London: Oxford.

Powell, S., & Tod, J. (2004). A systematic review of how theories explain learning behaviour in school contexts. In *Research evidence in education library.* London: EPPI-Centre, Social Science Research Unit.

Reece, I., & Walker, S. (2003). *Teaching, training and learning: A practical guide incorporating FENTO standards* (5th ed.). Sunderland: Business Education Publishers.

UCU. (2013). *Classroom management: UCU continuing professional development.* http://cpd.web.ucu.org.uk/files/2013/07/CPD-factsheet-6.pdf

Vizard, D. (2012). *How to manage behaviour in further education.* London: Sage.

Wallace, S. (2002). *Managing behaviour and motivating students in further education.* Exeter: Learning Matters.

Wallace, S. (2007). *Managing behaviour in the lifelong learning sector.* Exeter: Learning Matters.

Wallace, S. (2013a). *Doing research in further education and training.* London: Learning Matters.

Wallace, S. (2013b). *Managing behaviour in further and adult education.* Exeter: Learning Matters.

Wallace, S. (2017). *Behaviour management: Getting it right in a week.* St. Albans: Critical Publishing.

Wong, H. (2009). *The first day of school: How to be an effective teacher.* Mountain View: Harry Wong.

CHAPTER 3

Entering the Classroom

THOSE OPENING MOMENTS...

This chapter explores the initial problems of entering a classroom and a succession of strategies that teachers have used for dealing with these opening moments, particularly when students were not 'learning ready' or immediately resisted the teacher's wishes. There is an analysis of four case studies on teachers entering classrooms and facing extreme and unnerving problems of class management. This is really a key moment of teaching.

How might the teacher operate in this situation? Is the process of opening the classroom door the same as opening a door in a work, domestic, social or other situation? What strategies have trainees and teachers used in the past? What do theorists recommend and what happens/ed when these ideas were put into practice?

Typically, it is recommended that teachers might set ground rules in their first session, set tasks immediately on arrival, explain the relevance of the tasks, make connections with individuals and develop the inexplicable quality in themselves called 'presence' as a way of creating an 'aura' of being an authority, in charge, a facilitator or manager of learning (Rogers 2015). Having interviewed over 40 trainees about that moment of entry into the classroom, most describe feelings of fear and the rise of adrenalin. Psychological or emotional preparation seemed to involve some tutors steadying their nerves before this key moment. Some practised at home; carrying out body language gestures in front of a mirror was important (Cuddy 2012). Visualising oneself in the classroom the

© The Author(s) 2017   49
M. Lebor, *Classroom Behaviour Management in the Post-School Sector*, DOI 10.1007/978-3-319-57051-8_3

day before can create a sense of psychological preparation rather like training for a sports' event. This might work for some. Self-talk is crucial; learning to project is a significant skill (Goyder 2012). There was a feeling of excitement and anticipation, a wish to meet and be engaged with students. Others viewed it in a less emotional way as the functional activity of entering a space in order to 'deliver' skills or knowledge. This can be a question of individual temperament, context, experience, culture and attitude.

Writers recommend that the teacher arrives before the students and controls the space, sets up resources, arranges the desks or chairs as best suits the nature of the session and/or welcomes the students at the door into the classroom as if the class is their home environment into which students are being invited (Rogers 2015). The classroom should be tidy. There should be no litter on the floor. However, often teachers have to enter rooms where the previous teacher is either still at work or the students have been left in the classroom until their next tutor arrives. In other words the teacher can be seen as an alien figure, trying to make an impression, begin the learning process and forge relationships with a group that is already in place. The class can have their own culture from which the teacher might be made to feel excluded.

In this chapter I observe and interview teachers on how they create this teacher/student relationship in the opening of a session, but also reflecting on my own experience. I explore the openings of different sessions, analysing what happened, what was successful and worked, but also what failed. Why did it fail? How could trainees or tutors have improved that relationship with their students?

Trainee teachers' understanding of how to enter the classroom might well be conditioned by their own educational history, but also the behaviour of more experienced teachers whom they have shadowed or observed within the institutions where they work. The tone adopted at the beginning of the session marks the point by which the rest of the lesson can be characterised. What do we say after our initial words? Is it best to start with aims and objectives or can this in itself be alienating? Is it better just to write a numbered list of activities, which students can mentally tick off as each item is accomplished? Preparing teachers for the challenges of how to face the opening moments of a classroom, their fears and hopes is critical to understanding a range of inter-reactions within the learning process.

THE THREAT TO SURVIVAL

Initially, I discuss my work mentoring two trainee teachers, looking at the options available to them on entering classrooms where students displayed disruptive behaviour. In both cases trainee teachers involved in Cert Ed classes wanted to discuss this issue more than any other topic related to teaching and learning, because they said this was the most worrying and threatening to their survival as teachers (Rushton 2010), but also it was the most significant aspect, they said, that affected their self-esteem, identity, confidence and class interaction in delivering the curriculum.

Both trainee teachers were faced with situations where they had limited control over their students' behaviour, particularly in the first few minutes when they entered the classroom, but the issue was also how that behaviour impacted on later aspects of the lesson. The context of these two sessions took place during my work as a mentor for two trainees at a college anonymised as the Duncimore Institute. The wider context is that Ofsted show little tolerance for disruptive behaviour during an observation and lessons where disruption occurs are considered 'inadequate.' In their *Framework* Ofsted say that colleges are evaluated partially on the 'low level disruption' that takes place. They suggest that trainees need to 'develop strategies to promote and manage good behaviour successfully and tackle bullying, including cyber and prejudice-based bullying' (Ofsted, ITE 2015, p. 38). They determine that 'outstanding training in behaviour equips trainees with the knowledge, understanding and skills to promote and manage behaviour effectively and create an excellent climate for learning' (p. 40).

But how can negative behaviour be stopped, if it is there immediately on the teacher's arrival? Is the teacher responsible for what happens, if they have never been in that classroom before by themselves? What sorts of behaviours at this moment are or are not acceptable? What happens if students are simply not 'ready for learning'? How is it possible to make that transition of a class, from behaviour which is not conducive to learning to a systematic engagement with a learning culture? If the disruptive behaviour is merely chatting or a lack of engagement in the subject, this is very different to jeering, shouting or violence directed towards the teacher or other students (Parry and Taubman 2013).

There is a wide spectrum of disruptive behaviour, spanning from challenging questions to challenging the very nature of being in college (Mitchell et al. 1998). When disruption happens in a dramatic way, there are differences of context and culture which impact on the whole learning situation. However, the teacher must somehow overcome their own feelings. The teacher has been acculturated into education. He or she believes in education, otherwise they would not have been able to become a teacher and yet in these situations their very existential being can feel under attack. It can feel quite traumatic. The problem is that there is sometimes such a vast difference between the culture of the teacher and students in terms of ethnicity, class and educational background, that teacher and students can feel quite alienated from each other.

In these case studies, the first set of disruptive activities were arguably directed against the teacher. The second was accumulated, problematic behaviour, provoking constant low-level interference with the progress of the session. A third follows the narrative of a deeply problematic class. The fourth is an unambiguous success story.

It could be argued that trainee teachers should not be placed in settings where disruptive behaviour is widespread, but this would merely protect trainees from the realities of normative teaching (Milne 2010). Often trainee tutors, where in-service, are already in post or put into placements on pre-service courses, covering their required hours per week when they sign on for their Cert Ed. or PGCE. As part of the requirements to be assessed as competent of the teacher qualification, trainees have to teach a number of hours each term. Teaching practice placements are a key element of gaining professional teaching qualifications and status. Occasionally placements are changed because student behaviour is so problematic that the training cannot be sustained. Usually many classes do have elements of behaviour not 'conducive to learning' operating either beneath the surface or as a direct confrontation. Therefore opening discussions of strategies for dealing with these issues, especially regarding that key moment of entering the class seems critical.

CASES STUDIED

As mentor to over a dozen staff that particular year, my role was to observe teachers throughout college and assign grades to their performance. In my teachers' training role, I had to support trainee tutors who were on teachers' training placements from a local university. When observing their lessons at that time, I was responsible for saying whether trainees had passed their observation and attach a grade to different aspects of their performance.

SCENARIO 1: A MOTOR VEHICLE CLASS

I observed Mac's Communication session with a second year motor vehicle group. He opened the classroom door and all 15 desks and chairs were immediately thrown to the floor by students with a dramatic, crashing sound. It was a shock. The majority male and two female students had apparently planned this as an act of defiance. It was supposed to cause maximum drama and subversion. It was disruptive behaviour in that it was a defiant rejection of learning. But how should Mac react? He could have walked out, informed the course tutor and brought him in to regain control, or even refused to teach the class. Mac decided to stay in the classroom. The main vocational teacher might have had some sympathy with the students and been negative about Communication Skills. Mac looked in a state of shock; he stared at me, but I didn't respond. I moved to the back of the class, picked up a chair and settled down to write my observation report as was required. In the last chapter of this book, I suggest a different role for observers in these situations.

Mac didn't have a loud voice, so could not shout. He moved round the classroom with dignity, asking each student to pick up their chair, desk and work. He had regained his equanimity. He spoke in a firm voice and students responded. Slowly each student picked up their chair as requested. He began writing the session's undifferentiated objective on the board, namely that:

1. All students should be able to write a customer report on a selection of repairs made to a range of cars.

There was a handout with different car names, their faults and what had to be done to put the fault right. He gave hand-outs to the students, but the students were not yet settled. They were still making challenging comments. 'Had a crash then have we, sir?' The word 'sir' was notable. In the aftermath of such an extreme rejection of learning, this was good-natured bantering. Mac didn't answer. He could have remained silent until he had the complete attention of the class (Vizard 2007, p. 19). Instead he gave instructions, but there was still resistance. Mac made the decision to go down the non-adversarial approach as advised by Jones (2007). He moved around the classroom, asking each student about how they felt. Why were they so angry? What had gone wrong?

Mac now saw not reacting to the dramatic opening as the best policy. Tapping into students' feelings (Goleman 1999) made students feel important, understood and validated. This was a humanising dialogue. Mac rejected the authoritarian option. Striding around the class or clapping for attention as recommended by Petty (2014) was not his style. The students said they had been working hard all day; staff had shouted at them. They felt humiliated. This was revenge for other teachers' previous sessions. Anyway, they were there to work on cars, 'not write things', that's what they'd done at school. It was now 4.30; the fact that Communication Skills had been timetabled so late showed the subject wasn't respected. Students had turned on Mac because he was the weak link; he was, after all, 'only' a trainee teacher. But Mac asked; didn't they need communication skills to deal with customers who turned up at their garage? Wouldn't students have to fill report sheets? Hadn't they done this on placements? The lesson was beginning to sound relevant.

Slowly Mac was retrieving control. Reluctantly, the class began filling sheets and discussed cars they had worked on either in college or at work. There was now a buzz in the room and students were active getting through the forms. There were differences of ethnicity, religion and race, but these did not seem to matter in the new atmosphere. Mac corrected spellings and helped with expression. Enthusiasm grew. The students were now on task. After 40 minutes they had completed what was required. In the last five minutes Mac consolidated the session by asking 'What have you learnt?' The answers came back 'how to fill in reports,' 'they don't tell us that at placement.' 'What other lesson have you learnt?' asked Mac. The students seemed embarrassed. Eventually, the response came back as 'professionalism.' They couldn't just let out their frustration on whomever they liked. There were standards of behaviour. Just as in the garage they had to fit in with work culture, so in college the same was expected.

Scenario 2: CVs or Not CVs, That Is the Question?

The second situation also occurred at the beginning of a session, but here Ham was supposed to teach *Curriculum Vitae* (CVs) to a level 1 Foundation Studies group. I was the mentor observer. Ham opened the door and we were greeted with a scenario where students were all socialising or on their mobiles. The ambience was a mixture of boredom, antagonism and what could be described as an un-co-operative atmosphere. Should Ham remain silent until there was some order as Vizard advised (2007)? Should he shout? Make a second entry? How should he draw attention to the fact that he was in the room and the lesson had started? He tried Petty's three claps (Petty 2014). Someone mimicked him, but he was essentially ignored.

I sat at the back. Ham turned on his presentation. This was a more technologically engaged/professional lesson. There were aims and objectives on the screen. He had a session plan, scheme of work, profiles of all the students in the class as required and up-to-date resources all in place (Dixon et al. 2010). Everything he had been told to do during his training course was well prepared. The topic was CVs. He gave instructions. But the class just weren't listening. There was no relationship.

'Today, we are looking at CVs.' The letters CV were flashed across class consciousness via the presentation, but the class were not interested.
'What are CVs?' said one student, at least aware that this was the topic.
'*Curriculum Vitae*, it's the Latin for the history of your life!' Ham answered.
'Why do we have to learn Latin?'
'You don't!'
'You don't want to know the history of my life, mate!' yelled another student.
'Why not?' Ham asked, still clicking through the slides.
'Borstal mate!! Time inside!'
'CVs are boring!' said another 'We've done loads at school. We're sick of them and we're not doing them!! Do you get it?'

A small minority of students were now engaged with the teacher, but there was mostly indifference. This time it was not a physical reaction to the teacher's presence, but more obstructing the session's progress. It could be argued that some of the students' comments were exploratory or even helpful, questioning the task, the old-fashioned language, personalising the task to themselves and exposing the fact this had been taught many times before. The students' criticality and resistance could be seen as positive engagement or a questioning, challenging dialogue that might lead to deeper understanding of the socialisation process of getting employment. However, the major problem was that the majority of students were just not interested in what the teacher was saying.

Ham showed he was upset… 'Listen!' he screamed. But they didn't. He started walking round the class giving out handouts. 'What's this?' said a student, disturbed from his social life. 'It's work,' answered Ham. 'We can't do work!' 'Why not?' asked Ham 'It's not cool!' 'Is it cool to be powerless?' No–one replied to this challenge. 'We just don't understand this!' someone moaned. Ham had simplified versions of a CV with a basic task that he'd assumed everyone in the class could do. Paradoxically, the work had been done previously, was 'boring', 'not cool,' but was also apparently too challenging.

> 'Can't you just fill out this form?' Ham asked. 'Please!'
> 'Yeah, man! Just stop hassling us, can't you!'

Again, slowly students started to engage with the teacher. In a reluctant, un-co-operative way students began to fill in the form with their names and addresses. They then progressed to the next task which was looking at model CVs which students were asked to criticise. The students began constructing their own versions. Some students reverted to their conversations or phones; others carried out the set tasks. When the hour was finished, a student said, 'Good that's over, I can get on with my life,' as if 'life' and education were entirely separate. It was ironic that they had been studying *curricula vitae.*

Ham switched off his presentation, collected student papers, said 'thank you' and left the room. Sadly, no one acknowledged he had gone. It was almost as if the lesson had not taken place. If learning was defined as a transformative experience or involving inner change, then it was as if nothing had even ruffled these students' consciousnesses. Ham's lesson did not involve quite as dramatic a rejection as the first scenario, but nevertheless it was problematic in that the students showed little reaction to the tasks. Forms had been filled, but depending on the definition of learning, it was not clear whether any had taken place in this lesson.

He Needed a Vacation More than a Vocation

Both sessions contained substantial disruptions to learning. Both were problematic in that the planned learning had been subverted. The question for teachers is what advice could be given on how to deal with these challenging situations? Both classes could be said to suffer from what Willis (1977) identified as 'working class' young people taking on a counter-culture in opposition to the values, curriculum and attitudes of what were both self-identified as middle-class teachers. The students' subversive joking would, according to Willis, continue into the workplace. However, both classes consisted of male and female students from a range of social and ethnic backgrounds, so there was no simple co-relation between specific groups and disruption. Some of the auto-mechanic students' parents were garage owners; the foundation students' parents owned shops or properties. In each class nearly 50% were black and minority ethnic (BME) students. There was a culture clash between students and teacher, but not necessarily based on class, ethnicity or socio-economic identities. Nevertheless, Mac was able to help students realise that there was some relevance in doing communication skills. Ham didn't really manage to break through into a relationship with his students on this occasion.

In the *post-mortem* Mac said he wanted to walk out and refuse to teach this group. The 'crash' of furniture was so traumatic, such a deep attack on his whole psyche that he felt like giving up teaching, but then he realised that trying to communicate with these students was actually what he was committed to as a career. However, as a trainee teacher, he was in an awkward situation in that if he admitted to failure, he might not be allowed to replace this group with another on his timetable. This would compromise the number of hours he would accumulate in order to fulfil required teaching time as a trainee. It would be a sign of failure. He would also be admitting his own vulnerability and lack of control over students. Would this show he couldn't stand up for himself, couldn't be trusted or wasn't fit to be a teacher? The questions might creep in as to whether he was suitable for the job. Should he pass (Lambert-Heggs 2011)? Would he be employed by the college if he refused to engage with certain classes? How would this incident be interpreted?

Mac realised that he had to demonstrate to the students why the lesson was relevant for their placements and future careers. This seemed to be key to progress in this situation. By contrast, the problem seemed to be that Ham hadn't made the case that CVs were important for these learners. There can be a feeling on vocational courses that students are being prepared for careers in subjects where there is little possibility of work (Simmons and Thompson 2011). This can engender a deep sense of cynicism, undermining their reason for being there. It is also problematic that students have been schooled for many years already, the purpose of which other than getting a job is not always clear to the students themselves. What is the point of learning about CVs, if there are no jobs or the jobs available might not even need CVs? Why are they in college?

Explaining the relationship between teacher and students in terms of the increasing commodification of education or analysing the economics that underpin the power structure between managers, teachers and students could help to understand the context of this relationship (Simmons 2009; Avis 2009). But the trainee teacher needs help with the practicalities of gaining control, setting boundaries, ground rules or creating locally negotiated learning space for their students (Kyriacou 1998). It could be said that writing CVs are a vital part of the employability curriculum, but if so, how could Ham have started the session in a more effective way?

In his practical guide Petty does discuss 'Creating a working atmosphere in the classroom' (Petty 2014, p. 102). He suggests setting up the classroom before students arrive; Vizard advises arranging classroom geography beforehand into a horse-shoe, (2007) more geared towards facilitating adult discussion than the serried lines of 'pedagogic' class control. However, the assumption again is that the teacher can be in the room before the students. Both trainee teachers arrived in classes that were already in position. Petty advises getting silence in the first five minutes of the session by giving instructions (2014, pp. 104–105). Ham gave instructions for students to work, but they didn't. As Willis says, instructions are the voice and ideology of the institution; humour and subversion are the counter-culture of resistance (1977). So how could Ham have engaged with this class? Petty suggests.

> Get silence first and make sure the class are all looking at you. Some teachers especially those who must compete with noise from machines, have a routine way of attracting attention, such as clapping three times. Be brief clear and positive. (ibid., p. 105)

Ham tried clapping, but it didn't work. The students merely clapped back at him.

Marzano suggests setting down rules and clear procedures early in the session.

> Before addressing specific rules and procedures with students, it is useful to have a discussion regarding the fact that many situations in real life involve rules and procedures. (2003, p. 26)

These are general truths in teacher education, backed, for example, by Hannah who discusses: 'establishing explicit rules and routines, providing students with clear choices regarding their behaviour and starting each day with a clean sheet' (2012).

Setting ground rules are often a key element in the opening discourse of teacher education. Neither trainee did this. However, these tactics assume that there is at least an initial dialogue between tutor and students or that this has happened previously. Wong counters an authoritarian, disciplinary model with a managerial style where negotiation with students is central to the class dynamic (2009). Mac followed this route, negotiating directly with students, humanising them, seeing it from their point of view. The challenge to his 'authority' was more extreme, but his ability to regroup and create connection with individuals seemed more effective. Theories of classroom management suggest making 'a strong first impression' through posture, power and greeting position (Vizard 2007, pp. 18–19). Again, the classic text Petty's *Teaching Today* advises trainees to:

> Stride about the room as if you are absolutely confident of your ability to control the group. Appear to be self-confident, relaxed and in control – especially when you are not. This is particularly important in your first few lessons or when you are coping with difficulty. (Petty 2014, p. 98)

There have been many lists of strategies; thus, in *The Guardian* it was suggested that teachers remembered to smile:

> '... and greet your classes, even the groups you dread.' (Hannah 2012)

Ham's smile was more like a grimace.

Kounin offers a preventative approach, setting up positive expectations in the culture of lessons (1977). No matter how positive Mac's approach, it would be difficult to understand how he could have prevented the furniture crashing. Brophy suggests strategies to make learning meaningful, supplying extrinsic and intrinsic motivation (2010). This was a potential direction Ham could have taken, asking about jobs students wanted or maybe questioning the students on why they thought they were in college. However, questions can be counter-productive, forcing the student into silence. Questions about jobs can become loaded where none exist or where students feel out of their depth in the world of work. Another approach might have focussed on activities students enjoyed, an audit of their skills, what they had done in the past and where they saw themselves in the future. Students might have given subversive, humorous or pessimistic responses, but at least there would be dialogue, connection and hopefully a cognitive engagement in the trajectory of their lives.

Ham might have tried to harness the technology that the students were using anyway and make use of Mitra's self-organising system, the 'hole in the wall' (2010) experiment. Mitra offers computer-based, self-directed learning to children in a New Delhi 'slum', setting up a self-motivating system that offers learning without pressures and conflicts with teachers. The children are poor, curious and become enthusiastic learners. Mitra demonstrates that interest in learning is not related to poverty. However, his perspective assumes that there are computers in every classroom. This was not the case in either context. As with much literature on motivation and class management, Mitra's approach is geared towards younger pupils. Engaging disaffected adolescents and countering their culture of negativity might involve a different narrative. If Ham had asked the students to look up CVs on their phones, there might have been a mixed response from teaching theorists and authorities who could view cell-phones as a distraction from class-work. But would this instruction have given the students licence to go on social media?

I Need You…

I observed another class in the same college where the students had not carried out their homework. The tutor asked all 18 students to get out their phones to research various companies. All 18 students from a range of different ethnic and economic backgrounds immediately took out their phones as a research tool. No matter how poor, in UK classrooms, the vast majority of students seem to all have cell phones.

The benefit of technology, as always, depends on how it is used.

Dreikurs (2005) believed that teachers should move towards democratisation, classroom discussion or student-centred approaches that shift power away from a teacher-led stance of a conformist, authoritarian class-ridden society. The problem is what happens when this authoritarianism breaks down and is replaced by other less mediated social structures. The assumption is that there is sufficient relationship between tutor and students for 'adult' learning to take place (Knowles 1975). It was difficult for Ham to occupy that mid ground between authority and friendliness. It posed an almost existential question about the teacher's beingness in the classroom. Dreikurs' perspective is that there are 'logical consequences' to 'misbehaviour.' This 'control' ideology has been rejected by Kohn (2006), whilst more self-directed or progressive approaches (Avis 1999) could or should emerge. However, if Ham had been 'progressive' and allowed the students more self-direction, then possibly no work would have been achieved at all. The hour might have been spent socialising, texting and phoning. His problem was that he couldn't exude authority. It just wasn't in his personality. He needed to develop more 'presence.' But how?

After the observations all these issues were discussed. What did the trainees want? Apart from military support they said they wanted an exploration of options, feelings and attitudes about these fraught situations. The more they heard about the range of responses available, the more they said this developed their sense of what was possible in different situations. These discussions were ways of developing trainees' emotional, psychological range of responses, but also their ability to act in appropriate ways. Both trainees had eventually managed to get their students to carry out set tasks. Ham was actually referred because his students did not seem to engage at all with tasks on that occasion and his students showed no involvement with the session, the learning or any interest in educational or vocational issues. Mac's solution of connecting with individuals, asking them about their feelings of rage and ultimately humanising them by taking their concerns seriously seemed to offer a powerful message. Teaching was concerned with listening to the reality of students' lives. This approach seemed to privilege human interrelations and personal discussion above content.

What strategies could both trainees use in the future? They might have set ground rules from their first session, set tasks immediately on arrival, explained the relevance of the tasks, made connections with individuals and developed some inexplicable quality in themselves called 'presence' or authority (Rogers 2015). Nevertheless, by having a discussion with Ham about these strategies and suggesting that he connect with students turned out to be crucial and helped his personal development. He was subsequently able to re-enter that classroom and successfully engage with the whole group, explaining why CVs might just be useful for their futures. He also got them to produce some excellent examples through using large-scale versions of CVs to which sections on employment and skills could be attached.

In accordance with Bill Rogers (2015), he started to say: 'I need you to take out your pens,' rather than 'you must..' or 'get out your pens' or 'please get out your pens.' He began to say 'thank you' after students had done something he had asked, instead of 'please' beforehand. This seemed to work.

So how do teachers overcome that initial challenge and develop 'presence'? Discussing concerns and feelings with mentors or tutors and reflecting on what happened and how it could be different if other behaviours are adopted seems critical. Teacher 'presence' in class might come through watching other classes, reflecting on what went well and what needed development, experimenting with other aspects of personality, maybe role-playing incidents, using acting techniques, discussing options available and self-reflection on what works, but also experience and confidence in carrying out the above. When Mac began to connect with his students, show interest in their lives, and explore their personal reactions, their attitudes changed and they became far more co-operative and motivated to engage in learning.

Scenario 3: Some Very Basic Skills

In this section I explore what happened to me personally in a particularly challenging literacy class, where strategies for controlling disruption only started to emerge over a period of several months. The problems stemmed from how the lessons started, but this self-reflective account looks at a deeply negative situation, which I faced, that lasted many sessions. The question was how is it best to deal with chronic classroom situations that are not easily resolved?

I was part of a support team in a class of over 20 'literacy skills' students. They were 17-year-old males without qualifications, failed throughout school, mostly anti-authoritarian, angry and dissolute and yet now attending a vocational training programme at a college. Although they were in a classroom and all came to every lesson in order to claim money, their behaviour was relentlessly obstructive to learning.

I was assigned to work as literacy support for two individuals. There was another support worker in the class and two lead teachers present. There was a high staff-student ratio, but in reality each individual in the class had so many psychological and social problems that each student needed individual counselling and support. The fact that more teachers witnessed the constant chaotic behaviour in class did not seem to make a difference as to how the class reacted. It should be said that the teachers informed line managers, vocational area managers, senior managers and security, but the presence of these managers made only a brief incision of stunned silence into the general negative behaviour in this class. The classroom was placed in an annexe on a corridor away from the rest of the college. The college itself, anonymised as Navarre, had over 8000 students, ranging from Basic Skills/ESOL to level 3 A level and BTEC students in business, ICT, Health and Social Care. These Foundation level students were supposed to be preparing to enter one of these three vocational areas.

As we entered this 'skills' classroom, the students immediately started pelting us with objects, such as pens, paper darts and board rubbers. It did not matter that we were all rated as very good teachers and had prepared ground rules and a systematic lesson plan with tasks and activities. We had been given written profiles of every student, their background, education, psychological problems and aspirations. This did not help.

This direct attack seemed to imply a complete rejection of education, teachers and our authority. Some chairs were kicked over. Uproarious laughter followed. We four tutors stood in shock. This was our first introduction to Foundation Studies N2. Immediately a physically large student jumped on the table, ran over a line of computers and punched another student for being 'teacher's pet.' The so-called 'pet' had not thrown anything or smashed his chair down. He had apparently been instructed to attack us, but had not mustered the courage, motivation or belief that he should be part of this onslaught. A fight broke out. Our lead teacher screamed for order. There was a lull in the proceedings. Learners were asked to fill in a work sheet about their personal details. They refused to do so and laughed. 'I'm not doing that, that's baby work!'

'We've done all that years ago!!' 'Borrring!' came back the chant. One student was already on his computer downloading ring-tones onto his phone 'This is skill work!' he claimed. Another was now rocking back and forward to music on his headphones, oblivious to the demands of the lead teacher. My two students were from Mozambique and now sat meekly or bewildered trying to fill in personal details obediently. They were treated as traitors by the class for not joining the attack. This was my first meeting with them and I asked them why they had come to the United Kingdom or, for that matter, this college. They said, 'We came for the education...' The irony of this statement deepened as a missile flew across the class and hit one of them on the head.

'I will have order!' screamed the lead teacher.
'No you won't!' yelled back the ring-tone fancier.
'We'll send you to the principal!'
'But if we're not here, you'll be out of a job!' chimed in another comedian.
More laughter ensued. We each tried to speak to individuals or small groups, but no one was interested.
'Why are you here?' I asked.

'Got to be, haven't I?'
'What do you want to be?'
'Nothing...'

As the time came to 4.30, our first session with N2 ended abruptly and all students made a charge for the door, knocking over furniture and leaving only the Mozambique duo in their wake, who were still quietly putting the final flourish to their personal details.

But now we four tutors had to work out our strategies for the next session. How could we counter the apathy, antagonism and complete lack of interest or engagement in anything resembling what we understood as learning. The curriculum was literacy skills. But how could we ever get these students to sit down, let alone write anything? The lead teacher said, 'We need to get them to set their own rules of behaviour.'

That sounded dangerous.

We decided that the next lesson was going to involve getting the students to work out ground rules on the board and we would then point to the chart every time they broke one of the rules they themselves had suggested. At least this was going to be the plan as suggested in the text books (Petty 2014; Gravells and Simpson 2014). Then we might ask what they wanted in terms of their careers and how they intended to achieve their goals. It was all classic strategy and just to make sure it went to plan, we were to report all incidents and individuals to college management. However, after speaking again to line managers, it became apparent that they were less than interested. Their view was that, if teachers made the sessions relevant and interesting, then the students would be engaged in what we were teaching. They also had a strong view that the student was a valuable asset that brought money into the institution, whilst we as staff ironically were told that we were a drain on the college resources. If we were not being entirely efficient in carrying out our teaching, it was viewed as a 'problem of our own making.'

In other words, we were on our own.

The following week when we entered the classroom, the students were, this time, indifferent. They acted as if we were not there. No drama, no confrontation, just no interaction. Lead teacher asked for rules.

1. Don't speak while others speak!
2. Listen to teacher!
3. Don't break...furniture, computers, other people's mobiles...

4. No throwing objects....!
5. No fighting or spitting!

The rules were pinned up, but the students still weren't listening. They were on the computers, doing research into games, gismos and girls. One asked me to join him on 'jihad.' 'You and me Mr. Lebor, we go to Afghanistan together!!' It seemed like an attractive offer to escape this group, but I declined. The Prevent agenda had not yet been invented. Then the syllabus kicked in. We had to measure all class members and write out their weights, heights and ages in a table of personal details. The aspirant Mujahedeen was over 20 stone and became heavier when one of his colleagues jumped on his back. But was all this happening in the name of education?

'Get off him!' screamed lead teacher. A fight broke out. There was running on the desks and kicking of computers. The rules were being broken.

'You are breaking the rules!' screamed teacher, but the situation had gone beyond rules. 'Call security!' But, in the name of austerity, security had been made redundant. Eventually, after the excitement, the class settled down to an atmosphere of indolent hostility.

'Stop bothering me...' was said by a student, but that attitude pervaded the room.

The following session I suggested we record the students speaking. This was perhaps an early version of the body camera. The students all seemed happy with this; they wanted the attention. I was going to interview them vox-pop style, ask them why they were on the course and what they wanted. I set up the equipment and started recording. This seemed to attract their attention as nothing previously had.

'We have better equipment at home!' was the comment.
'But why do you want to study?'
'So I can take over my dad's business?'
'What's that?'
'Drug mule...man.' Others mentioned garages, shops and a building business.

I turned the recorder to the Mozambique duo. Why had they come here? What did they want? Well, they had studied Latin in Mozambique and wanted to further their understanding of the English language here, so they could become teachers in their own country. But were they learning anything? They were trying their best, still working hard on their personal statements. 'We will try and finish this work, sir,' they explained respectfully.

Only Connect!!

I swivelled the recorder round the room to speak to the other teachers and support worker, but they were slumped against the wall, half-collapsed from exhaustion. I was taking the class by myself. I went around the class speaking to each individual student. My philosophy was E. M. Forster's watchword 'only connect.' In other words, find something as a teacher that you have in common with the students. There will be large areas of teachers' and students' lives that do not overlap, but the key skill is to find one element that overlaps with the student's world, whether it is experience, interests, geography or emotional or psychological attitudes. Showing some element of empathy or experiences in common can be critical for the teacher/learner relationship to take place. Although our cultures were totally different, some connection was made.

In the following session I took each individual student out of the class and played back the tape of what they had said during the previous lesson. Each student had to justify why they had screamed, wasted time, ripped up task-sheets, fought other students or broken equipment. They laughed when they listened to the tape.

I re-played it. 'This is boring!' they said. 'Well your behaviour isn't so interesting. What would your parents say if they heard all this?' They looked embarrassed. The implied threat kept them slightly on edge for a few weeks. Was this behaviourism? Was it a potential punishment? Hadn't I said parents were only relevant in the school context? However, this change in their attitude inspired us to start a new systematic, planned approach for countering disruptive behaviour in this class. We needed to change our whole outlook to this session. We realised that we had to stop seeing the students as a hostile enemy group and start trying out the connection philosophy with them. But how were we going to put this into practice?

We had meetings where we worked out rules for ourselves. Firstly, we would act as if we were not fazed by rude or aggressive behaviour. We would start to build relationships with students one-to-one as if each learner was acting in an adult way. Secondly, each of us would speak calmly and directly to the class; the other three would always support or back whatever had been said by each teacher.

We did some role-play outside the class, acting out scenes we had witnessed and taking on the roles of students, whilst enacting better outcomes. We tried to hold our bodies in a more relaxed, but commanding stance, like actors aligning the neck and head (Goyder 2012). Thirdly, we were going to try and connect with each learner in the class. Communication was going to be the key to success.

After this planning we entered the class with a new attitude. We acted as if we meant business (Jones 2007). Before we had been almost overwhelmed emotionally and psychologically by the class behaviour, but now we were turning the tables on the students not in terms of power, but from the point of view of connecting with them as a way of helping them become adults. We asked them about their time at school. What were their best and worst moments? What were their triumphs and challenges? What had they liked and disliked? What did they want from college, teachers, adult life? What were their dreams, hopes or preferred futures (Iveson et al. 2012)?

Two described how when they were first in school, they had hated being humiliated or shouted at. They hated the way adults were rude and hurtful to them. We began to talk to them about each personal situation. They hated being told to 'get off the desks and get on with the work!!! It was so boring.' It was like they were still children or being treated as animals. But weren't they acting as if they disrespected teachers and other students in the class now? They did not answer. So why did they act in such an extreme, negative way? It seemed it was a kind of revenge for how they had been treated previously. They discussed and then began to write about their experiences at school; what had gone well and badly. How they had overcome problems or difficulties in the past.

Our personal interest in them helped to open them up, trust us and began to produce some relevant written work. The flow of language that had started orally now also operated on paper. Yet some still acted up, walking round the room, talking and disrupting other students. 'Why are you bothering to do this, you know it's pointless….?'

This seemed a new direction where the students were starting to question the point of each learning experience. This actually raised some difficult existential questions about why they were studying. At one level this was possibly a ruse in order to avoid work, but at another level this could be understood as a deep question, going to the root of why education was needed. The problem for the teachers was engaging with these issues in such a way as to open the dialogue with students and help support their self-esteem. If the question was merely understood as asking about the need for education, this would ignore the emotional element. The conversation went as follows:

ME: Why do you think what we're doing is pointless?
Rom: It is pointless…we just don't want to do it.
ME: Do you only do things you want?
Rom: Mostly…
ME: What do you like doing?
Rom: Football, cars, girls….
ME: In that order?
Rom: Yes…this is not exciting.
ME: But in all those areas you need to know how to understand, speak, read and communicate…
Rom: And if I can't….
ME: It's a way of being successful doing that stuff…..

This was not a model, good or arguably 'best practice', but it was making a connection, starting the conversation with a student, even if this might lead to nothing, no work or no progress. Rom was probably trying to distract me as teacher from forcing him to get on with the task. However, the conversation began to open up the relationship between teacher and student.

In a reflection session, the teaching staff said that they wanted to start shouting at students because of their behaviour. The main teacher, Capulet, had feelings of disgust for the students. However, if we had started shouting at them, that would have ended up intensifying what they had already experienced in school. We were definitely acting more assertively, but also trying to treat them in a more adult and humane way; it was a question of attitude, trying to make individual connections. We then asked the 'Wanderer', Mont, what was going on for him? The students expressed their feelings or views and then settled. The questions operated as a kind of counselling.

Cap: What problem are you having with this work?
Mont: I hate this work…
Cap: Why do you hate this work?
Mont: It's boring.
Cap: What would you like to write about?

Mont: Kung fu.

Cap: Well, why don't you write about it then?

The point here was that this was a way of engaging the student and getting him to start the process of writing. The discourse on Kung fu could be re-directed towards the task of writing personal statements. Mont began to explain his interest. His enthusiasm for his subject could be transformed towards more formal writing as a statement in terms of possible career paths. At least this was the theory.

The question was how did our preparation change us? What was the secret of this new attitude? The students now did what we asked. They worked on their personal statements. Why did they want to do this now, but not before? It seemed that the combination of assertiveness, treating the students as adults and engaging with their personal concerns, hopes and ambitions started to make all the difference. The Humanist argument seemed to work.

At a simplistic level, they were respecting us because we were showing respect for them. It seemed to be the connection. We were making an effort to speak their language. We now spoke in a clear direct way to the students. If they didn't do what we said, we started questioning each individual. They sometimes preferred to work than carry out these personal interviews. Sometimes they did want to talk about themselves. We used typical differentiation processes of preparing material that functioned at various levels to engage everyone in the class.

There were also a range of techniques for confrontations and encouragement.

When Brad said, 'I'm not doing this!' we held ground.

We began to ask students what they found interesting and why. Instead of adopting the broken record technique of 'You will do it!' ad infinitum, or even 'I need you to do this' (which didn't work with these students), we delved into their personal reactions, how they responded in different situations at school and at home or at other times when they had been asked to do something and they did not want to do it.

Leon: What do you feel when teachers ask you to do tasks?

Brad: Humiliated. We didn't have to do this before!

Leon: But we are trying to help you become adults....

Brad: I don't want to be an adult!
Leon: Yes it's scary...but this is the first step....
 Frei: Why are we doing this?
 ME: Why do you think you are doing this?

At no stage in the class were there easy answers. We now tried to be as honest as possible. What benefit would this activity have for this particular student? Would it help them to get a job, fit in with working life or develop them socially with their family or in relationships? We tried to show in each instance how each piece of written or spoken work was relevant to the future world of work or adult life.

The key question was: 'What would be of benefit to the students when they moved out of Navarre College?' It dawned on some students that the answer might be a job or more training. In other words this was establishing the relevance of what they were doing, challenging their sense of self-righteous arrogance or possibly low self-esteem through which they dismissed the adult world because they could not cope with it. It also proved that they still had many lessons to learn.

We began to develop some pre-prepared statements for the students, such as:

1. 'My main skills are...' followed by a list of possibilities.
2. 'At school I was part of a group that achieved ...'

The problem here was that the skills or achievements they had managed either individually or as a group were extremely limited. Models of CVs were produced that could be adapted and individualised. Yet our control over the group was growing, more through personal discussions on what each individual aspired to rather than by any authoritarian hold or class management techniques as such. There was some realisation that the students needed us in order to move beyond college and develop themselves for adult life in the future.

Questions emerged about the realistic career choices students were offered (Wallace 2007). Once the control grew, we began to connect more with each individual. 'What are you really interested in doing Lea when you've left college?' 'If you had the chance of doing the job you really wanted, what would it be?' Answers were sometimes unrealistic, but students were finally engaged in discussions.

Would these methods have worked if we had started with these strategies? Possibly, but the relationship had grown out of initial failure and an inability to create a relationship between teacher and student. There were four of us and we were with a relatively small group, but in principle, the point was that we were all trying to connect with these young people and help them move into the adult world of work, making the link between their personal lives, what was happening in class and their future. The key was communication and this seemed to help start the move from adolescent rebellion and aggression towards being in social communication with others.

After interviewing the other tutors involved it was agreed that the strategies we had used included:

1. Not being fazed or reacting to insolent or disruptive behaviour.
2. We tried to speak calmly and directly to the class.
3. We felt that the effective teacher holds their body so that the students understand who was in charge.
4. There had to be an attempt to communicate or empathise with all students.

All tutors involved said that often the best way to cope with really difficult classes was to come in with a forceful attitude and set fairly mechanical work initially so that the students had a task which they had to carry out. It was said that the students had to be ordered in a firm but friendly way to carry out required tasks and once the students had begun to be engaged, the tutors could start to make relationships with individuals. However, all this had not worked in this context. The break-through with this class seemed to come when tutors asked students to write about their experiences of school; the questions were asked as ways of finding out what made each individual in the class operate in a positive way. Only then could the teacher respond to what students said in terms of what was appropriate for their level and understanding.

It was particularly problematic in this case study for support staff and/or students because there were few structures within Navarre College where this class took place to offer a framework for progress to be made. This was a desperate situation. Institutional indifference did not help.

Scenario 4: Some Good Practice in an ICT Class

By way of contrast I am now going to outline a class observed and teachers interviewed where a support framework was in place to ensure that difficult/disruptive students were able to use their time at college in a productive and creative way.

This class took place in the large, multi-site inner city Arden College, where there was special provision for disruptive students who attended a range of vocational courses in a specialist locked-in floor with a suite of highly digitalised, modern rooms that offered a range of different visual images on the wall for supporting progress, with sayings, such as 'Be the person you want to meet.' Or 'today's the beginning....'

I was let in to the locked corridor for a lesson observation, was shown to a modern, pleasant room that was equipped with computers, white boards and other electronic equipment. There were also 20 students present and the teacher, Ezra, was working alongside only one support worker, Cal. It was a GCSE ICT class. The student profiles in the teaching file showed that the students had been 'difficult' or 'disruptive' at school, had achieved very little in terms of previous qualifications, were generally 'noisy' and did not co-operate in sessions.

The trainee Ezra had a strong presence in class. He spoke clearly and projected his voice so that the group had no alternative but to listen to what was being said. He managed the group effectively from the beginning, greeting each individual as they entered the room. He had also prepared for the session in considerable detail, dealing with students who found it difficult to concentrate by starting with a series of questions, allowing each individual the opportunity to speak. He planned the session in terms of activities that kept the students engaged in tasks, such as working on a story board, breaking into two groups of ten to share information, firstly standing up to do this, saying 'listen up now!' and then allowing Cal to take the second group. Students did not have a moment to become bored or dissolute because they were moved quickly from one activity to the next, which helped to create this productive learning environment.

Once in their two groups, each student spoke, explaining their views in a more public forum on different versions of commercial adverts, justifying the choices they were going to make in designing a poster in terms of colours, content and style. They wrote down their thinking about their motivation for choosing different directions which they later expressed as arguments. Students felt confident enough to speak and then act on their decisions to create posters on their individual computers. Each section of the session was timed. A large digital clock was on the screen. Music enhanced the activities which allowed students to relax and concentrate on what was required. At the end of the session each student had to present the poster they had created to their group.

Why had this session worked so well, whilst the earlier case study where I was personally involved had only succeeded after much struggle and effort? The similarities between the two classes were that both had 20 students; both contained 'low level' students who had failed/been failed by school; both classes had been designated as highly disruptive. However, the second class took place within a highly supportive framework. This college environment was structured so that the students felt appreciated and understood. The students were going into an environment that felt safe, productive and purposeful from the beginning. Management had set up this section of the college so that the students felt comfortable that they were going into an area that was protected. The pleasant decor meant that the students felt valued. This was especially important where issues of low self-esteem predominated. By way of contrast the first class felt bleak and desolate. It was not surprising that at Navarre College it needed four members of staff to try to contain the restless energies of these students. The lack of direction and initial purpose of the class was not well managed.

In the end the difference was in the initial direction and energy of the teachers, instructing the class to carry out tasks in a highly organised way. However, one might have described the class leadership in the Arden class as somewhat macho, constructing teaching as command and obedience or conformity, whereas the earlier session offered a version of teaching as dialogue. Initially, the first session in Navarre had been, by any standards, a complete failure. Nevertheless, the relationship between teacher and student had eventually developed into a more interesting engagement. Students had slowly emerged from a process of constant under-achievement and blind rage into something approaching adult relationships.

Some Suggested Strategies

1. Prepare for confrontational classes in front of a mirror at home. Developing presence can be done by experimenting with words, facial gestures and stances. Teaching can, arguably, be seen as a form of acting.

2. Role play scenarios with other trainees or friends, taking on the role of both teacher and student, so as to become more flexible about how you can be in the classroom.

3. Begin classes by working out democratic ground rules. This can open a discussion of shared values and attitudes between teacher and student.

4. Act as if you are not fazed by rude or aggressive behaviour. Speak in a clear, calm way.

5. Asking students about their previous experiences of education and what they enjoy/ed doing validates their lives, shows engagement and interest, but also builds up knowledge of students and what happened to them in the past and how this can be transformed in the future.

6. Speak more as if you are having a conversation with the class. This tends to feel more personal. If you lecture **at** students, this can have an alientating effect.

7. Only connect. Find elements of the students' experience, family, geography, career aspirations, interests, that overlap with your own. This could be a source of connection and/or empathy.

BIBLIOGRAPHY

Avis, J. (1999). Shifting identity: New conditions and the transformation of practice–teaching within postcompulsory education. *Journal of Vocational Education and Training, 51*(2), 245–264.

Avis, J. (2009). Whither further education: Econimism, instrumentalism and Class. In J. Avis, R. Fisher, & R. Simmons (Eds.), *Issues in post-compulsory education and training: Critical perspectives* (pp. 371–378). Huddersfield: University of Huddersfield Press.

Brophy, J. (2010). *Motivating students to learn* (2nd ed.). New York: Routledge.

Cuddy, A. (2012). Your body language shapes who you are. *TED Global.* https://www.ted.com/talks/amy_cuddy_your_body_language_shapes_who_you_are

Dixon, L., Harvey, J., Thompson, R., & Williamson, S. (2010). Practical teaching. In J. Avis, R. Fisher, & R. Thompson (Eds.), *Teaching in lifelong learning: A guide to theory and practice.* Berkshire: OUP.

Dreikurs, R., Cassel, P., & Dreikurs, E. (2005). *Discipline without tears: How to reduce conflict and establish co-operation in the classroom.* Hoboken: Wiley.

Goleman, D. (1999). *Working with emotional intelligence.* London: Bloomsbury.

Goyder, C. (2012). How to voice projection. You Tube. https://www.youtube.com/watch?v=ynmemxQicQk

Gravells, A., & Simpson, S. (2014). *The certificate in education and training.* London: Sage.

Hannah, V. (2012). How to teach behaviour management. http://www.guardian.co.uk/education/2012/aug/27/pupil-behaviour-management-teaching-resources

ITE = Initial Teacher Education. https://www.gov.uk/government/publications/initial-teacher-education-inspection-handbook. Last updated: 9 Sept 2015.

Iveson, C., George, E., & Ratner, H. (2012). *Brief coaching: A solution focused approach.* East Sussex: Routledge.

Jones, F., Jones, P., & Jones, J. (2007). *Tools for teaching: discipline, instruction, motivation.* Santa Cruz: F.H. Jones & Associates.

Knowles, M. (1975). *Self-directed learning. A guide for learners and teachers.* Cambridge/Englewood Cliffs: Prentice Hall.

Kohn, A. (2006). *Beyond discipline: From compliance to community* (2nd ed.). Alexandria: ASCD Books.

Kounin, J. (1977). *Discipline and group management in classrooms.* New York: Holt, Rhinehart and Winston.

Kyriacou, C. (1998). *Essential teaching skills* (2nd ed.). Cheltenham: Stanley Thomas.

Lambert-Heggs, W. (2011). The 'F' word: Conflicts and tensions in a community of practice when mentors confront the possibility of failing a trainee in teaching observations. *Teaching in Lifelong Learning, 3*(1), 29–39.

Marzano, R. J., Marzano, S., & Pickering, D. J. (2003). *Classroom management that work: Research-based strategy for every teacher.* Alexandria: Association for Supervision and Curriculum Development.

Milne, F. (2010). Top tips for trainee teachers: Get work experience in more than one school. http://careers.guardian.co.uk/top-tips-for-trainee-teachers-get-work-experience-in-more-than-one-school

Mitchell, C., Pride, D., Howard, L., & Pride, B. (1998). *Ain't misbehavin'. Managing disruptive behavior.* London: Further Education Development Agency.

Mitra, S. (2010). The hole in the wall. http://www.ted.com/talks/sugata_mitra_the_child_driven_education.html

Parry, D., & Taubman, D. (2013). *UCU whole college behaviour management: Final report.* https://www.ucu.org.uk/media/5693/UCU-whole-college-behaviour-policy-project-report/pdf/UCU_Whole_College_Behaviour_Management_Final_Report_June_2013.pdf

Petty, G. (2014). *Teaching today: A practical guide* (5th ed.). London: Oxford.

Rogers, B. (2015). *Classroom behaviour* (2nd ed.). London: Sage.

Rushton, I. (2010). Managing Meat One: Perceptions and anxieties of trainee teachers as they enter the learning and skills sector for the first time. *Teaching in Lifelong Learning, 2*(1), 15–22.

Simmons, R. (2009). An overview of the lifelong learning sector and its 'condition. In J. Avis, R. Fisher, & R. Simmons (Eds.), *Issues in post-compulsory education and training: Critical perspectives.* Huddersfield: University of Huddersfield Press.

Simmons, R., & Thompson, R. (2011). *Education and training for young people at risk of becoming NEET: Findings from an ethnographic study of work-based learning programmes.* London: Routledge.

Vizard, D. (2007). *How to manage behaviour in further education.* London: Sage.

Wallace, S. (2007). *Managing behaviour in the lifelong learning sector.* Exeter: Learning Matters.

Willis, P. (1977). *Learning to labour; how working class kids get working class jobs.* Aldershot: Ashgate.

Wong, H. (2009). *The first day of school: How to be an effective teacher.* Mountain View: Harry Wong.

CHAPTER 4

What Do Experienced Tutors Advise?

Up to now this book has contrasted a range of theories with practice, but also different approaches within classroom settings. In this chapter I interview experienced teachers, asking them about the interventions they made when faced with difficult behaviours during their careers. What were some of the worst situations they faced and what strategies did they use in order to overcome these difficulties? This small-scale qualitative research inquiry investigates a sample of experienced teachers dealing with disruptive students in their classes. I wanted to listen to what they said about their experiences interfacing with negative student behaviour. I firstly discuss a research instrument for collecting data on experiences and classroom strategies.

It seemed important to hear from experienced practitioners rather than relying on what textbooks advised. I wanted to outline the findings that interviews and questionnaires elicited in terms of key negative incidents that these teachers had undergone and the strategies they had deployed to overcome the social and emotional challenges of disruptive student behaviour. I briefly summarise these tutors' perspectives on the support they felt they did or did not receive on these issues from their management. I conclude this chapter by questioning the problematics of this research, its meaning, validity and possible application in other contexts.

© The Author(s) 2017
M. Lebor, *Classroom Behaviour Management in the Post-School Sector*, DOI 10.1007/978-3-319-57051-8_4

THE DATA COLLECTION TOOL

In order to widen this research, I wanted to formulate a data collection tool which would gather qualitative research into how individual tutors identified examples of negative student behaviour in their careers, but also how they dealt with these situations and obtained support in facing sometimes traumatic events. Again I use a range of words to describe these situations, such as 'disruptive', 'challenging', 'aggressive', 'difficult' and 'negative' behaviours (Cf. Mitchell et al.). It could be argued that challenging behaviour should be encouraged in order to provoke questioning; possibly promoting creative, non-conformist attitudes, maybe challenging authority in a positive way. However, the classroom behaviour analysed in this chapter is more anti-social rather than either merely high-spirited or deeply questioning of the teacher's authority for any overriding ideological or intellectual agenda. The key characteristic of the disruptive behaviour described is that it is not conducive to learners' learning, and also creates an unpleasant atmosphere for all present in these classrooms. It should be said that no teacher referred specifically to students with mental health problems, ADHD, autism or having Specific Learning Needs amongst the data sampled, so the disruptive behaviour was characterised by the teachers as part of their 'normal' teaching groups where students refused to co-operate with the social norms of being in a classroom.

There is an assumption that learners wish to learn and that they will conform to required classroom behaviours (Beere 2012). The question that underlies this chapter is what happens when learners refuse to co-operate or simply do not collude with the contractual/managerial expectations model of teaching (Dreikurs et al. 2005). As a result of this concern, I again question what has been done in the past and what might tutors do in these adverse circumstances in the future (Paton 2012).

I developed a series of open questions in order to 'capture the specificity of a particular situation' (Cohen et al. 2011, p. 382). I wanted to know about the worst behaviours these experienced teachers had encountered in their careers. What sort of explanations did they attribute to 'difficult behaviour'? Did the teachers manage to stop the disruptive behaviour? What support was available from the organisation within which they worked? What advice would they give to tutors just beginning their careers? However, my main focus was the underlying questions of what students did in disrupted sessions and how teachers dealt with these problematic situations.

Firstly, I needed to identify a sample of teachers to respond to these questions and how I would approach them in order to achieve authenticity as to the veracity of their narratives, whilst staying within the limits of the British Educational Research Association (BERA)'s ethical boundaries. Could I have merely itemised a list of negative behaviours that tutors had encountered (Cf. Parry and Taubman 2013)? Could anything be learnt from exploring these circumstances through qualitative research? Would the tutors' strategies be helpful for application at a more generalised level of praxis? Had the entire sample of tutors selected experienced some form of disruptive behaviour in their classrooms during their careers? How 'bad' was it?

These were all problematic questions to answer.

This was small-scale research; the focus was qualitative, exploring attitudes, behaviours, 'states and processes' (Flick 2006, p. 109). I felt it was time to focus on this issue in short narrative-based localised contexts. The fact that this research focused on a small sample might have meant it did not achieve 'generalisability' (Cohen 2011, p. 242), but the opinions of experienced teachers could nevertheless be valuable as this would elicit a range of potential solutions, modelling how to deal with these situations in the future. It would open the discussion in terms of personal experiences, attitudes and feelings.

The sample was made up of 30 teachers, all working within the Education and Training sector whom I had spoken to on this topic and they wished to participate in this study. They all had worked in a variety of educational institutions and organisations. I was known to all respondents. My first question was how many years had the interviewee been in teaching. The majority had been teachers for over 10 years, and many for 20 or 30 years. For the purposes of this research, I discarded respondents who had worked as teachers for less than 10 years, because I wanted to focus on experienced teachers who could offer a wealth of helpful strategies to less experienced tutors just entering the profession. However, it could be said that because the time-scale of the respondents being involved in teaching was longer, more incidents of negative behaviour were likely to have occurred. I also did not make any distinction between different geographic or socio-economic backgrounds of teachers or their students. As the research progressed, I heard about disruptive student behaviour in classrooms that had taken place in Further Education colleges, training centres and PRUs.

In order to conform to ethical considerations, I anonymised all responses and asked all contributors to fill in a participation ethics form (Cohen et al. 2011, pp. 91–93). There were greater numbers of women (60%) than men, but also some representation of black or ethnic minorities (over 10%) and due to the 10-year experience criteria used, all respondents were aged over 30. It should be noted that whomever I asked was passionate about contributing to this discussion, primarily because they said they felt it was an aspect of teaching that was institutionally unacknowledged. Generally, they wanted to express their views on a topic which they felt had, for too long, been taboo in many staffrooms or not spoken about in any depth during Teacher Education sessions or training days. As mentioned earlier, few books seemed available to discuss these extreme situations in any depth outside the school context, and teachers wanted space to explore some of the narratives that had occurred during their careers.

'The Worst Behaviour'

I questioned what teachers considered to be 'disruptive behaviour' in their sessions and asked them to list some of the worst behaviour they had witnessed. These simple questions elicited an extraordinary and extensive list of aggressive behaviours. At the more palatable or normative end of the spectrum all 30 of these teachers spoke about students talking in class, verbal interruptions, refusal to co-operate, confrontational encounters, disrespectful remarks or attitudes, disruptive mobile phone activities, students walking round the room, persistent lateness or students not carrying out required tasks. Learners were reported to have sworn and walked out of the classroom. One student refused to remove his balaclava and reveal his face.

When asked about extreme behaviours, nearly all teachers had stories at the next stage of intensity, whereby students rejected the classroom norms of learning behaviours and started throwing objects such as, in one case, a stapler. One student threw their hat in the air whilst the tutor was being observed; another threw a cheesecake. They swore aggressively, were involved in shouting, tables were knocked over, some students verbally bullied others, whilst some carried out acts of violence and fighting in the classroom; sometimes this was boys, sometimes girls. Teachers had faced deeply confrontational situations. A tutor reported on 'absolute chaos' in one of his classes, where regaining order was impossible. Security was called. There was aggression against other students in some classrooms, but also on the way in or out of the classroom. One tutor was physically attacked as a student aimed to hit another student. Tutors spoke of 'gang cultures' where students threatened other students with weapons, both in and outside the class. One tutor described a set of class notes being set on fire; another tutor commented on a pen being burnt on a table in the classroom. A student threw a chair at a tutor and later stole and hid the tutor's car keys. In one PRU a student was kicked in the stomach. In another, one tutor was goaded with threats of violence, whilst another student filmed the results. In one large college, there was a constant feeling of violence in the public areas. One of the female tutors said there had been a constant stream of inappropriate/sexual remarks. A teenage pregnancy group had drunk alcohol before the lesson and defiantly spoke during sessions about having unprotected sex earlier and having similar intentions for the future. This was an explicit subversion of the class.

I had asked questions about how long these behaviours continued. Was it every lesson or large sections in the session? Were these events one-off experiences that were not repeated? In fact some of the above behaviours were frequent and had to be continually battled; others were single incidents. A multiplicity of complex reasons were offered as to why students acted in these ways, ranging from poverty, an anti-education culture and parents' break-ups to large groups, long-term unemployment, frustration, prison backgrounds or the natural ebullience of young people. For the purposes of this chapter, the focus is on strategies and responses which these tutors adopted as ways of countering these difficult scenarios.

Some Suggested Strategies

Some tutors admitted that they had failed to stop the disruptive behaviour. Other tutors felt at times quite ineffectual and just could not control the class behaviour in certain contexts. One tutor had to rely on prison guards; another contacted parents. In one case the tutor had to position himself purposefully between the learners to prevent physical damage.

Interviewees claimed that they had set up their classrooms so that situations did not further deteriorate. Prevention, though not always possible, was said to be 'the cure.' In other words, the best way was obviously to engage the class with tasks and keep order from the beginning. Thus, successful strategies mentioned were standard approaches, such as establishing ground rules either imposed or through negotiation, maintaining regulations and discussing issues with students outside the classroom. This was also phrased as 'one-to-one tutorials' without the class as an audience. Turning students into teachers, getting them to research information and present it from a position of power from the front of the class was said to be an effective method of students internalising information and skills by imparting what they had learnt to others. Other perspectives were: 'reinforcing mutual respect and empathy' and offering 'unconditional positive regard for all students' (Rogers 1961). Tutors suggested being persistent, establishing authenticity in relationships, but also through 'teaching the subject effectively' whatever that meant in practice. This translated into managing the classroom by always keeping the students occupied. Osmond stated:

> Start early at the first session, take control, be consistent, never threaten what you won't or can't accomplish and always follow-through with all sanctions and threats. Don't show weakness! Ground rules, consistency and respect are the key!!

Other tutors emphasised class rules, goals and rewards. Rachel argued that the key was relationships; building up connections with individuals, finding out about their lives, communicating the curriculum so that it was understood by students and supporting individual learners with their problems. Rebecca countered the challenge from disruptive students who had multiple social problems by:

> Getting the students to share how they felt about education, school and their difficulties, by spending time with them individually. In session one; get students to write an autobiographical piece about what their school or previous education experience was like, what helped or hindered their learning; how they felt about now being in college and hopes for the future. If they trust you, students tend to be more open about their experiences and you, as a teacher can gain a lot of insights into their problems and help them with resolving or at least being aware of what is happening to these individuals. This can help guide your approach in understanding and supporting individual students.

Another tutor, Emilia suggested that the use of learning outcomes, aims and objectives on the board was problematic as it gave the assumption that learning could take place if the outcomes were met by the teacher in the session. She said that this was counter-productive as seeing aims and objectives on the board at the beginning of the session was 'an alienating experience' for many of her students. The language of science where everything was measurable was having a negative effect on lower-level classes. She suggested that lessons should operate as chapters in a book. Learning could work better as a narrative. The problem with this approach was that it went against the philosophy and outlook of the college where she was working and, if observed, she might have been failed as not meeting learning objectives because in her class they did not exist.

Possibly a more broad-minded approach on this issue might prove successful in terms of student engagement.

Management Support

In this sample of 30 tutors, over half (17) said they had no support on these issues from managers within the institution where they worked. The attitude that emerged was that if teachers had prepared their classes effectively, the events mentioned above would not have happened. Others said that they had had varying amounts of support from managers, depending on the specific team and institutions where they worked. For example, managers offered help with the removal of disruptive individuals from classes, but also suggested the possibility of staff development and training. Colleagues, peers and friends were better positioned than managers to offer emotional support. In one institution, teachers processed all incidents of student disruption in staff meetings. This team approach was seen as very productive by all staff involved.

300 Years of Solitude

This research revealed that all teachers interviewed had encountered difficult and disruptive students at some point in their careers; the behaviour was more extreme in certain contexts, such as classes for ex-prisoners, PRUs and with those students who were not in employment. Was this atypical? If the sample was expanded to a national level, would it show that these problems were just as bad everywhere or was this behaviour only in certain colleges and contexts? Was this a DNA of what was happening in the post-school sector as a whole? Was the sample merely a sample? Did it only represent those particular teachers and students or if other variables had been introduced would less or more extreme behaviour be evidenced (Cohen et al. 2011, pp. 186–187)? What would have happened if tutors had been selected who worked in leafy suburbs, or if the study focussed only on teachers working with students at level 3 or above? Or say I'd interviewed members of the Bullingdon Club at Oxford? Would they report on their A level years as ones they had spent in monkish, silent study?

The sample was random in the sense that I had no idea beforehand what the teaching experience or specific contexts were of these tutors? In fact, all teachers in the sample worked in urban environments; a variety of city colleges or training units. The limitations of this research might be perceived that it focussed on the negative side of teaching. Thirty teachers is a small sample, but their accumulated experience of at least 10 years each represented a minimum of 300 years potential teaching time under question. This meant that there were likely to be more examples of disruptive incidents during this lengthy time-scale. The questions focussed on the negative sides of these teachers' careers and therefore emphasised what went wrong rather than what went well during this period. It should also be said that all the teachers were still working in the sector at this point despite the negative events in their careers which they recounted. However, the data could also be interpreted that for most teachers in this sample these stories represented one or two dramatic events that were particularly memorable during a lifetime career. In some cases where tutors were working in more challenging environments, the time-scale of disruptive behaviours was relentless and formed a normative part of their everyday experience.

There was also the possibility that only teachers with very negative experiences would want to articulate their narratives of difficult classes as some kind of self-validation, justification or therapy for coming to terms with fraught situations. My questions allowed some anonymised relief, occasional humour or acknowledgement of the difficult and challenging times that teachers faced. When I asked teachers to contribute to this research, I had little idea of the specific disruptive situations that they had faced during their careers. The 10-year teaching criteria increased the possibility that all participants had had negative experiences.

VALIDITY QUESTIONED

This turned out to be the case. Everyone in the sample had experienced some element of disruption in their classes, and most had had to deal with situations which were disturbing and confrontational at some point in their career. The time element of how many hours, weeks or years this had continued depended on their context. Was this element of the research valid? Was I asking questions to which I already knew the answers? The fact that the participants knew me meant that there was trust. The participants came from at least 15 different colleges or training units. If I had gone into a college where I was unknown and asked these questions anonymously, there may well have been suspicion as to what was going to happen with the results. On having the opportunity to speak on this subject to teachers at a college where I was unknown, I was told that lecturers had to log all incidents of disruptive behaviour and these were seen as performance-related events to be discussed by teachers with their managers at appraisal. This showed the sensitive nature of this research and how asking about teachers' experiences often had implication in terms of how they were perceived in their institutional environment and that there could be repercussions on matters of career and pay.

Was anyone in my sample likely to say that they had never had any disruption in their classes? As explained earlier, there could be strong motivations for not revealing negative events in the classroom. It must be repeated that I was known to all respondents in this particular research either as students from different colleges on degree courses, professional colleagues in other institutions or teachers whom I knew through meetings at conferences. They knew my positionality that I was involved in Teacher Education and they had, in some cases, read previous articles and knew that they could trust me to anonymise their responses. Of course, the questions 'have you had disruptive classes and how did you deal with them?' might have a very different resonance and answer if deployed at a job interview or again at an appraisal meeting than in the context of educational research which had the aim of supporting teacher and trainee development.

It is true that I suspected that teachers would have their stories, but was not expecting the extraordinary level of intensity or dramatic nature of what many teachers actually experienced in their daily jobs.

Was the research valid? It could be questioned on grounds that there was not sufficient random sampling. It was a small sample. However, there are several problems with respect to random, anonymous sampling on this sensitive issue. Firstly, these questions provoke such a strong reaction that they go to the centre of all teachers' professional identity. Thus, questioning teachers with whom I had no prior relationship might well have drawn a blank on sharing such significant information. Respondents might well question what the data was being used for. Why would teachers trust a stranger asking them about their competence in such a sensitive area? Would Ofsted, management, other institutions or governmental bodies have access to the answers? Was this just more surveillance (Ball 2003)? The teachers I asked had to trust me as a researcher that this information was going to be used for academic purposes that might benefit other teachers and trainees.

Why was it significant that I briefly outlined the strategies that teachers suggested? Surely a more systematic approach to these questions is offered by Wallace (2017), Cowley (2014) and Vizard (2012)? The point is that in this chapter we are hearing the authentic voices of teachers recounting their experiences, strategies and students' actions, defining their own individual reactions to difficult situations they personally encountered rather than the generalised advice of textbooks. The strategies could be used in the future by other tutors, knowing that these were research-informed approaches.

Finally, I have to say that this research has confirmed yet again my belief that teachers are the unsung heroes of our society, battling constant government changes and bureaucracy, but also the day-to-day fight with many unwilling, resistant students.

Conclusion

The question as to what happens in classrooms where there is disruptive behaviour is a highly complex series of events. This chapter opened an investigation into the disorder problems and challenges that a sample population of teachers faced during long careers. It turned out that all the respondents had experienced disruptive behaviour. However, there were some key strategies suggested for trying to overcome these problems; namely the application of consistency, ground rules, communicating the curriculum effectively and making connections with and supporting learners through oral and written activities. Although support for teachers was generally not in evidence in any formal way for dealing with these challenging situations in most respondents' accounts, an excellent strategy did exist of talking through problematic classes in blame-free staff meetings. This was effectively used in one institution as a strategy of sharing difficulties, supporting staff who faced challenging situations and discussing approaches to individuals and classes. These are all possible ways forward to help teachers improve practice.

Some More Suggested Strategies

1. Offer a consistent, systematic approach in lessons, supporting learners with their individual issues and problems.
2. Possibly plan lessons in terms of chapters in a book, rather than aims and objectives. Presenting information as a narrative is more likely to engage the minds of students rather than basically a business plan.
3. Get students to write or talk about their experiences of school and the learning methods they liked and disliked. Begin to implement more of what they like.
4. Students to research information and be put into the role of teachers themselves, imparting knowledge to the class. This forces students into a position of authority and responsibility. It also improves their learning and social skills.
5. There should be space for teachers to talk through problematic classes in a blame-free supportive staff room/meeting environment.

BIBLIOGRAPHY

Ball, S. (2003). The teacher's soul and the terrors of performativity. *Journal of Education Policy, 18*(2), 215–228.

Beere, J. (2012). *The perfect Ofsted lesson.* Carmarthen: Crown House Publishing.

Cohen, L., Manion, L., & Morrison, K. (2011). *Research methods in education.* London/New York: Routledge and Falmer.

Cowley, S. (2014). *Getting the buggers to behave* (5th ed.). London: Bloomsbury Education.

Dreikurs, R., Cassel, P., & Dreikurs, E. (2005). *Discipline without tears: How to reduce conflict and establish co-operation in the classroom.* Hoboken: Wiley.

Flick, U. (2006). *An introduction to qualitative research.* Thousand Oaks: Sage.

Parry, D., & Taubman, D. (2013). *UCU whole college behaviour management: Final report.* https://www.ucu.org.uk/media/5693/UCU-whole-college-behaviour-policy-project-report/pdf/UCU_Whole_College_Behaviour_Management_Final_Report_June_2013.pdf

Paton, G. (2012). Bad behaviour in schools 'fuelled by over-indulgent parents'. http://www.telegraph.co.uk/education/educationnews/9173533/Bad-behaviour-in-schools-fuelled-by-over-indulgent-parents.html

Rogers, C. (1961). *On becoming a person: A therapist's view of psychotherapy.* London: Constable.

Vizard, D. (2012). *How to manage behaviour in further education.* London: Sage.

Wallace, S. (2017). *Behaviour management: Getting it right in a week.* St. Albans: Critical Publishing.

CHAPTER 5

Testing Times: What Is the Role of Assessment?

THE INTRODUCTION

This chapter presents a series of case studies exploring the problematics of assessment and how this can alienate students, cause disruption and ultimately undermine learning. There is one major case study, followed by five brief encounters where classes were alienated from the assessment process. The first section is an auto-ethnographic, self-reflective study based on a one-to-one encounter with a very challenging individual on an Access course and a series of strategies for getting him through a demanding assessment programme.

The assumption is that those who carry out violence and disruption are at a low level academically or are from deprived backgrounds. What follows is a counter-example case study that explores how a tutor engaged an individual student who was abusive to teachers and would not carry out set coursework assessments. It explores strategies to overcome barriers to achievement, particularly where a student resists assessment. The research is based on observation, interviews and a narrative of my involvement in the situation. It outlines strategies that worked with this particular student, concerning the 'improvement' of his behaviour. It argues a case for personal engagement, solution-focused, cognitive behavioural and humanist strategies. It ultimately argues for the complexity of understanding the key relationship between teacher and learner.

The other case studies involved questioning or observing individual teachers on their experience of dealing with students from different economic

© The Author(s) 2017   89
M. Lebor, *Classroom Behaviour Management in the Post-School
Sector*, DOI 10.1007/978-3-319-57051-8_5

and ethnic backgrounds who also showed anger and violence in the face of being assessed. Why did they react in this manner? What behaviours would help support them to stay within the educational system? Interviews, questionnaires and open questions might all elicit complex information about the motives and reasons for individual students resisting assessment. The question is whether it is ultimately possible to explain challenging behaviour. This goes to the centre of the nature of explanations and how well they cover, rationalise or deal with phenomena.

In the context of students now coming into colleges from diverse backgrounds, many with 'deep-seated learning difficulties' (Wolf 2011, p. 117), this chapter is an investigation into teaching individual students who display different types of learning difficulty. Whereas most literature on this topic has looked at these issues within the school sector (Haydn 2012) or within Education and Training as an issue of whole class management (Vizard 2009), this chapter is concerned with a storied account of individuals (Shacklock and Thorp 2005) who refused to co-operate with teachers. Much research into disruptive, vulnerable students (Atkins 2013; Bathmaker 2013) has also been focussed on level 1 students from poorer backgrounds, operating in alien classroom environments. However, in the first study the particular student was working at level 3 and was self-described as coming from an affluent household (Cf. Bates and Riseborough 1993). The question was how I as a tutor/mentor or 'teacher/researcher' (Nisbet 2013, p. 40) could possibly engage this Access student who had been violent and un-co-operative. What strategies could be used to help him complete tasks for his qualification within a deadline of six weeks? This account involves self-reflexive pedagogy of my role and relationship with a particular individual and how this evolved.

THE BACKGROUND NARRATIVE

The construction of the life story of an individual is not unproblematic. Character and personality are fluid. What or whom do we believe? How do we interpret the construction of what students or teachers say (Winter1982)? The problem of exploring lives also has ethical risks attached. The more we specify details of an individual's biography, the more they become recognisable and raise issues of confidentiality, anonymity (Cohen, ibid., pp. 91–92) and research ethics (Gallagher et al. 1995). The college and my line manager at that time gave me institutional permission (Lankshear and Knobel 2004, p. 102) to research issues of disruption because this was seen as a key college priority. The student, henceforth anonymised as Bard, was over 20, signed a consent form, allowing me to use his case study as the basis of research (BERA 2011). As with all research in this book the names of all persons and institutions involved have been anonymised; all persons spoken to signed consent forms. However, details have been changed so as to be able to reflect on the underlying issues of disaffection without intruding on the lives of individuals (Lankshear and Knobel, ibid., p. 109).

Through interviewing Bard, it emerged that he had GCSE passes with high grades. He described himself as living in an affluent area with parents; his father was a lawyer. He said: 'there is so much pressure on me to succeed.' He said, 'I dropped out of my AS course at [the anonymised] Lindsdale private school at 17.' He said: 'I was on drugs; I spent nights clubbing and the day in bed.' At the age of 20, he said 'my parents enrolled me on this Access course,' at what will henceforth be anonymised as Great Dunstain College. He said, 'I am now near the end of my Access course, but I haven't done anything...' When I met him there were six weeks before his coursework deadline set by the exam board. Bard had refused to do assignments. He had missed most classroom sessions. He came to college sporadically and a report on him said that he was seen to have been kicking a car in the car-park. He showed much anger (Vizard, ibid., p. 70). No damage was done and therefore the police were not called (Cf. Mulholland 2012). He verbally threatened one teacher (Townend 2013). His tutors wanted to expel him; his continued stay at college seemed impossible. 'Each time it comes to the crunch,' he said, 'I do the bare minimum work; my Dad comes in and sees the managers.' The pressure on college budgets to maintain numbers was critical in allowing Bard to remain on the course. However, four major pieces of work were outstanding, including a 5000-word research essay. At this point he was referred to me as student/staff mentor.

A Self-Reflexive Account of Myself as Researcher

How are researchers affected by their understanding of themselves as participants (Barnes 2001) in the interrogation of students as both subject and object of teacher research? As teacher/researcher, I had a background of working as an outreach ESOL tutor in several different marginalised and vulnerable, ethnic communities. I currently had responsibility for mentoring 20 members of staff and several individual students. I was an external moderator at other colleges on the Access course, but was not working for the exam board to which Bard was attached.

According to Vizard many students enter colleges 'disaffected from the learning process' (ibid., p. 1). For the purposes of this chapter I define disaffected as a 'dislike' for learning (O.E.D.), whilst disruption is 'interrupting,' 'shattering' (O.E.D) or stopping one's own or others' learning taking place (DFE 2012). However, disruptive behaviour can be seen as a socially constructed notion, the parameters of which could be viewed as highly changeable and complex, depending on boundaries as to where and how learning is situated within an institutional context (Prasad and Caproni 1997). This might be true, but does it help teachers working with difficult or disturbed students?

I had some superficial similarities with Bard. My own life-history involved going to a grammar school, albeit in the state sector. My father was also in Eraut's terms 'professional' (1994). Both of us were originally from different immigrant backgrounds, hence the pressure to achieve financial and social stability. I was also in rebellion against middle-class expectations in my early 20s, but never threatened or used violence either inside or outside the classroom. I passed all exams, but against my parents' wishes, idealistically went into teaching as opposed to more supposedly 'lucrative' professions such as law (Evans 2008). I had worked extensively with a range of poorer ethnic communities, teaching ESOL, so had some understanding of working in a context of ethnic difference.

My ideological assumptions in work are that supporting individuals' well-being and academic progress improves results. My approach is Humanistic, offering unconditional positive regard (Gatongi 2007) in helping students to self-actualise (Maslow 1987). I am consciously opposed to the highly pressurised grammar school culture of academic achievement at any cost which I personally experienced in the '60s and which now seems to operate within private sector schools and possibly with government plans in the wider community. The problem is what happens when students fail to meet up to the expectations of this process.

I had training in mentoring, such as the GROW model, counselling (Rogers 1961), Cognitive Behaviour (CBT) and Solution-focus therapies (Iveson et al. 2012). Sometimes I used one specific model, occasionally an eclectic mix for the specific needs of individuals. According to Clutterbuck and Megginson (2004) classic mentoring puts the power with the mentee, is developmental, goal-orientated, keys into the mentee's vision for the future whereby the mentor acts as model for the mentee to progress, offering holistic solutions to personal challenges. Mentoring has been used as a deficit model for addressing the problems of those not achieving at college, offering a vision for aspiring young people in a variety of contexts (Colley 2003). In this case I was operating as a learning mentor, hoping to offer an individualised, therapeutic intervention to help address the socially situated phenomena of disaffection (Ecclestone 2012). Mentoring and coaching have been associated with improved student behaviours (Reinke et al. 2008).

The relationship between teacher and student can develop students' performance (Lawrence 2006), but can also involve an inter-reactive process of making sense of constructing each other's personal background, history or the other's belief framework (Child 2004). Life histories are constructed (Prasad and Caproni, ibid.) and understood through 'connectedness' gained (Palmer 1998, p. 118) by expressing the language of self and what has happened to the narratee as much as narrator. Both are fluid entities, not easily framed within language.

THE NARRATIVE ARC

Through the window I saw Bard driven into the college car-park in his parents' four-wheel drive. He got out and I witnessed him viciously kick the door closed. His father drove off without further interaction. Bard came into my room, sat down and sprawled on the sofa.

His parents and tutors had insisted on him coming to see me; thus much of the power had been taken out of his hands and was located with the institution and me as mentor (Megginson, ibid.) and him as client. Hence this was not classic mentoring, but coaching someone with their work.

I began the encounter with a question:

'Bard, what do you enjoy doing?'

He answered, '[sic]hanging with friends and music.'
My second question was:

'Where do you have control in your life?'

After some discussion, I gave him a 24-hour week timetable sheet which he was asked to fill in, rating each hour separately in terms of how much enjoyment and how much control he had from each activity that he experienced during that hour. There was a 1–10 scale; 10 being the most control, 1 being the least. This was a CBT model of understanding behaviour (Greenberger and Padesky 1995). I thought if his week could be divided into hourly units, patterns could be established for him to make conscious choices as to what was helpful or important to him.

Large sections of his life were spent in bed or at night clubs. However, he rated these activities in terms of control and enjoyment far lower than mixing with friends. But were his answers to win approval for what he thought I might want to hear? I reflected on the question as to why my views might count.

Bard said, 'I'm surprised you're taking my enjoyment seriously!' I then asked what he wanted to do with his life. Were qualifications important? Yes. But then why wasn't he working now? He said 'there is too much pressure.' He said, 'I don't see the point; there are no obvious jobs or career opportunities.' He said: 'I don't know what I want to do...' In any case he said in a mocking, sarcastic way: 'I can always rely on 'Daddy' to pay.' He said: 'I want to be involved in leadership, buying and selling,' but a smoking gesture implied the product might be drugs. I asked whether drugs were a rebellion against his lawyer-father.

'I just do drugs,' he said.

His parents had 'grounded' him, but punishments did not work. So what would motivate him? Why did he kick cars?

'My parents won't pay for driving lessons unless I pass this course.'

So would he need 'intrinsic' and 'extrinsic' motivators? He had achieved everything before without working. But what about his self-esteem?

I started to ask about his course. What was the content?

He had to write essays on Edward Said's *Culture and Imperialism*, short stories, compare two newspaper adverts and a 5000-word research project on the media. He had six weeks, hadn't started and didn't seem motivated. I arranged to meet him twice a week for an hour for the next six weeks and told him to bring his laptop.

The next session he came without his laptop and fell into the chair, looking exhausted.

'So, Bard,' I began 'what do you know about *Culture and Imperialism*?' He talked about attitudes, prejudice, colonialism and post-colonialists, eastern cultures as exotic and the west's desire to control; he mentioned Said's book.

'Why are these ideas important?' I asked. This was the question he had been set in his assignment.

'Because this is about power; who controls whom.'

We began discussing our outsider status as both coming from ethnic minorities. Said's text seemed important because it related power and disempowerment to ethnic/cultural difference. This discussion seemed to connect Bard with the required learning. In my role as learning mentor, I asked him to write down what he'd just said.

He looked disconcerted.

My strategy was for him to write down just one or two sentences, a rough note, a word or diagram. I would then ask him to type this up. Once he had typed the initial phrases or sentences, I would then get him to print it out and start correcting or overlaying more ideas onto the first version with a pen. The reason for this strategy is that writing by hand offers a level of freedom or creative thinking; the typing represents steps towards the word count. Correcting by hand opens the dialogue between student, self and text (Cf. Bailey 2011). Adding words and phrases by hand, correcting what has been written brings in a level of self-criticality. It also breaks the tyranny of students believing that everything written in print or on screen is correct. It is a constructivist view of scaffolding previous knowledge and understanding (Bandura 1977).

If Bard had brought his laptop in, I would have asked him to type up what he had written. However, as I spoke to Bard, it emerged that he only wanted 'to get top marks,' but also 'I never want to write anything which is going to make me fail.'

'What is failure?' I asked.

'Not being top…' he replied.

He said, 'I want my work to be perfect.' The course tutors hadn't realised that he was, in his words, 'very clever.' However, he had never demonstrated this by writing any essays. He had attacked the teacher verbally when she 'asked me to write my essay.' I realised that this could be interpreted as striving for perfection, but also an assumption of privilege, sexism and could be understood as part of his disaffection mode. Bard had developed 'coercive relationships' with his teachers (Ladd and Burgess 1999). After questioning, it emerged that Bard had a problem writing the first letter on the page. Once that letter was there, it was a commitment to one word, perspective or what he felt was an unchangeable direction. Coursework has the dubious advantage over exams of offering much more time and many more possibilities for first sentences. The question always is; what if something better could be said? What if the first word was 'wrong'? Bard said: 'I have a mental block against writing that first letter.'

He said: 'I am worried if I write something down, it might be worth less than a distinction.' By writing, he said, 'I am going to be judged and I can't bear the possibility that my tutor is going to think, I am not intelligent.' The problem, as he expressed it, seemed to be that he had been told by his parents, his previous school and via the exam system that he was an A* student. He said 'if I'm not going to get the top grade, it's really not worth writing anything.'

I was anxious that he might turn violent on me. I was after all asking him to write an essay. My thought was: 'You take drugs, spend days in bed, kick cars, threaten teachers, don't do any work, yet you are worried about not writing the perfect opening sentence to an essay on *Culture and Imperialism*!'

Instead I said: 'Bard, you have got to engage in a dialogue with yourself and others, ultimately on paper, about the subjects you have been set. You have also got to start the process of writing somewhere; preferably it should be here now.'

'[D]isruptive behaviour has been viewed as a characteristic of the individual student, as resulting from a deficiency in the teachers' skills of classroom management' (Kaplan et al. 2002, pp. 193–194), but here disaffection was being constructed on an individual level as part of the dialogue between myself as tutor and Bard as student. A Humanist vision of learning and goal setting behavioural tasks that had to be done, were here being subverted. Bard started to write down the points he'd made earlier. The first essay on his course for that year had finally begun.

At the next session he brought the laptop and had written 1000 words. We printed it out and I asked him to look at the assignment outcomes and start to act as if he was an examiner, viewing the work in terms of whether it met the required outcomes (Skrbic and Burrows 2014). If given access to the assessment outcomes, learners are in a far greater position of control (Heywood 2000). Bard checked his essay, made several changes and realised that it fulfilled all criteria for a distinction.

We worked on a literature essay. The method was set. Bard started making notes, writing down single trigger words and a comparison diagram between two stories, the narrative arc. It was now difficult to stop him. The session was spent with Bard barely speaking, but relentlessly typing. By the next session Bard had finished both extended essays, done an exam and completed several outstanding shorter pieces. There were now two weeks left and he still had to complete a 5000-word research piece on reactions to news stories in the media. He produced questionnaires, gave them to friends and then discussed the problems of convenience sampling. He also carried out some phone interviews. He had led a focus group in his class. The deadline was nearly up and he had finished 3000 words.

It was Friday afternoon at 1 pm. I had my final session with Bard booked for then. The coursework deadline was 5 pm. But Bard had not turned up. Through the teacher's lens, I reflected that this might happen (Brookfield 1993). He was going to subvert the effort, qualification and meaning of the work he had done earlier at the last minute. The previous week he'd said: 'I don't want to be judged!' or later 'all this is only worth doing if I'm going to get a distinction.' I kept telling him to forget about the result and focus on the content. 'But I've lost faith in myself...' He also said: 'If a year's qualification can be done in six weeks, is it worth doing?'

But just then at 1.15, his father drove into the car-park. The father got out and came into the building, knocked on my office door and said, 'Bard won't come in. Will you speak to him?' I came out to the car. On the way he told me how violent Bard had been at home. They'd called the police because he had attacked his parents physically. Disaffection must be constructed as part of a reaction to the family (Cooper 2002). When we got to the car, Bard was sitting in the passenger seat. He had ear-phones on and looked half-asleep.

I said, 'Bard, do you want to speak?' But he didn't acknowledge me. He was sitting in a stupor, holding his laptop, but staring ahead.

'We don't have to do any work today. Let's talk about what's happening.'

He didn't move. I had made a paradoxical statement against which he could define himself. I told him he didn't have to work and this seemed to release him.

Without speaking he suddenly got out the car and walked with me into college. His father mouthed 'thank-you.' Bard sat in my office, staring ahead, not speaking. Then he said: 'I'm getting too much pressure at home...my parents only want perfection. They want me to get full marks.'

I said: 'So you don't want to finish this? Because if you did, you would actually give your parents what they wanted and that would be bad, wouldn't it...on the other hand if you don't finish it, you will turn 22 next year and your highest qualification will be your GCSE...It is, unfortunately, purely <u>your choice</u>.....'

My fear was that I was being manipulative or pressurising like his parents; nevertheless, it turned out to be one of those moments of disorientating realisation (Mezirow 2000). Bard briefly faced me, took out his laptop and started typing. I let him stay. He was obviously very articulate and wrote 2000 words in three hours.

He did it; handed in everything in time and got distinctions in all areas.

In an interview Bard said: 'The reason it worked with me was that before I felt isolated. I needed to connect with someone.' The fact that I shared my outsider status as ethnically different from his teachers in the college was helpful. Bard also said: 'You showed an interest in me. You weren't judgemental.... the writing technique helped break my need for immediate perfection.....'

UNDER ANALYSIS

This ethnographic research raises issues of how we carry out case studies. There are problems of objectivity where 'partisanship is an essential ingredient' in educational research (Carr 2000, p. 439). My engagement with this student meant that the nature of experience was affected. In ethnographic research there is always the possibility of interpreting deep engagement as collusion. The evidence of the findings came from my own construction of a story about teaching an individual. Is there a different way these events could have been captured in writing if perceived from another angle or if written from the perspective of the student or a 'neutral' observer? Are these experiences beyond formulation in an academic context? The core aspects of the findings are the elements of dialogue, actions and strategies. The dialogue was written in a teaching log at the time. The actions were the specific events of the case study (Van Wynsberghe and Khan 2007). The strategies I had previously used successfully on a number of occasions were here particularly effective.

The research might be questioned in terms of ethics. Is it right to research an individual student's experiences? There was consent, but the critical aspect is whether formalising and publishing the relationship between tutor and student in a book is somehow making public the inter-personal (Denscombe, ibid., pp. 329–342). This might only be justified by the need to explore practice, whilst protecting confidentiality. All research, particularly that based on teacher/student experience, must be subject to strict ethical controls (BERA); its rationale is the ability of the researcher to explore these experiences in the hope of learning how to improve and develop practice for others.

It could also be argued that the use of CBT assumes a medical model, whereas this was supposed to be mentoring a student through academic work. In fact there may have arguably been a case for therapy and this was suggested, but Bard had rejected this route. Depending on our understanding of models and versions of therapy, transference, projection, power relations and a welter of other psychological complexities, much of how we understand one another as teachers/learners must remain unacknowledged. Is education quite separate from psychological interventions (Hyland 2006)? If psychology is essential to being a teacher, which models of psychology or therapy do teachers use? If they employ Freudian-based systems, are they aware of transference? If CBT-influenced, do they use every detail of that system? Or do they use an amalgamation of different theoretical psychology systems? Is it a chaotic jumble of different ideologies? Is education separate from therapy? Which theories work in practice? Ultimately, I argue a case for personal engagement in the teaching/learning situation, offering an overall Humanist approach.

Another question is whether the research could be replicable? The CBT form is used regularly in therapy, whilst I have used the writing strategy as an effective teaching tool in many different contexts. The problem is more how we understand the psychological interaction between tutor and disaffected student and the extent to which individual solutions to the problem of disaffection are impacted upon by wider contexts of economy, power, the continuing diverse nature of the student body and complexities of constructing an understanding of the individual in terms of their family, education and community.

However, the specifics of the tutor/student relationship, Bard's particular problems, his perfectionism, the nature of his relationship with his parents, the wealth factor all make this a highly individualised case study which cannot be generalised. Nevertheless, in terms of improving teaching and learning, nuanced discussions of privilege and strategies for encountering disaffection might raise issues of the tutors' feelings of anger at the student. This can only be mitigated by self-reflective practice and self-analysis, plus the complexity of being a teacher/researcher seeking understandings of the learning process, all of which need constant self-scrutiny.

How Else to Resist Assessment…

The Language of Science

I interviewed a newly qualified science teacher Cleo who was working in a large inner city college, anonymised as The Forest Academy. I asked her how formative assessment took place in her sessions. She replied that she tried to ask questions to 17-year-old students about their knowledge of the language of science. In a class of 15 students, five were late, two absent, three were on their cell phones and four students were engaged and answering oral questions successfully in class. How could this situation be turned around so that positive experiences of learning took place? I suggested the tutor divided the class in two and got them to prepare a Lego-like model which they built and then wrote down instructions within a given time. The groups swapped and then each team had to build the structure following the other's instructions. In order to develop this idea, scientific language could be developed through a power-point about cells (the subject matter), gap-filling cloze exercises, glossaries and asking students about the relevance of this knowledge to their understanding of the human body.

Teaching Numeracy

I observed Olivia for a level 1 Maths group of 8 white students equally split between male and female. She had a strong, confident manner, communicated effectively with all learners initially, testing them on their Functional Skills through using a standard assessment paper. However, the students were quickly bored. They said they could not do the tasks. Three were using cell-phones beneath the desk. Two more students came in late. They were not challenged, sat down barely knowing what tasks were expected and immediately took out their phones as a kind of comfort toy. Teacher control had not been thoroughly implemented at the start. The dialogue between teacher and learner needed to be more robust. There was litter on the floor. The learning environment should have been prepared like a home in order to establish the idea that this was a welcome, clean place of study. The arrangement of desks could have been spaced so that Olivia had complete knowledge of what was happening for each individual. Doing Maths calculations on the board seemed to lose the students' attention. Getting individuals or pairs to explain their calculations could be seen as good practice for empowering students. It was only when Olivia asked the students to carry out numeracy problems on the board themselves that the class started to come alive.

Communicating the Communication Exam

I interviewed Donna, who had tried to bring order to a level 1 basic skills class, by putting on a CD of popular beat music. Most students had their ear-phones on and did not want to listen either to the choice of music selected by the rest of the class or to the teacher who was talking about the Communication Functional Skills exam. The 18-year-old students said they were in college to socialise. What were the solutions to Donna's problems? Ironically, I suggested more communication; discussions about music, careers, life histories, what they liked and disliked. Enlarge an exam question on a Prezzi, put the students into the teaching position. How would they teach this question? If they were the examiners, how would they ask students to prepare for their careers? What did they think was crucial in their lives and how could it relate up to their chosen vocational area? What would they like to write about?

The answer could come back as 'nothing.' But then even this started the dialogue.

The World of Beauty

I interviewed Sally who was teaching a group of 10 young women and one man, all aged 17–19, all beauty students. All students in this group had failed exams in academic subjects at school. They formed cliques. It was eight against three; the young man was in the group of three. The students were struggling with basic written material. They had failed GCSE English and Maths and had to do Functional skills at level 1 in this particular class. They did not concentrate, had music on in their classes, mostly socialised in their self-determined groups. Bullying was happening. The Functional skills exam was the background for more vital confrontations over personal issues.

The boy was being taunted because it was said that when it came to the world of work, he would not be allowed professionally later to do a 'bikini wax' and therefore it was pointless him being on the course. The clique of eight started to sing 'happy birthday' to him as a way of mocking him. This was a complex situation. Sally was trying to introduce formative assessment, question and answer in class. She began to challenge the sexist views of students in this classroom by explaining that there could be other career paths in the wide commercial and professional sector known as 'beauty.' Using questioning as a challenge to deeply held prejudices was an effective way of starting the dialogue with this class and beginning to shake their understanding of gender roles.

An Angle on Maths

I observed Portia, teaching a group of eight 'disaffected' students who had failed Maths GCSE three times at school. This was their 'last chance' at college. They said they hated Maths; they had hated school. They did not know why they had to study something they disliked so much. They never concentrated in lessons. 'This is boring,' they repeated. They were all white; a balance of five males and three females. One of the boys had to sit away from the group because he had a 'social phobia.' There were two support workers in the classroom because two students needed specialist help. The students entered in a lack-lustre way, barely showing any recognition that they were in a classroom. All were on mobiles, swinging on chairs, disengaged.

Portia had prepared a series of exercises on Pythagoras for their GCSE exam, but before she started the class, she cleared the space in the middle of the classroom and started playing physical party games with music and sitting on chairs. This physical episode seemed to give the students some energy. They were jumping round the room for five minutes and then they sat. Portia started questioning them on working out the hypotenuse of right-angled triangles. Students had to form themselves into shapes up against the wall as a way of embodying the Maths problem in a physical way. It was quite extraordinary to witness how the students became engaged with abstract ideas once they had been freed from the conformism of always sitting at desks for Maths sessions.

CONCLUSIONS

If we are not exploring and debating the issues of how to improve the work of disaffected students in the context of their assessments, then the value of what it means to assess students becomes diminished. Possibly involving students in writing the assessment or reading the specifications can help students understand what is required. These case studies open up some complexities of working with students who come from a wide range of backgrounds. There were also the complexities of interaction between tutors and students, plus contextual issues of power, differences in culture and gender in a range of contexts. Ultimately, our understanding of students is constructed and we can only make limited guesses at how individuals operate or are motivated in learning situations. In the end this chapter argues for teachers as reflective practitioners/researchers, endlessly testing strategies, interacting within highly complex social worlds that must be continually probed and explored through ethnographic and other research methods to gain some understanding of ourselves and our interactions with students from a wide range of cultures.

Some Suggested Strategies

1. Helping students at the appropriate level read the exam specifications, so they know what is required. Get them to mark each sentence or paragraph of their own work, using the criteria. This can transform results. Students need to know what is expected of them.
2. Coursework could be written as a mixture of typing and hand writing on top of the typed text so that students develop a self-critical attitude to their work and are not tyrannized by the typed versions of what they read on their screens. They type in their hand-written corrections.
3. Use a self-reflective tool for students to work out how they are spending their days in terms of each hour's enjoyment and control. It helps students regain some power over the chaotic elements of their lives.
4. Sometimes it is important to get students away from the boringness of sitting at desks and instead carry out some physical activity to release their energy.
5. Always have high expectations of your students. However, if they are deeply oppositional, this might be best expressed in a paradoxical way; saying the opposite of what you want, so as to get them to do what is required.

Bibliography

Atkins, L. (2013). Researching 'with', not 'on': Engaging marginalised learners in the research process. *Research in Post-Compulsory Education, 18*(1–2), 143–158.

Bailey, S. (2011). *Academic writing: A handbook for international students* (3rd ed.). London: Taylor & Francis.

Bandura, A. (1977). *Social learning theory*. Englewood Cliffs: Prentice- Hall.

Barnes, D. (2001). Research methods for the empirical investigation of the process of formation of operations strategy. *International Journal of Operations and Production Management, 21*(8), 1076–1095.

Bates, I., & Riseborough, G. (1993). *Youth and inequality*. Buckingham: Open University Press.

Bathmaker, A. (2013). Defining 'knowledge' in vocational education qualifications in England: An analysis of key stakeholders and their constructions of knowledge, purposes and content. *Journal of Vocational Education & Training, 65*(1), 87–107. doi:10.1080/13636820.2012.755210.

British Educational Research Association. (2011). *Ethical guidelines for educational research*. London: BERA.

Brookfield, S. (1993). Through the lens of learning: How the visceral experience of learning reframes teaching. In D. Boud et al. (Eds.), *Using experience for learning*. Buckingham: Open University Press.

Carr, W. (2000). Partisanship in educational research. *Oxford Review of Education, 26*(3), 437–449. doi:10.1080/713688539.

Child, D. (2004). *Psychology and the teacher* (7th ed.). London: Continuum.

Clutterbuck, D., & Megginson, D. (2004). *Techniques for coaching and mentoring*. Oxford: Elsevier, Butterworth-Heinmann.

Colley, H. (2003). *Mentoring for social inclusion: A critical approach to nurturing mentor relationships*. London: RoutledgeFalmer.

Cooper, P. (2002). *Effective schools for disaffected students: Integration and segregation*. London: Routledge.

DFE. (2012). Pupil behaviour in schools in England. *DFE-RR218*. https://www.education.gov.uk/publications/

Ecclestone, K. (2012). From emotional and psychological well-being to character education: Challenging policy discourses of behavioural science and 'vulnerability'. *Research Papers in Education, 27*(4), 463–480.

Eraut, M. (1994). *Developing professional knowledge and competence*. London: Falmer Press.

Evans, L. (2008). Professionalism, professionality and the development of education professionals. *British Journal of Educational Studies, 56*(1), 20–38.

Gallagher, B., Creighton, S., & Gibbons, J. (1995). Ethical dilemmas in social research: No easy solutions. *British Journal of Social Work, 25*, 295–311.

Gatongi, F. (2007). Person-centred approach in schools: Is it the answer to disruptive behaviour in our classrooms? *Counselling Psychology Quarterly, 20*(2), 205–211. Routledge, Taylor & Francis.

Greenberger, D., & Padesky, C. (1995). *Mind over mood*. New York/London: Guilford Press.

Haydn, T. (2012). *Managing pupil behaviour: Improving the classroom atmosphere* (2nd ed.). London/New York: Routledge, Taylor & Francis.

Heywood, J. (2000). *Assessment in higher education; student learning, teaching, programmes and institutions*. London/Philadelphia: Jessica Kingsley Publishers.

Hyland, T. (2006). Vocational education and training and the therapeutic turn. *Educational Studies, 32*(3), 299–306.

Iveson, C., George, E., & Ratner, H. (2012). *Brief coaching: A solution focused approach*. East Sussex: Routledge.

Kaplan, A., Gheen, M., & Midgley, C. (2002). Classroom goal structure and student disruptive behaviour. *British Journal of Educational Psychology, 72*, 191–211.

Ladd, G. W., & Burgess, K. B. (1999). Charting the relationship trajectories of aggressive, withdrawn, and aggressive/withdrawn children during early grade school. *Child Development, 70*, 910–929.

Lankshear, C., & Knobel, M. (2004). *Teacher research: From design to implementation*. Maidenhead: Open University Press.

Maslow, A. (1987). *Motivation and personality*. New York: Harper and Row.

Mezirow, J. (2000). *Learning as transformation: Critical perspectives on a theory in progress* (pp. 3–34). San Francisco: Jossey-Bass.

Mulholland, H. (2012). Millions paid out to teachers for classroom assaults and accidents. *The Guardian*. http://www.guardian.co.uk/education/2012/apr/05/teachers-classroom-assaults-accidents

Nisbet, J. (2013). What is educational research? Changing perspectives through the 20th century. *Research Papers in Education, 20*(1), 25–44. doi:10.1080/0267152052000341327. Routledge.

Palmer, P. (1998). *The courage to teach: Exploring the inner landscape of a teacher's life*. San Francisco: Jossey-Bass.

Prasad, P., & Caproni, P. (1997). Critical theory in the management classroom: Engaging power, ideology and praxis. *Journal of Management Education, 21*(5), 284–291.

Reinke, W., Lewis-Palmer, T., & Merrell, K. (2008). The classroom check-up: A classwide consultation model for increasing praise and decreasing disruptive behaviour. *School Psychology Review, 37*, 315–332.

Rogers, C. (1961). *On becoming a person: A therapist's view of psychotherapy*. London: Constable.

Shacklock, G., & Thorp, L. (2005). Life history and narrative approaches. In B. Somekh & C. Lewin (Eds.), *Research methods in the social sciences* (pp. 156–163). London: Sage.

Skrbic, N., & Burrows, J. (2014). Specifying learning objectives. In L. Ashmore & D. Robinson (Eds.), *Learning, teaching and development strategies for action* (pp. 39–69). London: Sage.

Townend, M. (2013). Massive rise in disruptive behaviour, warn teachers. *The Guardian*. http://www.guardian.co.uk/education/2013/mar/24/schools-disruptive-behaviour

VanWynsberghe, R., & Khan, S. (2007). Redefining case study. *International Journal of Quality Methods, 6*(2), 1–10.

Vizard, D. (2009). *Meeting the needs of disaffected students*. London: Network Continuum.

Winter, R. (1982). Dilemma analysis: A contribution to methodology for action research. *Cambridge Journal of Education, 12*(2), 161–174. Taylor & Francis Online.

Wolf, A. (2011, March). *Wolf review of 14–19 vocational education*. London: DfE.

CHAPTER 6

Could Class Management Be a Management Issue?

ENDEMIC PROBLEMS

The background of this chapter is that after investigating classroom management for many years, I was asked by managers at different colleges to speak to staff about strategies for counteracting the problems tutors faced in many classes on a daily basis. A question that emerged was how might managers in the Education and Training sector support lecturers in coping with stressful situations. My research methods aimed to determine managers' views, using a survey to find out a sample of perspectives. This led to focus groups with managers opening up exploratory discussions, followed by an interview with an experienced manager working with challenging classes. The purpose of this interview was to review model strategies that might be used to help managers support staff to create more effective learning environments in the future. The next stage was to subject managers' suggestions to the views of teachers. What did tutors think of managers' suggestions?

The findings showed there were endemic problems in many colleges where this research took place. Managers from different institutions wrote to me, saying that in their areas there were 'regular fights between students...', 'endless niggling behaviour.' Students were 'coming back from breaks late,' 'eating in class', 'getting up and wandering around', 'feigning illness and going home whenever they feel like it,' 'accusing each other of swearing,' 'calling each other names' 'boys putting their arms on the backs of girls' chairs....'

© The Author(s) 2017
M. Lebor, *Classroom Behaviour Management in the Post-School Sector*, DOI 10.1007/978-3-319-57051-8_6

I initially surveyed 38 tutors from over 30 other colleges. All said they regularly experienced low-level disruption in classes, including constant socialising, endemic use of mobile phones 'under the desks' and lateness. However, many spoke of violence between students or non-co-operation with teachers. Extreme cases mentioned were the level 1 male student who had physically attacked his girlfriend. There was the adult female student who had tried to strangle another learner because she 'didn't like his taste in music.' This incident lasted 15 minutes of class time. I personally witnessed an ESOL adult student who came into class late and started yelling loudly in her native language until calmed by the tutor and told in a gentle way to sit down three times, which she eventually did. Most tutors from this sample said the support from managers was virtually non-existent, but would be highly welcome.

There has been little research exploring this issue from the point of view of how managers might support tutors who face these unpleasant and sometimes dangerous situations. There have been many critical attacks on manageralism (Avis 2002), but these pieces never address the problems that individual managers actually face in their roles. The term 'manager' is open to much debate (Gold et al. 2010, pp. 4–9), but for the purposes of this research, a 'manager' in education is defined as someone with responsibility for organising teaching, training or 'controlling the activities' (O.E.D.) of other teachers. Most managers questioned were in charge of departments or areas in colleges. This study was concerned with hearing their voices. Some recommendations were formulated so as to offer examples of good practice in departments when faced with challenging situations.

WHAT'S ETHICAL?

My interest is to explore what managers thought. I was also concerned with validity issues (Cohen et al. 2011, pp. 179–199). Was I sampling managers who would make a representative contribution to this discussion? Would the findings be generalisable or would the samples have the individual characteristics of case studies (Cohen et al. 2011, pp. 289–94) which would only have relevance in the context of the colleges where this research took place? Again the problem which arose was that the more one identified particular characteristics of a situation, i.e. the more it was authentic, the more problematic it became in terms of outsiders or insiders being able to identify individuals, colleges and departments. In order to avoid these problems, I got permission to research this issue in a range of institutions. All participants were asked to sign a permission form, allowing me to use their views in research and were given the option to withdraw from the research, whilst in line with BERA requirements all managers and colleges remain anonymous (2011). My overriding sensitivity in this research was not to expose any particular course, college or area as undergoing the problems associated with disaffected behaviour, but rather to be able to suggest ways of supporting departments and teams to work out strategies that would overcome these challenges.

MY METHODOLOGIES

Qualitative research was used to explore managers' views on disruptive classes and make recommendations by which managers could improve support for lecturers in their department. Mixed methods of research were used as the apparatus for triangulating data from college managers. I mainly used a non-probability sample survey to work out managers' attitudes, but also opened a more general discussion on this topic through two focus groups and then had an in-depth interview with an experienced manager who had worked for many years successfully in two colleges with many disaffected students.

Just as the unions understood management as needing to put in place strategies to overcome student 'bad behaviour' (Parry and Taubman 2013), managers could construct difficult students as the fault of teachers for not producing sufficiently engaging lessons. Hopefully, because of their experience and position within colleges, managers might offer helpful strategies for dealing with these problems. They could suggest ways in which they could support staff. Were there any innovative ideas that could be shared, so that tutors and students would be beneficiaries from this research? Deploying key questions might elicit data rich responses on these issues. Ultimately, so as to check whether these recommendations were potentially helpful to practitioners, a different sample of 43 teachers were later surveyed and asked which recommendations were most likely to be of use in practice. They then rank ordered what they felt would be most effective in supporting their own classroom practice. Their views were significant from the point of view of triangulation in that they all worked in different colleges or training organisations; 28 female/15 male coming from different cultures across the North of England. Class management was an important issue for all those teachers questioned.

The first question was to ask if managers had been approached by tutors to discuss disruptive classes. This question revealed whether tutors felt comfortable approaching managers about this issue. The problem might be that tutors could sense that they would be victimised or viewed as poor teachers if they admitted that they were experiencing disruptive classes. It might show that they could not cope with their job and that they were exhibiting weakness in that they needed help.

The second question posed was: what did teachers 'describe as problematic' in their classes? This question was a method of exposing the sorts of problems that teachers 'said' they were experiencing in classes; or at least these were the problems that tutors reported back to their managers. I next asked: 'what did the students do that stopped learning taking place?' The fourth question addressed to managers was: 'what strategies did you suggest to the tutor?' This was an opportunity for managers to explain their advice as to how tutors should deal with disruption in their classes. The next question was whether the strategy worked, whilst the final question was whether the manager had more strategic suggestions so as to help tutors overcome the challenges of difficult students.

Similar questions were put to the focus groups and the later interview with some variations which were due to the dynamic of the groups, follow-up questions and how points evolved through discussion.

What Were the Findings?

It was significant that all 37 managers questioned from different areas, departments and colleges answered in the affirmative that all had been approached by tutors to discuss disruptive students. When asked what stopped students learning, there was a wide range of activities that included students being 'confrontational', giving 'verbal abuse', 'shouting out of turn,' 'rude behaviour', 'sexually suggestive comments', 'asking inappropriate questions' and 'swearing.' There was also 'drunkenness,' 'throwing paper', 'use of mobile phones,' and 'refusal of students to engage in sessions,' 'ridiculing' or refusing 'to undertake planned activities.' Sometimes students 'diverted the tutor and the rest of class onto other topics.'

Drug issues were mentioned in several contexts, which caused 'mood swings' and 'erratic' behaviour in class. However, most common were students' 'attitude', 'late' arrivals, low-level 'talking', 'disrupting others', 'non-submission of assessments' or just not turning up. One manager spoke about how cohorts of 14 year olds from schools came to their college and wrecked the facilities. These were, he said, 'students whom the schools found un-teachable.' They were sent to college to work in film studios. They broke equipment in the photography dark room. The reason the college accepted them was that it boosted funding, familiarised younger students with colleges and therefore operated as a kind of marketing regime for the future. It was also supposed to help younger students mature and understand the careers they might wish to enter later in life. Unfortunately, it was deeply distressing for adult degree students in the same building. The degree students wanted to come to college to be in an adult, creative environment. The introduction of young school children was counter-productive from their point of view.

Keep Calm and...

The next question asked managers about the strategies they suggested to tutors. Some answers were specific to individuals. Thus in one case, the 'tutor got upset and broke down in tears.' She was told 'to keep calm....' and 'walk out of the room,' but not 'get into a shouting match with the student.' Another manager, Barnaby suggested 'recognising some learners may not want to do planned activities, so they should identify their own objectives.' A third manager, Aviva, was less sympathetic to the 'student-centred approach' and asked the tutor to 'get learners to meet learning objectives.' Some managers advised the tutor to discuss the problem with 'key players' in the group on a one-to-one basis away from the rest of the class, where 'student improvement plans' could be worked out. Others 'supported the tutor', 'met up with the student group' and issued 'warnings' as required. 'Ground rules', 'disciplinary procedures,' focus on 'learning contracts', changing 'seating plans' or the lesson's 'activities,' asking students to leave the class and ultimately imposing suspension were all perceived as critical weapons in the managers' list of strategies. At other colleges, managers introduced 'strict policies on attendance and punctuality' whereby students were forced to 'catch up on sessions outside their normal timetable.'

Well-planned lessons with excellent resources, combining theory and practice in an effective way or even short starter activities seemed to be a way for stopping problems from developing. One suggestion was the idea of 'removing tutors' own 'pre-conceptions of individual students and starting again.' One manager felt it would be helpful for her to act 'as a sounding board for the tutor's frustrations.' Occasionally, this discussion took place in staff meetings or staff-room peer support sessions. Other managers made it clear that because of Ofsted requirements, there should be 'zero tolerance for disruption' and as a result tutors should use methodologies like the 'questioning of students' needs.' Certain managers offered more positive ideas, such as sending digital texts to learners about 'future classes', but also sending texts to students after class, feeding back as to how well the students had done during sessions. Managers told tutors to get students to 'teach each other', tell the students to 'do something as if it was a given' and then thank them when the task was completed (Rogers 2015).

One manager, Christine, reported on the use of lanyards and ID pictures with different colours for each academic or vocational area worn by every student in their institution. The purpose of this was to ensure that no non-students were in the building. The ID cards operated as swipes to enter college premises electronically. Security guards operated the entry systems. The coloured lanyards were a method of identifying students with particular areas of the college, militating against the impersonality of the large size of the college and developing a more corporate identity and loyalty for students associated with their specific area. If or when students 'mis-behaved' they were reported on a computer data system, thus alerting other tutors as to what was happening to their students in public areas outside the classroom.

But Did These Tactics Work?

Many of these strategies were said to have been effective, but it was 'hard work.' Learners needed 'repeated reminding.' In a particular class the tutors gave students a warning about bringing in drugs. This worked. Sometimes managers had 'one-to-one discussions.' This helped in the short term. However, bad behaviour crept back with 'students experiencing frustration.' In one situation a student was suspended for one day and then returned to act out his bad behaviour the next. It was as if there was no learning or development. Some strategies created more problems; 'an example was sending a student out of class only for him to smash furniture outside…' Some managers 'continued to provide a listening ear' to staff. Tutors tried 'everything,' but a handful of students remained impervious to their efforts and seemed to relish disrupting lessons.

WHERE ARE THE BOUNDARIES?

The next survey question asked for more strategic suggestions as to how tutors might overcome the challenge of disruptive students. This question asked for wider approaches rather than localised conundrums faced by particular teachers. Thus more general suggestions emerged such as 'don't take it personally,' 'establish rapport with individuals,' 'make sanctions known and follow through,' 'always praise good work, especially of disruptive students' to reinforce the benefits of student achievement. Ten managers said they constructed themselves as neutral personas to 'discuss issues with both tutor and student.' But some managers thought about the issue in a wider context and realised that there needed to be a 'whole organisation approach,' (Cf. Parry and Taubman 2013) 'training in how to de-escalate' problems (Cf. Rogers 2015). In-house training as to how to challenge 'students appropriately' was suggested. Teachers needed training in 'classroom strategies,' and had to understand that they 'should take control of the class regardless' of student behaviour. But the question remained 'how was this to be done?' If 'all failed, tutors should set clear boundaries' and then 'go back to the class contract.' Other managers were clear that 'tutors needed to be aware of the college's procedures and policies.' 'Peer mentoring' systems, 'consistency,' 'not challenging 'everything,' but pick your issues,' 'finding out the real cause of the problem,' and talking 'to the students as people rather than products' were all mentioned as ways of solving these situations.

One manager, Angela, said that a tutor had approached her about an Access class where there were 29 students. Seventeen students were highly committed, wanted to go into 'the professions,' took detailed notes, carried out all tasks and were generally on track for success in their assessments. One student always engaged the teacher and took up much attention with detailed questioning, displaying needy, emotional behaviour. Five students were late or did not turn up to class. Six students were constantly on their phones, reggae dancing at the back of the class or insulting the teacher on grounds that the work was either too hard or too easy. The manager started to come into the class, observe what was happening and occasionally took measures against particularly difficult or unpleasant behaviour.

FOCUS ON THE FOCUS GROUPS

The two focus groups operated as open discussions of the problems departments faced rather than offering more strategies. Both discussions were sections of meetings on other topics, as well as a prelude to filling in the above-mentioned survey. Managers wanted to explore these issues because of the way they impacted on all aspects of teaching and learning in their departments. They said that it would be preferable to discuss this issue via structured delivery of training to their staff. But what did they suggest should be the content of that training?

In the first focus group there were five managers present and the discussion turned to a critique of the 'the culture of blame.' It was said that lesson observers were unfair to blame tutors for disaffected classes when often it was a question of time-tabling, i.e. who had been given which group. Sometimes a particularly effective tutor could 'turn around' very badly behaved classes through deploying resources, group psychology, voice, presence and setting effective tasks, but occasionally the behaviour was so 'appalling' that it was hard to use 'normal strategies.'

One teacher was perceived as 'weak' by one set of managers because he had the security guard's number on his cell phone, but other managers present viewed this strategy as eminently sensible. It was also agreed that managers were increasingly under pressure to become more involved in issues of disruption. This was either to support teachers off-loading their emotional reactions to these situations or carrying out disciplinary actions with respect to students. 'Restorative practice' was suggested as a solution; not seeking to blame, but finding ways of progressing situations without criticising individuals. This was planned as an approach to be disseminated and used across the whole of one particular college.

This focus group expressed a strong view that standards were not met in observations because of disruptive behaviour, but that 'support had to be in place' that was meaningful for the teacher to ensure they could cope with and ultimately improve performance. Often the same tutor could teach motivated classes and produce 'outstanding sessions.' The problem was 'the situation they were put in' rather than their ability as teachers. In an optimal context students were engaged, wanted to succeed in their careers or were intrinsically motivated because of their interest in the content of a session and therefore achieved at high levels. One manager said:

> There is no universal solution as it is all context specific and disruption is inevitable in some classes, but must not be allowed to continue unchecked.... it would also be useful if management worked more co-operatively with teachers to help address problems rather than seeing the problem as belonging to the tutor.

For the second focus group of ten managers disruptive students were a concern. They debated techniques for trying to alleviate the situation for tutors in their departments. In some cases there was a feeling that tutors should be producing good lessons, but there was acknowledgement that occasionally staff had to change material mid-way through sessions because they had to focus more on what was relevant or needed by learners.

The main problem seemed to be with mandated students sent by Job Centres, but who, for a variety of reasons, had no interest in the skills that college tutors offered. There were also problems with students who had been excluded from school and felt empowered when they disrupted other students' learning. The solution seemed to be that particular tutors built up a rapport with individual students and could help them settle and develop. Communication and interest in the lives, hopes, needs and aspirations of the class was crucial. This was particularly difficult to establish where there were 'rolling groups' every two weeks. Tutors had to create sympathetic relationships quickly in order to make the content and skills of lessons relevant and effective for each different group. There were assumptions that these students had had negative experiences in education and therefore would take a challenging attitude towards being in a learning situation, returning yet again to a place where they had previously failed. Often these students had major literacy problems and therefore found the moment of being exposed publicly with their lack of ability to read deeply threatening. There was often a need for literacy support to be in place.

Four managers present insisted that tutors had to take ownership of the problems they faced. This was part of their job surely? They couldn't 'keep running to the managers' with each difficult incident. However, other managers in the room saw the role of both tutors and managers to 'offer nurturing' where this had not been given previously either to teachers or students. The overall solution seemed to be greater co-operation between managers and tutors.

WHAT DID A SUPPORTIVE MANAGER SAY?

An hour-long phone interview was arranged with an experienced manager, anonymised as Juliet. She was manager of a large successful department in Montague College where there were major problems with disaffected students. Similar questions were asked as previously, but this time to a specific manager whom I knew had developed a range of approaches to managing staff in the context of disruptive students.

The opening question was whether she was approached by staff about disruptive student behaviour. This happened frequently because 'there was so much challenging behaviour in classes' that had to be acknowledged. Her view was that behaviour, such as 'swearing,' 'fighting,' 'lack of respect,' 'use of cell phones in class' and other negative behaviours, were 'widespread' and had almost become 'the norm' of every day teaching. When cell phones were confiscated, often students had an extra phone secreted away in their bags. Staff frequently experienced 'challenging events.' They often came to Juliet for advice. In this interview she spoke of several supportive strategies that she deployed within her area in order to help staff and students. She placed much emphasis on constant staff development and support through individual one-to-one sessions, staff meetings and training events where these issues were often discussed. She had instigated a recording system through which all significant incidents were logged so that all staff in the department developed a systematic approach.

Juliet was often called into classes to speak to individuals or the whole class 'about their behaviour.' She 'buddied more experienced with less experienced' staff, but teachers 'with more challenging students came to her quite often for a rant.' This they could do 'without recrimination.' She was 'non-judgmental in her attitudes.' Her view was that 'if one strategy didn't work, then tutors needed to try something else.'

When called to classes Juliet would attempt to work out the student's problem. If it emerged that the student had 'additional learning needs', then she would arrange for extra support, but often she would be trying to 'help the student understand what was required in this particular learning situation.' Sometimes this was a question of 'negotiating ground rules.' This was framed in terms of 'the ideal tutor' and 'ideal student' from the student's perspective. The rules were more likely to be sustained because 'dialogue had been negotiated' and therefore students had a vested interest in its success.

Tutors negotiated with students whether disruptive behaviour was recorded and whether they were at the stage for their first warning or not. This tactic involved students in 'decisions that were being made about them.' Tutors were also asked to make strategic use of 'teaching assistants' so as to explore 'the key issues for their learner before class.' They used a 'swear chart in each classroom, so that the student's name would be ticked when they swore.' The idea was 'to raise awareness in a non-condemnatory way...' how many times they swore per hour. It was a method of preparing students for the world of work by making them aware of using appropriate language. Most students seemed unconscious of how much they swore in general conversation.

Students often did 'not have examples at home' of appropriate behaviour and therefore it was critical to give them the 'norms of social discourse.' Juliet's tutors were told to use 'positive strokes' and 'celebrate success.' Especially, 'difficult students were welcomed at the door of the classroom' and a 'seating plan was in place.' Very disruptive students were 'moved around' so as to re-locate them from 'where they caused trouble.' Occasionally, competitions, games, starter activities, quizzes and ice-breakers were useful, but it was important for teachers to be flexible and 'change if the strategy didn't work.' Tutors had to ask students what 'they enjoyed and try to make the work relevant for the students' lives.' These different tactics meant that there was a bank of resources from which tutors could draw, as a result of which they were 'not afraid to try something new with the students' each lesson. However, the question was if these strategies were so successful, why were there still problems? Juliet's answer was that the problems were social, economic and endemic.

Highly Recommended?

The main recommendations from these managers were that a whole organisational approach needed to be taken to ensure that there was a systematic attitude across the institution. Significant incidents of disruption were recorded in each department so that a consistent approach could be adopted by all tutors. Ongoing training ought to be developed, focussing on appropriate interventions. Buddying or mentor relationships were set up between experienced and inexperienced tutors. Time and space, such as staff meetings and training sessions were opportunities to discuss strategies that worked or didn't work in a blame-free discussion. Joint practitioner research could be offered where managers, tutors and students would be involved in working out solutions to these situations together.

The final stage in this process was to ask a sample of tutor practitioners whether any of these suggestions were useful in their own contexts. The rationale for involving practitioners was that since the research was ultimately for their benefit in teaching their classes effectively, it was crucial that at least a small sample of 43 practitioner views could be heard commenting on managers' recommendations. To achieve this, I approached a completely different group of tutors from a wide range of Education and Training contexts and asked them firstly whether there were disruptive students in their classes, whether they felt well supported by managers to deal with challenging situations and finally to rank order which of the six recommendations above would they find most helpful in their current work.

Twenty-three out of those sampled, in other words over half, said that they had 'challenging' students in their classes. Whilst the majority of those tutors sampled previous to this research, mentioned earlier, mostly from Further Education colleges said they were not supported by managers, this sample was based in smaller training units and here there was a more mixed response to this question. Slightly over 50% said they were supported by their managers in these situations. The majority thought that the key recommendation was to 'develop spaces of time and place such as staff meetings or training sessions where managers and tutors could discuss strategies that worked in an open blame-free environment.' The second most important recommendation was that institutions should offer staff more training in 'appropriate interventions' and then the 'whole institutional approach' had significant support. The space for other suggestions mostly re-iterated ideas already discussed as classroom strategies in this chapter.

ANALYSE THIS

It could be argued that questioning managers who were already involved in difficult classes meant that the project was predisposed to uncover evidence of disruptive behaviour (Denscombe, pp. 34–36). It was also known that these problems were occurring in the contexts of the individuals who were approached, so there was a strong possibility that the purposive nature (Cohen et al., p. 156) of the research meant that there was very little random selection of samples, nevertheless the evidence seemed to confirm again that there is a significant problem of disruptive students in the Education and Training sector. Private sixth form schools, for example, where students might be preparing for Oxbridge or Russell Group Universities were not approached; managers working in this context might have been questioned in order to balance the sample and show that the problems were specifically in Further Education contexts. I opened discussions with a wide range of managers from different institutions. I could not, however, offer, for example, longitudinal action research because that would have meant enforcing management recommendations on a whole institution and then testing before and afterwards as to whether there had been substantial improvement reported in students' behaviour.

One problematic aspect of the research was that the managers involved were from different institutions and therefore did not share a specific culture. This was helpful in terms of preserving anonymity of participants (Cohen, pp. 91–93) and presenting a wide spectrum of views, but if this had been action research for improving the practice of one college, the research could be said to have failed. The other problem was that managers generally answered as if they were teachers rather than managers, outlining classroom procedures they would use locally rather than attempting to formulate college-wide or even departmental strategies. Many of these suggestions were in line with literature on this topic, thus for example, Petty's classroom management ideas (2014), Curzon's helpful 'class control' list on preparing lessons, ensuring classrooms are appropriate and ultimately considering sanctions (2013) or Wallace's focus on communication, ground rules and celebrating success (2017) were all vindicated in what managers said. Is there a basic consensus on all these ideas? However, the views of managers are not discussed in any of these texts.

Some managers answered questions in terms of how they personally supported individual tutors, whilst others saw management as a quality control mechanism for checking tutors' outcomes. The central concern was to ascertain effective ways through which managers said they supported tutors encountering disruptive behaviour. Using three different methods for collecting data allowed a range of ways for managers to report on their approaches. The survey meant that there was an opportunity for managers to consider questions and write down views on their experiences. The focus groups allowed for unguarded open discussion, whilst the professional telephone talk was an exploration of how an individual, supportive manager understood her role.

The polarity of perspectives ranged from highly supportive, as evidenced by Juliet to attitudes in the focus groups and survey where there was a more judgemental attitude that it was the tutors' responsibility to produce effective sessions. The range of outlooks meant that the research findings were messy (Derrick 2011).

The most important strategic ideas that emerged were that there needed to be a more co-operative attitude towards this issue. After subjecting the main recommendations to a sample of 43 tutors for scrutiny, it was suggested by 21 tutors that the most important idea was that there should be open discussions in staff meetings and training sessions as an outlet for feelings, but also sharing good practice in a blame-free environment. Eleven tutors preferenced as first choice that there should be ongoing training on appropriate interventions. Eight tutors in the sample gave precedence to the recommendation that a college-wide or organisational approach was needed so that all involved had a shared understanding of values and culture. However, 18 tutors placed this idea as second in their list of preferences. Further down the list of the practitioners' priorities were that 6 tutors thought that priority should be given to significant incidents, systematically recorded, in order to keep a history of what had happened as a basis for consistent practice and training in departments. Managers in the survey saw this as a fundamental strategy that needed to be implemented in all colleges where the research had taken place. This idea was also confirmed as a significant second choice by twelve tutors in the triangulation survey. The content of training could be the strategies discussed, exploring incidents that had happened or working through the feelings of teachers in training sessions. The final idea that ten tutors placed second and managers agreed as highly significant was to involve students in discussions so that their views could impact on strategies and policies on learning and teaching (Coffield 2009).

CONCLUSION

This research shows yet again that disruptive behaviour is a problem for tutors and managers in many different institutions. The use of diverse methods of collecting information meant that a rich source of data was revealed on the incidents that were currently happening in classes and how managers perceived and dealt with these problems. A range of management behaviours were outlined from highly supportive to a more laissez-faire approach, but the overwhelming feeling was that communities of practice (Wenger 1998) located in staff meetings, staff rooms and training events where spaces for tutors and managers to talk had to be developed more systematically. A whole organisation approach where there was communication between managers, teachers and students was seen as the best way forward.

Some Recommendations

1. Develop spaces of time and place where managers and tutors can discuss strategies that work and don't work in an open and blame-free environment in each institution/department.
2. Where relevant ongoing training for staff involved in teaching disruptive classes, particularly focussing on appropriate interventions. The content could be sharing information about current classes where students are not co-operating with the norms of learning.
3. A whole organisational approach needs to be taken to ensure that there is a systematic attitude across whole institutions.
4. Significant incidents of disruptive behaviour to be recorded within each department so that consistent approaches adopted by all tutors and these situations used as case studies for training.
5. Set up buddying/mentor relationships between experienced and inexperienced tutors.
6. Offer more joint practitioner research where managers, tutors and students could be involved in working out how to resolve these situations together.

BIBLIOGRAPHY

Avis, J. (2002). Policing the subject: Learning outcomes, manageralism and research in PCET. *British Journal of Educational Studies, 48*(1), 38–57.

British Educational Research Association. (2011). *Ethical guidelines for educational research*. London: BERA.

Coffield, F. (2009). *All you ever wanted to know about learning and teaching, but were too cool to ask*. London: Learning and Skills Network.

Cohen, L., Manion, L., & Morrison, K. (2011). *Research methods in education*. London/New York: RoutledgeFalmer.

Curzon, L., & Tummons, J. (2013). *Teaching in further education: An outline of principles and practice* (7th ed.). London: Bloomsbury.

Derrick, J. (2011). The messiness of real teaching and learning. In J. Derrick, U. Howard, J. Field, P. Lavender, S. Meyer, E. von Rein, & T. Schuller (Eds.), *Remaking adult learning: Essays in honour of Alan Tuckett*. London: Institute of Education.

Gold, J., Thorpe, R., & Mumford. (2010). *Leadership and management development* (5th ed.). London: Chartered Institute of Personnel and Development.

Parry, D., & Taubman, D. (2013). *UCU whole college behaviour management: Final report.* https://www.ucu.org.uk/media/5693/UCU-whole-college-behaviour-policy-project-report/pdf/UCU_Whole_College_Behaviour_Management_Final_Report_June_2013.pdf

Petty, G. (2014). *Teaching today: A practical guide* (5th ed.). London: Oxford.

Rogers, B. (2015). *Classroom behaviour* (2nd ed.). London: Sage.

Wallace, S. (2017). *Behaviour management: Getting it right in a week.* St. Albans: Critical Publishing.

Wenger, E. (1998). *Communities of practice: Learning, meaning and identity.* Cambridge: Cambridge University Press.

CHAPTER 7

So Why Do Disruptive Students Say They Disrupt Classes?

NOT A MORAL PANIC

This chapter investigates data from over 100 students, exploring how 'disruptive students' themselves view challenging or difficult classes. Students were identified as 'disruptive' by their institution, department or teacher and then were questioned as to why they behaved in a disruptive way in sessions. The rationale was that if we could determine what 'difficult' students say they wanted, teachers would be better prepared to teach them. The problem was how to frame questions so that they were comprehensible for students at a range of levels and yet construct meaningful data from their responses.

Students in this sample were identified as having been involved in physical and/or verbal violence in their classroom. Disruption has been defined as activities that are perceived to stop learning taking place (DfE 2012). However, in this chapter, students are actually not just stopping learning, they are breaking ethical and social norms through their negative behaviour. These problematic scenarios might be seen as part of the teaching of groups marginalised from education. Questioning students who behave 'badly' is listening to student voices. The fact that I was doing this was meant to counter the idea that I was instigating a moral panic where students were blamed. Instead I was trying to listen to what students said they wanted.

Nevertheless, this research process has many complexities implicit in the dialogue with those who could be constructed as 'the cause of the problem.' Are we objectifying and therefore downgrading students through the research process? How should students classified

© The Author(s) 2017
M. Lebor, *Classroom Behaviour Management in the Post-School Sector*, DOI 10.1007/978-3-319-57051-8_7

as 'disruptive' be selected for research? Why would they want to be involved in research which after all is part of the academic system from which they feel alienated or which they reject? Would they tell the truth about their behaviour? Would they be ashamed and not wish to co-operate because they might be worried about being in 'trouble'? Or would there be bravado and false stories about carrying out dramatic or daring acts of subversion? What had alienated these students from education? Or was their experience of education so negative, they so damaged, that teachers had to use some form of therapy or counselling in order to attract these students into a more positive relationship with the learning process?

Is education quite separate from psychological processes? If an understanding of psychology is essential to being a teacher, which models of psychology and/therapy do or should teachers use? If they employ Freudian-based psychology systems, do they believe in oedipal theories or id/ego/superego and transference? If CBT-influenced, do they break every situation down into thoughts, feelings and actions; if Solution-focussed do they always ask about 'preferred futures' or how hopes are achieved? Do teachers apply these processes systematically? Or do they use a mish-mash of different theoretical psychology approaches? How have teachers been trained? Is education separate from therapy? There is a major question as to whether education should involve therapy for vulnerable students and if so which model of therapy could or should be used? If, alternatively, all disturbed students were merely referred for counselling, would the financial or resource implications be too vast to contemplate?

PHYSICAL VIOLENCE

The findings showed that the majority of students from these classes said that they had been involved in physical and/or verbal violence in class and that they rejected the learning that was supposed to be taking place in their environment. From this research it emerged that the sample of students from classes identified as 'disruptive' by their teachers said that their preferred sessions would be 'supportive', 'respectful', 'one-to-one'; they would learn more, be involved in discussions and generally enjoyed practical work. In other words all the features that would be associated with normative good practice in teaching and learning. The consequent challenge implicit in these findings is how to help teachers communicate these strategies, attitudes and values in a disruptive and challenging environment.

Yet many view these problematic scenarios as part of the teaching of groups marginalised from education (Atkins 2013). Like Wallace, it seemed important to directly question students who behaved in a way perceived by their teachers to be disruptive to learning. This would also be in line with the norms of college quality procedures of listening to student voices, even if students spoke about their own and other classroom experiences in a negative way. This could be understood philosophically as a highly complex process. Was the very act of answering questions for research displaying some level of collusion with authority? Or were these students' experience of education so alien; were they so vulnerable and damaged that teachers would have to use therapeutic approaches (Ecclestone 2012) in order to attract these students into a more positive or pliable relationship with the learning process? Was their involvement with the research part of that rehabilitation process?

How to Be a Disruptive Student...

As a teacher educator, there were some problematic aspects of carrying out research with students who were not actually in the researcher's classes in terms of practicality, ethical dimensions and selection of sample (Cohen et al. 2011, pp. 143–64). What paradigm of research should be used (Creswell 2013)? What were the definitions of disruptive students (Wallace 2003, p. 90)? Would students wish to identify themselves as disruptive? Was it a badge of courage or shame? What was their experience that stopped them co-operating with education? The solution for this chapter was that teachers had identified these classes as 'disruptive' and they or their managers wanted me to offer training on these issues. Despite potential commercial sensitivities, the managers and institutions concerned gladly gave me permission to research and speak on this area (BERA 2011). All students involved in the research were over the age of 18 and therefore did not need permission from parents or guardians to participate. The dilemma was ethically whether students might feel I was intruding on their lives or even wishing to punish them in some way for their non-conformist or misbehaviour (Cohen, ibid., pp. 170–171) rather than just questioning them on educational concerns with the purpose of ultimately working on ways to improve teacher/student relationships. In fact, all students and teachers engaged in this project gave their written permission to answer questions and be involved.

In my role as a lesson observer, I had watched many sessions where students were un-co-operative, impolite, or socially unpleasant. However, the catalyst for the proposed research and training were a series of incidents in classes at a range of different colleges where violence flared in sessions. Incidents described below could be interpreted as part of 'deficit' education, where vulnerable learners struggle in an alien system more in need of therapy than disciplinary regimes (Bates and Riseborough 1993).

Two teachers reported that a female student in her mid-20s attacked a younger male in their class; the physical conflict could not be disentangled for five minutes; a 30 year-old male student screamed abuse at a female teacher and stormed out. In an observation, I witnessed a student tearing up another student's work. A manager wrote me a long letter outlining incidents of verbal and physical violence in her department, mentioning 'regular fights between students...' Once it became known within various colleges that I was researching this topic, managers asked me to carry out training with their tutors, hence my wish to research the views of students in the hope of working out more strategies, solutions or humanistic and possibly therapeutic approaches to these situations.

The students selected for this sample were mostly level 1; many were aged over 20 on short, two-week, rolling, mandatory courses. Questionnaires were used as a way of taking a snapshot of students' perspectives without unnecessarily intruding into their lives or the limited time available to them in college. The advantages of questionnaires are that they offer a quick, economic way of questioning a group and accessing a range of attitudes, feelings and experiences. Their disadvantage is that the researcher cannot ask follow-up questions, explore the group's perspectives in depth (Denscombe 2010) or allow for an interchange between the group. Nevertheless this was a small-scale project set up through tutors and managers who asked me for training on this issue within their departments. There was little time or accessibility to the students themselves other than through their tutors.

However, researching students' views through questionnaires raised issues about the extent to which rich data would be produced. I was concerned that data might include fabricated narratives, bravado escapades or even ideas deployed to subvert or destroy the authenticity of the research. We are after all dealing with 'disruptive students.' However, it could be argued that even this 'fake' language would reflect students' life experiences (Shacklock and Thorp 2005) thus making the research meaningful (Cresswell 2013) at least in terms of hearing student discourse. Moreover, there were ethical concerns. As mentioned, I managed to get written permission from the various institutions concerned and asked students, teachers and managers to sign the relevant ethics forms (BERA 2011, p. 4). Permission was sought, ethics forms were signed by everyone involved; no-one was asked to participate against their will. The fact that students were mostly level 1 to 2, suggested a level of vulnerability (Atkins, ibid.), however, getting parental permission was not appropriate as many students were at least in their 20s, living independently or were sometimes parents themselves.

QUESTIONING STUDENTS

It was problematic producing an appropriate student questionnaire. The questions could not be too complex or too simple; they might be considered insensitive (Cohen et al. 2011, pp. 395–6) assume a negative, condescending tone or lead students into expressing material they would regret or that was fictitious, imagined or had no basis in reality. I gave my first pilot version of the questions (Cohen et al. 2011, p. 402) to 25 teachers who were currently working in the Education and Training sector and asked for their feedback before attempting to try the questions on students. They were critical of my first attempt, suggesting a series of improvements so that I could approach 'disaffected students' in a more sensitive way.

I decided to ask a mix of 'open-ended' and 'closed' questions (Cohen et al. 2011, pp. 381–3). The challenge of approaching students whom I didn't know was that anonymity could give them the confidence, licence and freedom to speak about their feelings freely, but they might also just consider the research as a continuation of the schooling process which they might be determined to subvert. In-depth interviews might have been a better way of approaching the problem (Cf. Atkins 2013), but the teachers' needs were desperate and time limited, and the students were in college for less than three weeks.

COLLECTING THE DATA

The challenge of writing a questionnaire to extract information, attitudes, opinions, thoughts and feelings from 'disaffected students' was going to be problematic. When speaking directly to students, difficult words or ideas would have to be re-phrased or made comprehensible to the interviewee, and follow-up or subsequent questions could be asked to determine nuances of attitude. But if these were given out as questionnaires, then words like 'disruptive' might be outside the normal language of the students. Hence, I decided to use a range of words, such as 'mess around', 'behave badly' and 'disrupt' to be synonymous with stopping learning taking place, so that the students would have a clearer understanding. I also did not want to start with negative assumptions or leading questions, so after a brief explanation that this was going to be anonymous research and that I was concerned with improving their teachers' lessons, my first question asked about what they enjoyed in class. The idea behind these opening questions was to present a positive frame of reference with respect to the classes they were currently attending.

Eighty percent of those sampled were mandated students who had to attend college or have their benefits cut. There was an assumption that they had not completely rejected education or refused to turn up, but that they had some engagement with teachers, representing the authority of college, schooling and education. Students with particularly negative attitudes might express anger, rejection or even a wish not to co-operate with this research, but at least through these questions I might give participants the freedom to respond 'in private, in depth and with honesty' (Cohen et al. 2011, p. 176). It was possible for the students to say that they disliked classes or consistent with BERA recommendations (2011) that they didn't want to participate in the research at all. It is notable that in Wallace's book (2003), disruptive students, when interviewed, were sufficiently co-operative to be able to say what they thought of their teachers (Wallace 2003, p. 23). The fact that Wallace's student samples were prepared to engage with the world of institutionalised education meant that there was some compliance with authority. Would there be differences in students' attitudes separated by time and location which in turn could reveal different results in my research?

On interviewing teachers of students mandated to attend literacy, numeracy and vocational classes or return to or start work, I learnt that these classes were described as often 'fraught.' Through interviewing several tutors teaching classes at a range of institutions henceforth known as The Venetian Institute, Tempest College and the Arden Academy, it emerged that there were violent incidents, student outbursts of anger, violence, fights between young men and women, and problems of class management (Cf. Wallace 2003, 2007). All eight tutors initially interviewed agreed with the statement 'we are being faced with difficult classes for which we have been insufficiently trained' (Cf. Bathmaker 1999). Thus even asking students from these institutes to fill out questionnaire forms might be difficult to achieve. Nevertheless, I wanted to proceed into the centre of the storm and ask difficult questions that would have implications for training, policy makers, strategies and theories of teaching and learning (Bathmaker 2013).

WHAT WAS FOUND?

I surveyed around 100 students from eight different classes and eight tutors from different courses and colleges. Sixty percent of the students were level 1 students; 40% were level 2 or above. All were over 18 and many were in their 20s or 30s. All were currently on basic literacy courses or in vocational training; 57% were male; 43% female. Their all-white teachers analysed the student sample as white European with around 10% from Black and Asian backgrounds. All research has an ethnic/race dimension either through inclusion or exclusion, but teachers did not interpret disruptive behaviour as being aligned with any specific ethnic or racial group (Gunaratnam 2003). These teachers said there were no statemented students (those with diagnosed special educational needs) in the research samples; merely that these were 'disruptive or difficult classes.'

The first question was open-ended and asked what the students enjoyed doing in lessons. The answers were surprisingly positive, varied and almost sounded like an intensely, vibrant model curriculum where students actually might like coming into college!! The anonymised students liked many aspects of college. Henry liked 'learning and thinking.' John enjoyed 'projects', Richard: 'practical work,' Harry: 'handson [sic] lessons'; Barbi 'more maths,'; Clarence: 'computers'; Ed: 'writing'; Isabella: 'workshops,';

Morti: 'writing stories,'; Staffi: 'learning in new ways'; Georgi: 'I like the whole thing'; Walt: 'getting on with my work'; Michelle: 'speaking and listening'; Glossi: 'grammar tests'; Suffi: 'discussion'; Carrie: 'work which makes you think'; Daff: 'learning as much as possible as I need skills and information to find good [sic] working place.' Denny said 'I enjoy staying in a lesson that I will learn from. The teachers smile and the help they give up to help ower [sic] work.' Winnie said 'nothing,' whilst Charles said: 'I don't enjoy lessons,' but these explicitly negative views were in a minority of two.

However, when asked whether they had disrupted their current class, 'messed around' or behaved in a 'disruptive way' most students replied that they had. Beatrice, Miri and Staffi admitted that they had been 'late', which they interpreted as disruption, but then Henry had thrown 'rubbers', Glossi threw 'putty'; Richard and Christopher 'stopped work,' whilst John and Charles 'argued with other students' or 'shouted out.' Reggie 'set fire to a bench,' whilst Jeanie, Edgar and Edmund admitted to hitting 'teachers,' but Ed had only done this at 'Hight School [sic].' Barbi had blown 'the Bunsen burner in the teacher's face.' Many said 'swearing;' for some, this was at teachers. '[F]ighting' or 'playfighting [sic]' was common; Cali threw a chair and told the teacher to 'f--- off.' Others had started fights or 'started with someone;' Ari: 'spoke over people.' Seb said he had 'stabbed a student in the neck....because he was annoying me.' Students said they 'laughed,' 'shouted,' 'disturbed others,' 'threw papers,' let their 'phones go off' and finally one 'fell asleep.'

When asked through a closed series of questions why they had acted in these negative ways, most answered that they were 'bored' or they 'didn't like the subject.' Walter had started a fight as a result of 'stress Because [sic] of spelling and writing.' Fighting was conflated with boredom in several instances. However, many explained their disruptive activities as resulting from 'anger towards another student' or 'anger towards the teacher.' The reason for hitting a teacher was identified as the fact that Ari had been 'bullied by two' [other students]. Another reason for disruptive behaviour was that Safi had 'things on [his] mind.' Sometimes the problem was that the student was feeling 'tired'; Cali was angry because of being 'teased because of [his] southern accent.'

Finally, when asked what would make classes better, answers were revealing. Henry, John and Harry said 'more help'...or 'one-to-one support.' Ed said 'teachers that help you learn.' Others definitely wanted more practical or physical work, whilst Georgi wanted 'more challenging theory lessons.' Several objected to 'teacher attitudes' in the department, whilst others wanted 'a better teacher', 'no teacher,' 'more professional teachers,' or 'more interesting lessons.' For some this meant 'more videos and presentations,' others wanted 'smaller groups', 'more resources available,' 'topics fit for daily life', whilst others were just 'not sure.' However, Nym poignantly said 'teachers should love teaching not just have it as a job' and furthermore they 'should talk with students like [sic] they are equal.'

When the eight teachers who had identified these 'disruptive classes' were asked about their responses to the student perspective in a focus group discussion (Cohen et al., ibid., pp. 436–7) during the planned training session, the salient points to emerge were Alfie saying that 'although we have all done Cert Eds., we feel ill-equipped for dealing with these challenging situations'. Adrienne said: 'we need much more daily support from managers and other staff in dealing with these problems.' Iris said: 'Can you please run more sessions going through strategies and interventions for coping with class management issues.' When asked which models of counselling these teachers had been trained in or even knew about, the answer, as with most teachers to whom I spoke during this research, was unanimously 'none'.

ANALYSE THAT

It must be admitted that there were limitations to this research; its small-scale nature, the fact that I had been asked to prepare training for the self-selected group of tutors meant that the sample of students was pre-identified and perceived by their tutors as 'disruptive.' This was a snapshot of student attitudes from classes, where I was asked to support a range of tutors who were involved with disaffected classes. The groups were characterised as disruptive, but there were individuals in each group who had been involved in the normative processes of learning and had not been identified as difficult members of the class. Nevertheless 67 out of 100 students did answer the question about disruptive activities they had carried out, offering examples of their own 'negative behaviour'. Was it true? Had they been as destructive as they said or was this boasting? Fabricated stories might have been interpreted as more subversion. However, when interviewed, their teachers confirmed that these abridged autobiographic incidents were true and that they had witnessed much of this behaviour in regular classes (Cohen et al. 2011).

There was an element of 'convenience sampling' (Cohen et al. 2011, pp. 155–162) in that I was aware of these classes and had spoken personally to all the teachers involved in these contexts. The questions that emerge are whether more 'random sampling' (Cohen et al., p. 153) would have produced similar results. An alternative method would have been to set up an online questionnaire for teachers to use with their students or I could have requested on-line/blog or websites for students to recount their perspective or views on the questions. However, the anonymity and lack of personal contact or communication with the teacher or students would have meant that the positive of more randomised research would have been fulfilled, but fewer methods of corroboration about the information transmitted being true would raise questions about validity.

Creating identities and events on digital media is notoriously the widespread outlet for fantasy fiction in our society. The problem with interviewing students in more depth was that this might actually have made the learning situation worse with little benefits for either the students or teacher (Denscombe, ibid., pp. 331–332). Crucially, there were time factors. Students were in college for limited periods, justifying spending it on interviews and more research was not really appropriate for students who were engaged so little in education. By using the limited method of a survey plus some extra interviewing and questions, before carrying out the required tutor training, was a simple and effective way of finding out information. Ethical issues of intruding into the lives of students were also minimised.

The outcomes of this research reflect an interesting range of views. Some significant strands to the survey emerged. Thus though many of these students had been involved in fighting, swearing, had thrown chairs at teachers, had hit teachers, most students had normative suggestions about how lessons ought to be conducted. They suggested smaller groups, one-to-one teaching, more practical sessions, more interesting sessions: all were positive ideas. Teachers should treat students as equals, act in a more professional manner and love their jobs rather than being there just for the pay-check – these seemed laudable aims. Nevertheless, some of the negative behaviours encountered now seemed to be far more extreme than that reported by Wallace (2003, 2007). This did not necessarily represent a worsening national situation, but could be understood in terms of different contextual circumstances, closeness of myself to the tutors involved in these situations, their frankness in explaining what was happening in their classes and the fact that the students were only in college for a limited period.

The positive outcome of this research was firstly that this was an example of student voice; students admitted what they had done in sessions, but also expressed what they wanted. Secondly, the significance of the research findings was that students who said they had carried out destructive acts in class were also the same people who said they wanted what amounted to engaging sessions, professional teacher behaviour and basically good individualised teaching and learning. In fact these students seemed to be vocalising the agenda of the key standard textbooks on teacher education (Petty 2014; Avis et al. 2015).

Eventually I used the research material in the colleges mentioned for training sessions to several groups of tutors. In the sessions I went through a range of strategies for engaging and building relationships with learners, working out support systems for staff, exploring case studies for interventions, but ultimately discussing students' perspectives and exploring teachers' ability and resilience to support students' personal growth and advance their academic and/or vocational careers in the sessions available.

CONCLUSION

The key aspect of this research was the focus on what students said. The findings were that the students surveyed said they had carried out some highly destructive acts in class. They gave a range of reasons why they had acted in this way, including 'boredom', 'anger' at other students and the teacher, provocation, stress, tiredness, dislike of the content of lessons and a response to bullying. It would be difficult to arrange all sessions so that none of these feelings emerged or legislate that classes could be set up that stopped any of these emotional or psychological events from taking place. However, it is reasonable that these students wanted to be treated respectfully, have engaging/interesting sessions, have more personalised learning and learn more about what was relevant to their lives and careers in their current contexts of study. The way forward in these situations might just be better communication between teachers and students, a more humanised approach and more training for interventions, all of which might bring out better results for both sides of the classroom desk. Achieving this should go to the centre of all debates on what it means to teach and learn.

Some Suggestions

1. This is difficult with large classes, but there should be some one-to-one tutorial time for each individual student, so that all students feel the teacher is concerned for their welfare.
2. Focus on the career aspirations of individual students. This makes the session seem more relevant.
3. Well-resourced, stimulating lessons can be an antidote to boredom.
4. Showing professionalism, love of the job, a positive, up-beat attitude, and being good-humoured can all counter the negative, hostile atmosphere in some classrooms.
5. Teachers need to be thoroughly aware of their students' vulnerabilities. Aggression and anger are defences against potential attack. Concern or sympathy might be useful strategies for defusing explosive behaviour.

BIBLIOGRAPHY

Atkins, L. (2013). Researching 'with', not 'on': Engaging marginalised learners in the research process. *Research in Post-Compulsory Education, 18*(1–2), 143–158.

Avis, J., Fisher, R., & Thompson, R. (2015). *Teaching in lifelong learning: A guide to theory and practice.* Maidenhead: Open University Press.

Bates, I., & Riseborough, G. (1993). *Youth and inequality.* Buckingham: Open University Press.

Bathmaker, A. (1999). Managing messes and coping with uncertainty: Reviewing training for teachers in post-compulsory education and training. *Journal of Further and Higher Education, 23*(2), 185–195. doi:10.1080/0309877990230203.

Bathmaker, A. (2013). Defining 'knowledge' in vocational education qualifications in England: An analysis of key stakeholders and their constructions of knowledge, purposes and content. *Journal of Vocational Education & Training, 65*(1), 87–107. doi:10.1080/13636820.2012.755210.

British Educational Research Association. (2011). *Ethical guidelines for educational research.* London: BERA.

Cohen, L., Manion, L., & Morrison, K. (2011). *Research methods in education.* London/New York: RoutledgeFalmer.

Creswell, J. (2013). *Qualitative inquiry and research design: Choosing among five traditions.* Thousand Oaks: Sage Publications.

Denscombe, M. (2010). *The good research guide for small social research projects.* Maidenhead: OUP, McGraw-Hill Education.

DFE. (2012). Pupil behaviour in schools in England. *DFE-RR218*. https://www.education.gov.uk/publications/

Ecclestone, K. (2012). From emotional and psychological well-being to character education: Challenging policy discourses of behavioural science and 'vulnerability'. *Research Papers in Education, 27*(4), 463–480.

Gunaratnam, Y. (2003). *Researching 'race' and ethnicity: Methods, knowledge and power*. London: SAGE Publications.

Petty, G. (2014). *Teaching today: A practical guide* (5th ed.). London: Oxford.

Shacklock, G., & Thorp, L. (2005). Life history and narrative approaches. In B. Somekh & C. Lewin (Eds.), *Research methods in the social sciences* (pp. 156–163). London: Sage.

Wallace, S. (2003). *Managing behaviour and motivating students in further education*. Exeter: Learning Matters.

Wallace, S. (2007). *Managing behaviour in the lifelong learning sector*. Exeter: Learning Matters.

CHAPTER 8

A Methodology for Supporting Tutors Who Face Challenging Classes

THE ANGST

In this chapter I will outline a strategy for supporting teachers outside the classroom in developing their ability to deal with disruptive student behaviour in their classes. I describe peer-reflective practice and demonstrate how this has been effective in impacting on helping teachers deal with disruptive groups. I explore a strategy for offering teachers support by sharing case studies of trainees' classes where students were disruptive. Some epistemological questions are raised as to the problematic nature of how teachers know whether improvements take place when an intervention is made.

There is much anxiety and concern amongst trainees and tutors about the issue of dealing with hostile classes. A group of 12 Cert Ed. trainees at a college, henceforth anonymised as Oldcastle College, said their main anxiety on their course was students' challenging behaviour and class control. This corroborates much extant research that students' bad behaviour is the key negative experience of being a trainee tutor. Many teachers have to face insulting and aggressive behaviour as part of their normal working lives (Townend 2013). This chapter explores ways in which teachers cope with these situations, develop resilience, receive support and offload the stress that disruptive classes pose for them. In this chapter a strategy for achieving this in a teacher education context is put forward and then used as a model for qualified teachers to follow.

© The Author(s) 2017   137
M. Lebor, *Classroom Behaviour Management in the Post-School Sector*, DOI 10.1007/978-3-319-57051-8_8

THE RATIONALE

I began to think about ways in which tutors could be supported with their anxieties. Would opening up about what happened in their classes make them more vulnerable? Does discussion of issues necessarily improve situations? Or is it better to be tough, show no weakness, pretend there is no problem by armouring oneself against the possibility of attack either by students, colleagues, observers or managers? I began to interview a group of 12 Cert Ed. trainees at Oldcastle College who again said their main anxiety on their course was students' challenging behaviour and class control (Cf. Hobson et al. 2009). I started asking them as to whether it would be better to discuss issues or keep them private. I wanted to help teachers find ways of coping with these situations, developing resilience, getting support and off-loading the stress that challenging classes posed.

But there was also an issue of trying to 'improve practice.' This meant that teachers' feelings, emotional states or the affective domain were within a social context of managerial control. The notion of 'improving' practice in post-school education is a dominant aspect of the discourse of surveillance (Ball 2003) where models of improvement assume that teachers are supposed to be continually getting better (O'Leary 2006). Is this possible? The new Ofsted regime of observing teaching and learning reduces all lessons to meeting standards. Disruption if understood as behaviour that stops learning taking place can range from students merely talking to obstructive, violent or subversive behaviour. Such behaviour leads to the 'requires improvement' grade. The belief that underpins this view is that if the educational institution had systematically set up a zero-tolerance attitude towards disruptive classes, then no student could breach the peace of the learning process (Ofsted 2012).

The context is also one of increased commodification of learning (Simmons and Thompson 2011) where an audit culture of checking 'value for money' is a key element. Teachers are constantly being judged on their performance (Avis 2002), whilst their teaching is taking place in geographic areas of poverty where exclusion becomes more likely (DfE 2012, Table 15) and there are no jobs and therefore the incentive to achieve is limited if their qualification is not going to lead to employment (Simmons and Thompson 2011). The reason these factors are important in exploring class management is because they all impinge on purpose, motivation and aspiration of students who do not see a future for themselves in training or jobs and therefore fail to see the point of more education if it is not going to become financially justified.

The question is how can trainees improve their teaching for the Cert Ed. if they are faced with a class of hostile students who will not submit to authority or almost seem implacable to class management or negotiation techniques? Are Marzano's establishing negotiated classroom rules (2003) sufficient to deal with aggressively negative views? Should we be modelling more neo-behaviourist, positive and negative reinforcement processes (Jones 2007) or more humanist attitudes (Kohn 1993) to help trainees deal with these fraught situations? If trainee tutors are teaching say Functional Skills to those who are daunted by numeracy (Ofsted 2012) or just don't want to be in class, is it carrot, stick or something else that can possibly motivate students in these contexts? How can teacher educators improve trainees' ability to cope with these situations, model appropriate behaviour in our teacher education classes to prepare, support and have a real impact on trainees who face these disruptive groups (Reinis 2013)?

There are again many questions that underpin even a superficial analysis of these issues. Is improving teaching in this context engaging learners, getting them to conform, achieve qualifications or merely quieten their noise? Is improvement judged in terms of when an observer happens to be in the room or the overall achievement rates of students? Can the immaterial nature of relationships between teachers and students be designated as getting better? What is the meaning of improvement? In this chapter I explore an approach towards acknowledging the problematic nature of teaching under difficult circumstances and offer a strategy for supporting teachers who find themselves in these situations.

WHAT STRATEGY?

The teaching strategy is a straightforward, but effective method for developing reflection possibly in tandem with the written reflective practice models associated with Gibbs (2001) and Boud and Walker (1998) where the feelings provoked by situations are open for exploration, but also moves towards an oral form of Brookfield's critical lens (1993). It could develop self-reflexivity (Cunliffe 2004) interaction or group critical challenge, offering support for trainees on an emotional and psychological level, suggesting a particular form of setting up a community of practice (Wenger 1998). I argue for a non-competitive class environment where trainees offer support for each other. I explore the effect of this strategy in two case studies. It must be said again that case studies have limitations in terms of their generalisability (Cohen et al. 2011, p. 184) nevertheless, they are a means for offering limited tests of ideas in practice.

It should also be said that there are major differences between the class-room environments of teacher education and the environment that train-ees have to face in Further Education colleges. Both are highly evolved cultures and densely layered with relationship that is difficult to unpick. The teacher education class in this instance was a group of 12 trainees, all devoted to improving the life chances, ambitions, careers and emotional-psychological development of individuals in their respective classes where they were based on placement. There were eight women and four men; two trainees were from BME backgrounds, the rest were white. In terms of class seven described themselves as coming from working class back-grounds, whilst the other five thought of themselves as middle class. Vocational and academic subjects represented by the trainees ranged from beauty, English, Functional Skills, Acting, Art and Animal Welfare to plumbing and hairdressing. They all consented to participate in this research; they were all highly supportive of one another. I had begun the two-year programme by saying that:

1. They were not in competition with each other.... (they all visibly relaxed at this point).
2. Their job during the year was to support one another via Critical Friendship Groups (Costa and Kallick 1993; Wachob 2011)

Could this be said in staff rooms?

The strategy was a vision based on social learning theories, such as Bandura (1977) and Vygotsky (1978). I was also very aware that what was being said in training sessions did not necessarily reflect the experi-ence of trainees being alone and outnumbered by a class of students; one person supposedly in control of many. Why should the students obey anything the teacher said? Modelling classroom behaviour in the training session was totally different to the trainees being in front of tough, dis-ruptive classes (Powell 2012). Being a self-reflexive practitioner, explain-ing every move I made in the classroom (rather like an advanced driving test) for trainees to follow would not necessarily be helpful. If a trainee started to act in this way in their own vocational context, of say plumbing, the students could become very aggressive and alienated from the learn-ing process, not wanting to hear about the plumber's personal musings or feelings.

Setting Up the Training Session

I set the training classroom out in a horse-shoe with myself at the centre in my role as facilitator. I also made it clear that trainees could and maybe should challenge my views. If I said something that did not apply to their context, I allowed critical discussions to take place. I again pointed out that trainees were not in competition with each other, but were there to support one another. Could they use this idea in their own classes or would open discussion be too threatening for both tutor and students? I said that the class operated as a supervision (Randall and Thornton 2001) whereby, in teacher education sessions, each trainee's teaching of the previous week was going to be discussed with me and the rest of the class in an emotionally supportive, hopefully sensitive, but possibly critical way. The final aspect of the strategy was that the class operated as a kind of think-tank, whereby each trainee offered supportive help or suggested solutions to other trainees' class-management problems.

However, the key defining characteristic of the strategy was that it gave primacy to trainees' experiences. In this respect it could be thought of as an empirical methodology in that trainee teaching experience was the focus of discussion; theory or a meta-language of analysis was used to define, explain, give some structure or interpret raw trainee experience. There was here a key issue of constructing experience using language, breaking up classroom incidents and inevitably interpreting them through narrative. The complexity of what had happened in their classes was explored through oral, critical and self-reflective practice.

The fact that I began by telling the class that they were not in competition with each other in the opening session had a demonstrable effect on all trainees. They immediately relaxed; faces visibly lowered in tension. Could this in turn have an impact in their classrooms? I deliberately did not use imagery of competition or even games which might bring in a competitive edge. The reason was that if trainees were to trust each other totally or were going to be reliant on one another for feedback and support, then there had to be an adult atmosphere of facilitative learning. Games and competition might detract from the atmosphere of reflection and authentic support. I was concerned that bringing in competitive activities (which other teacher educators used quite regularly) might encourage a more individualistic approach and undermine a supportive, communal atmosphere. I wanted them to be intrinsically motivated by interest in the nature of what went on in each others' classes. As Kohn argues intrinsic and extrinsic motivation are reciprocally related: as extrinsic goes up, the intrinsic most often goes down (1993).

I wanted an atmosphere where all trainees would feel comfortable about sharing difficult or challenging experiences, responding to social engagement, collaborative learning and dialogue (Pritchard 2009). I started each session with simple questions, such as 'what has gone well this week?' This was supposed to elicit confidence, building up a bank of good experiences, examples of 'good practice' or how trainees overcame difficult circumstances. It also was supposed to build an accumulation of activities where trainees had successfully engaged students, had overcome problematic behaviours or taught good or even outstanding lessons. Enumerating these experiences reinforced positive messages about teaching, built up community, developed a sense of resilience, particularly offering ways for trainees to operate in a challenging climate with clear ideas of how it was possible to be successful. However, the key question for exploring what was problematic was the question 'what challenges have you faced in your placements this week?'

The class were all teaching in a range of vocational and academic environments; private training companies, Further Education Colleges or community-based adult education. All were now willing to express their feelings and experiences, but also support one another in class. Why did they want to do this? Although they were all teaching in different contexts, they understood that they were part of a culture dedicated to improving student behaviour in their own contexts and wanted to gain skills by which this could take place. It benefited each trainee to be honest and receive and give support. Could this actually be a model for all staff rooms?

Once I had asked this opening question each trainee had five minutes to outline what had happened in their classes during that week. Some trainees needed longer when they faced more difficult circumstances and other trainees wanted to offer ideas or directions from their own experience. Each trainee explained their specific challenge and then other trainees or I would present theoretical models, ideas, possible solutions or explore how they would have dealt with that problem in their own context. The fact that the problem was out in the open and could be discussed or put under scrutiny started to have a strong impact on all trainees in the class. Everyone began to feel more confident to speak. This developed trainees' sense of self-confidence and ability to express themselves in public. Everyone felt supported by other trainees; everyone said they felt less isolated. This was crucial as a model for dealing with disruptive classes. Trainees said they looked forward to this weekly class because they felt they had a space where they could talk about professional issues and challenging class management problems. They said it was a space where they could speak about appalling circumstances, be listened to and be supported.

As facilitator I sometimes abnegated myself in order to make more space for the trainees' presence. I felt that if my personality was too dominant, then it would take power away from the students, but also give them less space to reflect on their classroom practice. However, I made it clear that this was not a session to talk about relationships, family or personal problems unless these impinged in some direct way on the trainee's ability to teach. The trainees' personal presence, self-esteem, reflection on self, emotional resilience was only important in so far as this impacted on their professional lives. The focus of all discussion was how to overcome difficulties coping with 'problematic' classes and students.

WHAT PROBLEMS DID TRAINEES FACE?

Trainee A, anonymised as Adrian, explained how he taught a Foundation Learning group in Social Care. The room was very large; he had a group of around 15 learners. There was a whiteboard at the front and the students sat on benches, but these were placed at quite large distances of over 10 yards from the front of the classroom. The benches were at disparate angles from each other. The students found it difficult to concentrate. They had fights outside the class. Chairs had previously been thrown round the room. One male student had head-butted his ex-girlfriend before the lesson. Both had been students together in this class. He was excluded as punishment; she had been hospitalised. The atmosphere in class was apparently sullen and tense.

Trainee B, anonymised as Bates, described his class where eight students sat in a computer room at a table. This table was in the middle of the room. They were supposed to be studying Functional Skills Numeracy. One student tore up another student's work, security was called and the student was excluded. Another student shouted out: 'He's ugly! I'm not sitting near him.' Another female student handed out condoms. One student settled to her work on a computer; the others talked or argued. Some carried out tasks, whist others disrupted the atmosphere with changing seats, texting or shouting 'You, W-!' The content of the lesson, 'subtraction,' was the last subject anyone seemed to be interested in. Someone asked: 'Why do we need to do Maths? I left school to get away from all that! Why are you making us do this?'

THE STRATEGY AT WORK

We began to discuss Adrian's class. Violence was no longer coming from teachers to students as in my experience, but was now from students to teachers. Adrian seemed relieved that the tension of coping with this fraught situation could be shared in the teacher education classroom. There was no condemnation that the class was basically not successful. Adrian had warned the fractious couple about dating whilst being on the same course. They had not heeded his warning. It was also ironic that this class was in 'caring.'

So what should Adrian do to improve the class atmosphere? The first point made in the discussion was that the geography of the class needed changing. Setting the teacher education class up as a horse-shoe might work in our training context, but would it work for disruptive students? Vizard (2012) and Petty (2014) advise teachers to set up classes where possible before the start of the session, but this is not always possible. Colleagues in the current session suggested that the benches should be positioned near the whiteboard at the front. Through discussion Adrian was beginning to model his class on what he had seen happen in our training class. But was this enough? Just because a strategy worked in the training context did not mean it would work when teaching students in their vocational settings. In class we were modelling Rogers' view of unconditional positive regard (1961), a Humanistic perspective on relationships between tutor and students, however, would this be of any use in a more aggressive environment (Powell 2012)?

We also used Knowles' andragogy approach (1975) in the teacher education context, where all trainees were treated as self-directed adults. However, again the problem was trying to bring this sort of relationship into Adrian's classroom. We debated how he might transpose the sort of civilised discussion we had in teacher education classes into such a fraught environment? The debate focussed on whether Adrian should apply other theories of classroom management, using behaviourist approaches of reward and punishment, such as negative and positive reinforcements as more effective in this brutal context? Maybe, this was the only language that the students understood.

Through discussion, support and analysis, Adrian started to build more confidence, self-esteem and presence in the training classroom. He was starting to take on the tone in training sessions that he was going to use in his own class. He was beginning to recreate this adult version of learning with his group. Students now sat in pairs and discussed an idea, as we had done in training sessions, or read a piece before they contributed to class discussion. We had a trainee education class discussion on authentic ways of embedding Equality and Diversity into lessons. Adrian reported that his group were particularly engaged in discussing this issue. The support that Adrian received from the teacher education class was beginning to have an effect on his teaching. Adrian said that class discussions were starting to be more meaningful and impact on his students' learning. He had introduced a non-competitive element into his class; students were beginning to open up and explore issues, just as we did in our training sessions. On many levels this was an 'improvement.'

CREATIVITY VERSUS CONTROL

Bates was using creative ideas to engage his students. He reported a range of activities, such as identifying coloured shapes on a power-point, offering a range of imaginative worksheets on number, innovation, goals and feedback (Hattie 1999). This was discussed in class, but not modelled in our sessions. The students were, however, resistant. In the trainee education sessions, someone suggested changing Bates's class layout, placing each student on a computer round the room and then putting them on a numeracy programme whereby they could build up their Maths skills and get used to ICT in a more controlled way. This was counter-intuitive or seemed retrograde in terms of inclusive learning, communication and stopping the isolation of students. Was this a control model, where students' creativity was being shut down? This strategy might 'settle' the students, ensure they were carrying out tasks, and involve them more directly in the culture and outcomes of their numeracy exam. But was it creative?

Should Adrian use behaviourist approaches to get results (Knippen and Green 1997)? Against the culture of our own training discussions, I suggested that Adrian could take on a more controlling approach to his students. I said that he might get more assertive, but should he follow Petty and pick on individuals (2014, p. 107) or bring in rules, sanctions and rewards. Was I suggesting this because of the disciplinary methods in my own background or because I was offering a provocative, alternative view? Or was it from my experience of teaching 'difficult classes' during my career, protecting Bates from the overwhelming stress of unresponsive students or the Ofsted context of not tolerating disruption? All these thoughts were in my mind.

Although I argued for a more controlled version of the classroom, both Adrian and Bates resisted my view very strongly. Both wanted to use person-centred teaching methods (Gatongi 2007) and did not want to treat their students in a behaviourist, controlling or negative way. They refused to treat students as objects because this completely contradicted their values and the reason why they had become involved in a teaching career in the first place. Was this a re-statement of my own motive for going into teaching, a valuing of the human above the requirements of performativity that so dominate our current environment? Bates had empathy for his students (Patterson 1980); they had been degraded or treated in a negative or demeaning way in their homes or schools. They were from poorer backgrounds (Freire 1972), had had limited access to education, development or progression in their personal lives or careers; their 'disaffection' had covered a 'wide range of characteristics, attitudes and dispositions towards home, learning and life' (Wellington and Cole 2004, p. 102).

The andragogy model had been internalised by the two trainees and they made it a principle that they were going to treat all students in a full, humanised respected way (Doyle 2008). They both said they were trying to connect, have congruence and empathy with their students (Gatongi, ibid., p. 206). Was the modelling of what we were doing in our teacher education classes being carried out in foundation learning classes (Powell 2012)? Or was it something else? When it came to observing these classes, by the end of the first term, both classes had 'settled' down. Both groups were carrying out tasks as required, becoming engaged in class discussion and, most important of all, beginning to speak to each other and their teachers in a more respectful way. Was this the method that had worked or did all classes start to acculturate into college routines? Was this just the process of immature students maturing? It was certainly an improvement.

Yet More Analysis

The question is whether there was direct causality between the reflective strategy deployed in the teacher education class and the 'improvement' in student behaviour in Foundation Learning classes? It could be argued that the students may have matured during the 10-week term under discussion anyway. They may have become acculturated into the more adult modes of college life, realised that there was a purpose to Functional Skills and that the alternatives to upgrading qualifications were even more grim than being in class. They may not have wanted to be excluded as had happened to other colleagues. The institutional framework, managerial attitudes and course requirements may have all begun to percolate into the students' consciousnesses.

We understand learning as constructed (Prasad and Caproni 1997). The assumption of this chapter is that learning takes place and there is development and change. The problem is how do we know what causes what? How do we know that the teacher education model of andragogy and focussing on trainee experience actually had or has an effect on the trainees and this in turn impacted on their classes? In other words, how can we be sure that teacher education or even reflection is effective (Cornford 2002)? All we know is that according to the trainees their students were initially un-cooperative. They were not interested in being in a learning environment. We know through my evidence of an observation that they were later on programme and when observed were 'engaged learners,' working on their required tasks. There was little, if any, disruption. Was the 'improvement' due to an observer being present which created a more productive lesson (O' Leary 2006)? Their 'improvement' might have been fear of an outsider coming into the class and possibly reporting on their behaviour? Or was the 'improvement' due to the growing confidence of the trainees? Was this in turn caused by 'the strategy'? There were so many variables.

However, the trainees themselves said that the support they had received from the teacher education class, the way that they had formulated their own values in this context and the space they had been given to experiment with possible approaches was crucial. The weekly supervisions had helped with working out a Humanistic approach to dealing with their respective, 'problematic' groups. Opening up and discussing feelings about classes had been, according to these trainees, a liberating and supportive experience.

Could this now work in staffrooms?

CONCLUSION

As suggested, case studies open debate on specific situations, but cannot necessarily be applied to other contexts. However, these trainees' teaching situations seem to be typical of the problems and challenges many tutors face in the foundation or basic studies learning sector. The debate around how best to deal with disruptive classes and individual students is an ongoing problematic issue that depends on the dynamic of each individual tutor, their relationship with their classes and the institutional framework within which they are trained and work. In this chapter I have tried to suggest a strategy, which could be used in teachers' training sessions for supporting trainees in these fraught situations and possibly extending this methodology to staff-rooms. In one instance learning at computers was seen as the solution. In the next chapter we will start to explore some of the problems of blended or digital learning before we move onto more research into what different teacher educators and trainees from many different colleges, universities and training organisations say on these issues.

Some Suggestions

1. Create a supportive environment through stating that other teachers/students/trainees are not in competition with each other in class.
2. It could be suggested that all students/trainees are there 'in order' to support one another. This could help to build a 'community of practice' in classrooms.
3. Create safe spaces where teachers can discuss what happens in their lessons, exploring what is going well and difficulties.
4. Be flexible enough to use a range of different strategies and techniques in lessons. Keep records of what works with which classes.
5. Teachers can develop critical friendship groups physically or online, helping each other with what is going on in their classes.

BIBLIOGRAPHY

Avis, J. (2002). Policing the subject: Learning outcomes, manageralism and research in PCET. *British Journal of Educational Studies, 48*(1), 38–57.
Ball, S. (2003). The teacher's soul and the terrors of performativity. *Journal of Education Policy, 18*(2), 215–228.
Bandura, A. (1977). *Social learning theory.* Englewood Cliffs: Prentice- Hall.
Boud, D., & Walker, D. (1998). Promoting reflection in professional courses: The challenge of context. *Studies in Higher Education, 23*(2), 191–206.
Brookfield, S. (1993). Through the lens of learning: How the visceral experience of learning reframes teaching. In D. Boud et al. (Eds.), *Using experience for learning.* Buckingham: Open University Press.

Cohen, L., Manion, L., & Morrison, K. (2011). *Research methods in education.* London/New York: Routledge and Falmer.

Cornford, I. (2002). Reflective teaching: Empirical research findings and some implications for teacher education. *Journal of Vocational Education and Training, 54*(2), 219–234.

Costa, A., & Kallick, B. (1993). Through the lens of a critical friend. *Educational Leadership: Journal of the Department of Supervision and Curriculum Development, N.E.A, 51*(2), 49–51.

Cunliffe, A. (2004). On becoming a critically reflexive practitioner. *Journal of Management Education, 28*(4), 407–426.

DFE. (2012). *Pupil behaviour in schools in England* (DFE-RR218). https://www.education.gov.uk/publications/

Doyle, T. (2008). *Helping students learn in a learner-centered environment: A guide to facilitating learning in higher education.* Sterling: Stylus.

Freire, P. (1972). *The pedagogy of the oppressed.* Harmondsworth: Penguin.

Gatongi, F. (2007). Person-centred approach in schools: Is it the answer to disruptive behaviour in our classrooms? *Counselling Psychology Quarterly, 20*(2), 205–211. Routledge, Taylor & Francis.

Gibbs, J. (2001). *A new way of learning and being together.* Windsor: Centresource Systems.

Hattie, J. (1999, August 2). *Influences on student learning.* Inaugural Lecture: Professor of Education, University of Aukland. Available from http://library.hud.ac.uk/summon

Hobson, A. J., Malderez, A., Tracey, L., Ashby, P., Mitchell, N., McIntyre, J., et al. (2009). *Becoming a teacher: Teachers' experiences of initial teacher training, induction and early professional development.* Final Report DCSF Research Report DCSF- RR115. https://www.education.gov.uk/publications/eOrderingDownload/DCSF

Jones, F., Jones, P., & Jones, J. (2007). *Tools for teaching; discipline, instruction, motivation.* Santa Cruz: F.H. Jones & Associates.

Knippen, J. T., & Green, T. B. (1997). Asking for positive reinforcement. *Journal of Workplace Learning, 9*(5), 163–168.

Knowles, M. (1975). *Self-directed learning. A guide for learners and teachers.* Cambridge/Englewood Cliffs: Prentice Hall.

Kohn, A. (1993). *Punished by rewards.* Boston/New York: Houghton Mifflin.

Marzano, R. J., Marzano, S., & Pickering, D. J. (2003). *Classroom management that work: Research-based strategy for every teacher.* Alexandria: Association for Supervision and Curriculum Development.

O' Leary, M. (2006). Can inspectors really improve the quality of teaching in the PCE sector? Classroom observations under the microscope. *Research in Post-Compulsory Education, 11*(2), 191–198. Routledge.

Ofsted. (2012). *The framework for school inspection from September 2012. Doc.* http://www.ofsted.gov.uk

Patterson, C. H. (1980). Theories of counselling and psychotherapy cited in P. T. Clarke (1994) A person-centred approach to stress-management. *British Journal of guidance and Counselling, 22,* 27–37.

Petty, G. (2014). *Teaching today: A practical guide* (5th ed.). London: Oxford.

Powell, D. (2012). *Teacher educators from the lifelong learning sector working together to develop the use of modelling in their practice: An action research project.* Consortium for PCET annual conference 2012 in association with Higher Education Academy Seminar Series 2011–12, Friday, 29th June 2012, University of Huddersfield.

Prasad, P., & Caproni, P. (1997). Critical theory in the management classroom: Engaging power, ideology and praxis. *Journal of Management Education, 21*(5), 284–291.

Pritchard, A. (2009). *Ways of learning: Learning theories and learning styles in the classroom.* Abingdon: Routledge.

Randall, M., & Thornton, B. (2001). Supervision and the three-stage model of helping. In *Advising and supporting teachers* (pp. 61–76). Cambridge: CUP.

Reinis, N. (2013). FE sector fights back over Ofsted. *InTuition, 2*(Spring), 12–14.

Rogers, C. (1961). *On becoming a person: A therapist's view of psychotherapy.* London: Constable.

Simmons, R., & Thompson, R. (2011). *Education and training for young people at risk of becoming NEET: Findings from an ethnographic study of work-based learning programmes.* London: Routledge.

Townend, M. (2013). Massive rise in disruptive behaviour, warn teachers. http://www.guardian.co.uk/education/2013/mar/24/schools-disruptive-behaviour

Vizard, D. (2012). *How to manage behaviour in further education.* London: Sage.

Vygotsky, L. S. (1978). *Mind in society: The development of higher psychological processes.* Cambridge, MA: Harvard University Press.

Wachob, P. (2011). Critical friendship circles: The cultural challenge of cool feedback. *Professional Development in Education, 37*(3), 353–372.

Wellington, J., & Cole, P. (2004). Conducting evaluation and research with and for 'disaffected' students: Practical and methodological issues. *British Journal of Special Education, 31*(2), 100–104.

Wenger, E. (1998). *Communities of practice: Learning, meaning and identity.* Cambridge: Cambridge University Press.

CHAPTER 9

What Could Possibly Be Problematic About Digital Learning?

The triggers for research in this chapter into the disruptive aspects of ICT learning, teaching and assessment were from several sources. In my work over many years as a Quality Reviewer/External Moderator, I have been highly conscious of many tutors' concerns around plagiarism in students' work. This was not merely copying and pasting material that could be picked up either through software, such as TURNITIN and URKUND, or by typing phrases into Google and finding that essays supposedly written by students came up verbatim on the Internet; this was something far more sinister.

THE GHOST WRITERS

I was asked at a conference on disruptive behaviour as to whether blended or digital learning dealt with many of the classroom problems that I had outlined. Students were now in Google, virtual or flipped classrooms or were involved in different forms of distance learning, so the problems of violence, aggression, insulting behaviour towards teachers, lack of concentration, socialising in the classroom or use of mobile phones were no longer relevant. Much college work was blended between physical and virtual classrooms. My answer was that unfortunately, some of the same issues, such as cyber-bullying (Agatston et al. 2007) and disruption of learning and even plagiarism on a large scale functioned within the digital environment. But was this true? I had heard much evidence through interviewing teachers within the post-school sector about students getting parents, siblings, tutors, colleagues or paid writers to 'ghost write' their coursework

© The Author(s) 2017
M. Lebor, *Classroom Behaviour Management in the Post-School Sector*, DOI 10.1007/978-3-319-57051-8_9

at GCSE, BTEC, A level and degree work (Anon 2014). Was this more widely true and could it be substantiated? What did a sample of teachers and students say? What was their experience of using digital technology in the post-school sector?

Despite notes of caution (Hennessy et al. 2005), there is an assumption that we are all part of a culture where ICT is deeply embedded into every activity that supports learning (Livingstone 2011). Yet there are many pedagogic concerns, such as the assumption that time online is necessarily spent carrying out learning tasks and that all students' work can be authenticated as their own, but also that abuse is not taking place within social media supposedly devoted to learning.

In this context of investigating students' activities that 'stop learning taking place,' it might be helpful to explore what a sample of teachers and students say is happening on this issue with respect to digital learning in localised situations and whether they can suggest any ideas to obviate the problems that they are currently experiencing. Was ICT useful as a method for countering class management issues? But who should be approached to recount or elucidate their experiences? Were students going to give authentic, reliable accounts? If they were plagiarising work, what would motivate them to acknowledge this? Why would they be believed? Why would certain tutors offer a more expert view than others? Would it not be better to approach the extensive literature on these topics? There are many complex reasons for plagiaristic behaviour (Park 2003). These include limited language abilities (Polio and Shi 2012), misunderstandings as to what plagiarism is (Jurdi et al. 2011), and even different cultural outlooks on plagiarism (Liu 2005). I argue that plagiarism and cyber-bullying are forms of abuse, disrupting digital learning.

This book is really centred on what students, teachers, managers, trainees and teacher educators say about their practice and how this is or is not compromised by disruptions of learning. It is a dialogue between theory and experience; that is, I quote authorities, but I am more interested in these ideas only in so far as they are put into use or classroom practice. Then the question is how do I know about teacher or student experience? Again all I can rely on are the traditional social science methods of extracting data. This is qualitative research focussed on what people say they believe or how they say they act. Hence, I have used interviews and surveys to find out about teachers' and students' views and experiences. In order to work with different samples I researched teachers and students at three different colleges and focussed on learning centres where ICT was heavily embedded. Again why not base the information on online data-collection surveys?

In fact I did carry out initial research in this way, but found much of the information unreliable. Total anonymity meant that people claiming to be teachers or students could make extravagant claims under the protection of secrecy. Why would students who plagiarised work be honest in a digital survey?

THE QUESTIONS REMAINED

Were the same problems of disruption happening in ICT environments either in digital learning centres or online? Were there any ways of countering these problems? These were the underlying questions of the research represented in this chapter. It is again small-scale qualitative research into the experiences of teachers and students, exploring the problematic nature of virtual classrooms, analysing the benefits and disadvantages of bringing technology into the classroom from the point of view of class management issues. It probes the surface of these issues. More systematic, triangulated research is probably necessary.

After an initial survey of over 50 teachers, it emerged that the main pedagogic concerns they faced were firstly the assumption that time spent online supposedly doing academic work was not necessarily spent learning. The second issue was that all students' work could not be authenticated as their own. Students signing authentication declarations did not mean that this was genuinely their own work. The third issue that they mentioned was that abuse was taking place within social media supposedly devoted to learning contexts. The research task was to survey a range of teachers and students investigating whether these claims could be substantiated in three different contexts and whether these ICT users could offer ideas for countering these problems.

The wider context of this research is the overwhelming consolidation of the importance of digital learning through many books (Palloff and Pratt 2007; Darlene 2014), academic papers (Granberg 2010; Underwood and Dillon 2011; Wood 2012) and practice (Sutherland et al. 2004) whereby ICT is now 'omnipresent' (Underwood and Dillon 2011, p. 317) in all areas of teaching and learning in the United Kingdom and beyond. There have been 'utopian' hopes for ICT as potentially stimulating an educational renaissance as digital technologies are now so thoroughly embedded into teacher practice (Fisher et al. 2006) that it is difficult to imagine the classroom without digital support. There is a widespread belief that technology in and of itself facilitates active learning and higher-order thinking skills (Swan and Shea 2005), but also, an acknowledgement that there are a range of opposing paradigms explaining the impact of ICT on education (Aviram 2004). Nevertheless, the belief is that ICT is now central to learners' experiences (Underwood et al. 2010) and blended learning is key to our understanding of how courses should be run from the point of view of economics, globalisation, increased learning and commercial innovation, but also as preparation for the world of work (Chowcatt et al. 2008).

Technology has a positive effect on student success (Yang 2008), but is also used effectively to enhance teaching by offering a digital environment outside the physical classroom that was not available to previous generations, involving e-mail, chat-rooms, blogs and online discussions (Szabo and Schwartz 2011). More discussion time, critical thinking and more direct interaction between teacher and student becomes possible. It has also been used to transform education and set up self-determining groups of learners, genuinely offering 'pedagogies for the oppressed' (Freire 1972) by radically opening up the lives of some of the most economically and educationally deprived students (Mitra 2010). As argued in *Harnessing Technology*, ICT is a social and cultural phenomenon (Chowcatt, ibid.) whereby digital technologies have transformed the ways we engage with knowledge (Kress and Pachler 2007). Central to these views is Further Education Learning Technology Action Group (FELTAG 2013), which seems to offer faith in new technology in Further Education as the future of teaching in the post-school sector. The problem is whether this technology is being abused and what is the experience of teachers and learners in this context.

Methodology

A possible approach to this question would be to ask large numbers of teachers how many times they had detected plagiarism in students' work or ask equivalent numbers of students whether they had been bullied online or what was the relationship in terms of time they spent carrying out learning or assessment tasks compared to time online for social purposes. It was more important for this book, in line with the qualitative methodologies already in place, that I explored teachers' and students' attitudes and feelings towards ICT. Thus, using qualitative research to explore attitudes and experiences (Wallace 2002, p. 81) it was important to triangulate their views on ICT (Denscombe, pp. 346–351) through using mixed methods of research (Cohen, ibid., pp. 197–8). Thus data was collected by asking another 40 teachers their views via a survey, but also exploring attitudes through in-depth interviews with eight teachers who had a particularly strong commitment to using ICT. Did it stop disruption taking place? A sample of 150 students selected at random from three ICT workshops at different colleges were also questioned as to their own positive and negative experiences of using ICT in learning in order to triangulate teacher-based information. The underlying question again was, from the point of view of this book, whether blended or ICT based learning could counter the problems of disrupting teaching, learning and assessment.

The aim of this small-scale study was not to undermine or question the use of ICT *per-se*, but rather to question some assumptions. Attitudes were investigated through a survey which in the first instance sequenced (Cohen, pp. 397–8) teachers' thoughts on the benefits of ICT. This was a way of engaging with the positive side of technology and reflecting on views which would probably corroborate much of the literature alluded to above. It also put the more problematic side of the research into a wider context, thus the opening question read: 'What do you see as the main benefits of using ICT in teaching and assessment?' This was a chance for teachers to extol the many benefits of using ICT and show that the problems of disruptive learning took place within a wider, highly positive context. The next question again asked about how ICT supported teaching. This initial positive opening was a way of not asking leading negative questions (Cohen, ibid., p. 396) or showing an expectation that the survey would be weighted towards wanting to hear negative information about ICT. The third question asked about the main problematic aspects of using ICT in terms of teaching and learning, whilst the fourth listed a range of possible problems, including being aware of students as victims of cyber-bullying or plagiarism. There was a box for anonymous writing about any of the above issues and finally a chance to suggest ways of countering these problems. The interviews with tutors asked the same questions, but there was a chance that tutors' answers could be explored in more depth.

The sample for the survey was chosen on the basis of tutors by sending out e-mails to a wide range of teachers who worked in a variety of colleges. In the end over 100 tutors were given the survey and they filled it in, discussed the content and signed ethical forms authorising their participation in the research (BERA). They worked in many contexts, such as universities, colleges, training units and charities.

The main interviewees were a sample of eight tutors who worked within different educational institutions. They all had qualifications beyond first degree, a strong commitment and/or vested interest in ICT. They were all highly literate in using ICT in teaching, but were aware of the problems and were in a position to express some criticality. This explored some of the problematic aspects of ICT in an open and candid way, offering an opportunity to discuss ways in which ICT enhanced, but also was subverted so that learning was ineffective, misused, disrupted or did not take place. In order to triangulate the findings of this research, it also seemed to be important to ask a range of students about their experience of using ICT. In what ways was it useful? But on the other hand, how was learning disrupted?

I have constructed a brief table of the tutor-practitioner interviewees so that the reader can see some spread of experience, perspective, training and background which might be taken into account when determining the positionality of their views.

THE EIGHT TUTOR-PRACTITIONERS

	Age	Gender	Highest qualification	Involvement with ICT
Abie	60+	Male	Phd.	Taught sociology at professorial level in HE; director of own digital technology company
Blanche	20+	Female	MA (CAM)	Consultant manager/trainer in digital technology company
Miriam	40+	Female	Phd.	Section leader of department; heavily committed to embedding ICT resources
Dennis	30+	Male	Masters/on doctoral programme	Manager of ICT systems in HE
Eleanor	40+	Female	Masters/on doctoral programme	Manager of HE programmes; heavily committed to ICT resources
Fabian	40+	Male	MA in ICT	Lecturer/trainer using applications of ICT in teachers' learning
Gavriel	50+	Male	BSc/diploma in information technology	Manager of learning resources at a college
Hal	50+	Male	MBE/engineering degree	Manager of ICT college workshop for 1000 students per week

What the ICT Practitioners Said

The opening two positive questions asking about the benefits of using ICT offered a surprisingly wide range of answers, highlighting points from the general literature on ICT applied to the tutors' specific contexts of experience. Abie said ICT 'helped students with research,' 'supported remote learning,' 'speeded up assessment' and helped 'students who could not attend classes for health or other reasons.' Blanche saw ICT more in terms of 'knowledge sharing,' 'lessons are more democratic because not under one authority,' information was unconfined because it could be 'accessed easily on a phone on the bus.'

Miriam said ICT 'prepared students for the global economy' and opened a 'plethora of resources.' Dennis was more focussed on 'the improved experience of learners,' whilst Eleanor spoke of 'extending the classroom, offering follow-up conversations,' but most importantly 'enhancing equality and diversity.' Fabian viewed ICT as related to a way of 'resourcing lessons more cheaply,' offering 'the flipped classroom as a good model for initiating self-directed learning.' Finally, Gavriel saw it as a way of 'constantly upgrading resources,' whilst Hal thought of ICT as a way of 'connecting the individual to the world.'

But what about the more negative sides of ICT? What were the drawbacks to using ICT in teaching, learning and assessment? Abie saw ICT as 'offering a huge opportunity for plagiarism.' This was not necessarily because of copying from digital sources which could be picked up by software, such as TURNITIN, but the anonymity of typed work. 'It could be written by anyone.' Abie had, in fact, during his career, challenged 'many dozens of students' for plagiarising work directly from books or journals without referencing. Blanche thought the main problems were 'information overload' and the 'constant distractions of commercialised advertising targeted to tempt students away from the focus of research because of what the student had previously browsed.' This was a distraction or even disruption of learning. Blanche thought there were also major issues of the constant re-appropriation and availability of other people's ideas' which were 'passed off by students as original.'

Miriam felt that the biggest drawback was the depersonalisation of knowledge; once alone with the screen, there was a problem that students could be looking at anything and had no access or help with interpreting 'what information actually meant.' The significance of this was that they spent much time online looking at material that was irrelevant to learning. But was this disruption of learning or merely self-sabotage?

Dennis said there was 'a need for facilitators to help mediate informa-tion.' Traditional approaches 'are now being forced into an ICT based delivery.' He said 'ICT is often failing to reflect the correct levels of learn-ing that have occurred.' The question remained as to whether having access to so much information meant that learning was undermined. Eleanor was concerned about 'vested interests controlling what could be learnt,' the way technology kept 'being updated,' yet 'this was not necessarily for the benefit of the learners.' But ultimately her main concern was 'the endemic plagiarism that went beyond what was discernible by software.' Fabian focussed more on the fact that 'teaching and learning was essentially about building human relationships.' He said that the positive 'outcomes of the hidden curriculum,' such as 'ethical behaviour were not easily captured because ICT embedded notions of performativity into learning agendas.' Students, in his experience, mostly focussed on their social lives.

Gavriel believed that students 'were now too reliant on technology,' but there was also a 'definite need still to explain the meaning of digital work to learners,' who tended to just cut and paste their work without understanding its meaning. Learning was continually being subverted. Finally, Hal's experience was that 'students were frequently distracted from their course material.' They were 'often lured into social media' and instead of 'staring out of an actual classroom window' were staring 'into multiple windows of far more attractive, virtual worlds.'

When asked specifically whether these tutors had knowledge of their learners suffering from cyber-bullying, none had direct personal experi-ence of their students being involved either as victims or perpetrators of this behaviour; all, however, were highly aware that this was phenomena reported at considerable length in the media. Nevertheless, again when asked about plagiarism, all eight tutors said they had 'experience of their students plagiarising work' which was an issue that seemed to present an ongoing battle for many tutors.

THE VIEWS OF 80 OTHER TEACHERS

This was a written survey, gathering information from 80 tutors who worked in many diverse areas of the Education and Training sector, rang-ing from University, Further Education, training units and charities to special programmes supporting apprentices or vocational training in the community. They were asked a similar range of questions, but wrote down their answers rather than being interviewed. They responded to e-mail requests for attitudes and views on whether ICT stopped the problems of disruptive behaviour or whether ICT generated its own areas of concern?

Their views on the positive benefits of ICT corroborated the literature and the outlook of the ICT 'practitioners.' Other points not addressed above were that ICT was particularly 'ideal for visual learners,' offered 'large amounts of instant information,' 'numerous articles were available,' it compensated for 'book shortages in the library' and could 'make material more interesting through Youtube and other film back-up.' Many other points were made, but all could fit under statements or categories already identified in the literature or explained by previous interviews. When it came to the negative sides of ICT, the 80 teachers offered a range of attitudes, a sample of which is recorded below.

Thus, ICT delivery is, according to Aaron, a licence for 'many of my level 3 and level 4 (degree) students....to plagiarise work. They just cut and paste from the Internet.' Alexander was aware that 'all 16–18 students' in his classes 'were always attempting to plagiarise work if given the chance.' Bruce said 'Google classrooms were just an opportunity for students not to turn up at lessons, copy the material and pretend that they had learnt something.' Gertrude said that 'too much information' was 'overwhelming' for her level 3 students. Students needed 'to be taught how to select material.' She said that they did not even understand the difference between plagiarised and authentic work.

Joshua was aware of 'constant data protection breaches,' whilst Barbara said it was 'easy to plagiarise information online; you just had to change a few words to fool plagiarism software or put in extra spaces.' She said 'working as an online tutor, I find there is a lot of plagiarism in answers given,' whilst Dean was aware of his students trying to 'carry out plagiarism or cheating in online assessments as the norm.' Simone said she was aware of students 'involved in cyber bullying.' Jeremy said his students were 'constantly distracted by Facebook and other social media.' Thomas said 'sometimes learners plagiarise their assignments,' but 'many were involved in social networking during learning time.' Bill needed to explain 'all digital content to students as they did not understand where their own work started and digital work stopped.' Finally, Malcolm knew 'of one online bullying situation,' but more generally found students 'often couldn't stay focussed because of too much information in front of them.'

The other 65 teachers in this sample continued with the themes of plagiarism, lack of focus, the problems of understanding or accessing technology, but only a couple referred specifically to their actual experience of knowing about perpetrators or victims of cyber-bullying. The main experience of teachers from a wide variety of institutions seemed to be mostly centred on plagiarism in terms of the problems of disruptive behaviour. This research seemed to suggest that merely moving to the digital classroom did not solve problems of disruptive or subversive behaviour in terms of undermining teaching and learning. But what did a range of students say about digital learning?

WHAT 150 STUDENTS SAID...?

Students using ICT facilities in three highly populated ICT workshops at different colleges were approached randomly and asked about their experiences of ICT on a questionnaire form. The questions followed the same pattern as previously, but were slightly shortened in order not to take up too much student time, but also to simplify the issues so that students from a range of academic levels could easily read and engage with the content of the enquiry. In fact out of the 100 students initially questioned 78 were on level 3 or 4 courses, in other words, A level or degree based learning equivalent. All were 18 or over as I was conscious of only using students aged 18+ to ensure that there were no problems of parental authorisation (BERA). All participating students signed a consent form.

The first question again focussed on the benefits of ICT. The responses reiterated much of what had been earlier stated in the literature, by the ICT 'practitioners' and the 80 teachers. This included some predictable comments on the 'fast' availability and 'easy access to information and more resources,' or that it was 'good for research' and 'communication.' However, other comments referred to aspects which were more specific to student life than the view of teachers, thus one student said that information was 'simpler online than in books'; another agreed that it often 'clarified complicated topics.' Others said engagement with ICT helped 'you keep up with technology'; ICT was 'useful for gaining skills for a career in the future.' Kahoot online quizzes, for example, were an effective way of checking learning. ICT gave 'efficiency' and 'offered free space to do work and access new data.' It 'allows flexibility and can be used for visual, verbal and interactive learning.'

There were two slots for students to explain their more critical views. The first space asked 'what do you see as the main problems of using ICT on your course?' The second asked students whether they were aware of themselves or other students (A) being a victim of or carrying out cyber-bullying. (B) Carrying out plagiarism or cheating in online assessment They were supposed to tick both, either or none of the options and possibly comment on any details.

Only two students ticked box A, i.e. admitting that they had been or knew of other students who were victims of cyber-bullying. Fifty-five students ticked box B that said they had knowledge of other students plagiarising. The following opinions were stated by interviewees.

Medical Science students Douglas said 'plagiarism and bullying are endemic,' whilst Dani said that 'plagiarism [is the] biggest problem.' Denny said 'plagiarism and cyber-bullying [are the] main ICT problem on [the] course,' whilst Don characterised the main ICT problems as 'bullying, plagiarism and slow computers.' A level Maths student, Mark, said 'distractions waste time....' All the above-mentioned students plus groups of students from Business Studies, Engineering, Sports, Public Service, Science, Health Studies and Wild Life ticked the plagiarism box as one of the main problems of ICT on their courses.

Access Business student Geoff said the main problem was 'the distractions.' An A level Law student, Fran, said 'I am aware of students cheating, but I do not know these students personally.' Health student Jan said 'plagiarism and cyber-bullying [are] the main problem.' Art and Design student Maggie said the main ICT problems were 'hacking' and 'catfishing' i.e. others assuming identities for fraudulent purposes. Helena said 'students just copy and paste from the internet.' Again all the above students identified plagiarism as the main problem of ICT on their courses. However, it has to be said that 12 students interviewed out of the 100 said that there were no problems with ICT or as one chemistry student, Gerry, expressed it … 'there are no criticisms of ICT at all.'

At a later date I surveyed another 50 level 4 vocational students, 18 of whom said they were conscious of other students being involved in plagiarism on their courses. Seven students from this sample mentioned that they were aware of cyber-bullying happening either to themselves or other students at varying levels of intensity. Ghost-writing was said by five respondents to be a key feature of current, academic practice where other people wrote students' work for them.

Even if this was a small-scale piece of research, involving only 150 students from different colleges, some of these overall findings must be seen as, at least, quite disturbing.

ICT Practitioners View the Students' Findings

After reading the comments of students and being aware of the relevant literature, what did the eight practitioners suggest as ways forward for dealing with the issues that were raised by these students? Abie felt that the plagiarism situation was 'going to get worse,' because there were going to be so many more opportunities for this in the future. He suggested 'more sophisticated software that can identify individuals through their style of writing and the characteristic use of repeated words.' The software would have to 'recognise who is writing what.' In Blanche's experience 'much online testing is being carried out by other people,' but that candidates for jobs and qualifications 'needed to be further tested in other non-virtual environments in order to check for the reliability of candidates' work.' She also suggested 'optics tests, Skype interviews or digital signatures connected to finger or palm imprints.' She claimed that these were all ways to counter the culture of plagiarism and the undermining of student authenticity.

Miriam wanted a return to more traditional forms of assessment so that students could be tested through 'class-based coursework or vivas for back-up testing as to whether individual candidates really understood what they were writing about.' Dennis said 'each scenario was different' and so planned to improve 'the overall experience of assessment in ICT' by offering further research into each context' ensuring that ICT was being 'appropriately applied so that it was reliably implemented in each situation.' Each assessment framework needed to be individually researched and put under scrutiny for 'the possibilities of plagiarism through quality assurance methodologies.' Eleanor wanted to know about 'assessment contexts.' She asked: 'Who is the assessment for? Why is it necessary in each context; what is it supposed to achieve?' Only in the light of these 'fundamental questions about assessment' could 'the place of coursework and digitalised testing be secure.' Fabian suggested that sites for learners should be 'as full as possible.' There needed to be 'follow-up time' where teacher interactions with students were seen as 'of immense value.' Learners 'needed face-to-face support.' According to Fabian there was now a 'greater need than ever for softer teaching skills in communication and interpersonal development.'

Gavriel said that 'training is the key.' He said 'educational institutes need to offer very sophisticated forms of support to FE and HE students' who often 'struggle with the interface between the digital and the human.' Finally, Hal characterised the 'modern student' as someone who was 'partly using complex digital technology' and yet was also 'developing their own personal and knowledge-based identity.' He said 'we are now living in a world of considerable flux in digital education and identity.'

The complex problematic nature of individuals interacting with digital learning, their own emerging identities as learners and the processes of teaching and assessment seemed to raise more questions about the meaning of learning and being assessed in an authentic, reliable way within a digital context. This added yet another dimension to the class management debate.

SOME ANALYSIS

The reason for opening up this area of research into ICT when the focus of this book is ostensibly issues of behaviour management was that the blended classroom or digital learning model seemed to offer a potential solution for teachers facing disruptive or disaffected students. However, even a brief glimpse into a small sample of current students' experiences, operating at the borderlines between post-school/pre-university and university education seemed still to involve a subversion or disruption of learning processes for a number of students whether through plagiarism, lack of focus on learning or in some instances through cyber-bullying.

Nevertheless, there were some limitations to the scope of this research. Firstly, the practitioners and teachers selected for this research, might have been more authoritative, widely published on the issue or come from a wider range of colleges and universities. There might have been a larger sample of practitioners representing ICT in more academic contexts, interviewed in a more detailed and systematic way. However, this was the point of the research. It was not necessarily the elite authorities on ICT who were questioned, but rather teachers and learners who regularly used ICT as a crucial element in their teaching practice.

The eight chosen figures represented a high level of commitment to ICT, current engagement with large numbers of students using ICT and were associated with management deployment of digital resources for teaching and learning: they were practitioners rather than experts as such. Again, a wider or more random sample of teachers using digital technology might have been selected. The sample could have been approached online. However, the sample of students, teachers and ICT specialist practitioners selected represented a wide range of subject areas and backgrounds from Further Education colleges, universities, and vocational training units, thus offering views and experiences from many areas within the post school sector. Finally, the 150 students were selected at random in three different ICT workshops, each of which was used by over 1000 people per week. They were either sitting in small groups, hence the clusters of subject specialism, or were seated by themselves. Each person was asked whether they were over the age of 18 and whether they would be prepared to participate in some research. All 150 answered positively to these questions. However, the sample could have been much larger, more anonymous, captured online or been carried out more systematically through interrogating large classes of students. The advantage of this particular method of data collection was that it highlighted perceptions and experiences of individual students through a mixture of discussion, filling a survey, but also represented students who used official ICT facilities.

The findings showed that that there was a perception that using ICT in assessment was fraught with possibilities for plagiarism and that many teachers and students were either aware that this was happening with their students in the case of tutors or in the case of students there was a definite perception that this was rife amongst colleagues. Types of plagiarism were not differentiated in this research. However, four students said they were aware of other students' parents or siblings heavily inputting material into colleagues' degree level work. One said 'her dad said he had to stay up all night so his daughter got a 2.1. and not a 2.2. on an assignment.' Was this behaviour being replicated more widely (Anon 2014)?

My own personal experience, when marking a third-year BA dissertation from a student named Jasper, was the line: 'In my recent book I argued the case for....' When I interviewed Jasper, I asked: 'What is this book you have just written?' Jasper said, 'What book? I haven't written a book....' I said 'So you didn't even bother reading your own plagiarised work?'

This then became a disciplinary matter.

Despite, cyber-bullying being a rising concern, only a few respondents in my research identified this as significant in their experience. Teachers and students both felt that there needed to be more human guidance or tutor interventions in explaining relevant material for their courses. In other words self-directed or blended learning had to be tempered with tutor input to help students understand what they were learning.

However, once humans were more involved in direct classroom interaction, then all the issues of class management and disruptive behaviour could again potentially emerge.

The findings corroborated the literature that ICT was thoroughly embedded into tutor and student practice (Fisher et al., ibid.), but was also central to students' learning experience (Underwood et al., ibid.). Teachers and students accepted that ICT put them in touch with the global economy, increased learning and was a preparation for work (Chowcat et al., ibid.). A range of these points were made by tutors, students and the practitioners answering questions about the positive effects of ICT. The digital world supporting the classroom was acknowledged as a key aspect of current teaching and learning (Szabo, ibid.).

Not so prominent in the literature are the problematic aspects of ICT as reflected in the views and experiences of participants. The normative 'solutions' to plagiarism are more sophisticated software. Cyber-bullying is usually 'solved' through vigilance, patrolling the internet and tutor interventions when there are abuses.

Discussing 'solutions' could trivialise highly problematic issues that impact on academic ethics, concerns about the nature of what is actually being learnt and whether blended learning can really be the 'answer' to issues of great social and interpersonal complexity. Questions proliferate; for example, is it learning to transfer material from one digital place to another? At what level does this material penetrate the minds of students? How do we 'know' which student is really saying what?

The reason for this chapter on ICT is a way of showing that the digital dimension has its own endemic problems that need to be addressed as part of an engagement in discussions on virtual and real classroom encounters.

Some Suggestions

1. There should be no tolerance for online bullying. If exposed, it should be clear that perpetrators must be excluded from college.
2. The complex nature of plagiarism needs to be explained in a very simple, straightforward way to all students. Possibly testing students on their ability to differentiate between original and plagiarised work needs to be embedded into every course.
3. Some oral questioning of students' coursework either through a physical interview or via face-to-face discussions online needs to be in place so as to determine the authenticity of student work.

4. Preferably, assessment needs to be multi-faceted, oral tests, course work, interviews, professional discussions, presentations and exams so that student achievement is not dependent on what has become an unreliable method of authentic assessment.

BIBLIOGRAPHY

Agatston, P. W., Kowalski, R., & Limber, S. (2007). Students' perspectives on cyber bullying. *Journal of Adolescent Health, 41*, 59–60.
Anon. (2014, October 1). I know students who buy essays online are being ripped off – I used to write them. *The Guardian.* http://www.theguardian.com/education/shortcuts/2014/oct/01/i-know-students-buy-essays-online-being-ripped-off-i-used-to-write-them
Aviram, A., & Talmi, D. (2004). *The impact of ICT on education: The three opposed paradigms, the lacking discourse.* Retrieved from Elearning Europa website: http://www.elearningeuropa.info/extras/pdf/ict_impact.pdf
Chowcatt, I., Phillips, B., Popham, J., & Jones, I. (2008). *Harnessing technology: Preliminary identification of trends affecting the use of technology for learning.* Coventry: Becta.
Darlene, C. (2014). *The successful virtual classroom: How to design and facilitate interactive and engaging live online learning.* New York: Amacom.
FELTAG. (2013). Paths forward to a digital future for further education and skills. http://feltag.org.uk/wp-content/uploads/2012/01/FELTAG-REPORT-FINAL.pdf
Fisher, T., Higgins, C., & Loveless, A. (2006). Teachers learning with digital technologies: A review and of research and projects. Futurelab Report No 14. Retrieved from http://www.futurelab.org.uk/research/lit_reviews.htm#lr4
Freire, P. (1972). *The pedagogy of the oppressed.* Harmondsworth: Penguin.
Granberg, C. (2010). Social software for reflective dialogue: Questions about reflection and dialogue in student teachers' blogs. *Technology, Pedagogy and Education, 19*(3), 345–360. Routledge.
Hennessy, S., Ruthven, K., & Brindley, S. (2005). Teacher perspectives on integrating ICT into subject teaching: Commitments, constrains, caution, and change. *Journal of Curriculum Studies, 37*(2), 155–192.
Jurdi, R., Hage, H., & Henry, P. (2011). Academic dishonesty in the Canadian classroom: Behaviours of a sample of university students. *The Canadian Journal of Higher Education, 41*(3), 1–35.
Kress, G., & Pachlere, N. (2007). Thinking about the 'm' in m-learning. In N. Pachlere (Ed.), *Mobile learning: Towards a research agenda* (pp. 7–32). London: WLE Centre, Institute of Education.

Liu, D. (2005). Plagiarism in ESOL students: Is cultural conditioning truly the major culprit? *ELT Journal, 59*(3), 234–241.

Livingstone, S. (2011). Critical reflections on the benefits of ICT in education. *Oxford Review of Education, August,* 1–16.

Mitra, S. (2010). The hole in the wall. http://www.ted.com/talks/sugata_mitra_the_child_driven_education.html

Palloff, R., & Pratt, K. (2007). *Building online learning communities: Effective strategies for the virtual classroom* (2nd ed.). San Francisco: Jossey-Bass.

Park, C. (2003). In other (People's) words: Plagiarism by university students–literature and lessons. *Assessment & Evaluation in Higher Education, 28*(5), 471–488.

Polio, C., & Shi, L. (2012). Perceptions and beliefs about textual appropriation and source use in second language writing. *Journal of Second Language Writing, 21*(2), 95–101.

Sutherland, R., Armstrong, V., Barnes, S., Brawn, R., Breeze, N., Gall, M., et al. (2004). Transforming teaching and learning: Embedding ICT into everyday classroom practices. *Journal of Computer Assisted Learning, 20,* 413–425.

Swan, K., & Shea, P. (2005). The development of virtual communities. In S. R. Hiltz & R. Goldman (Eds.), *Learning together online: Research on asynchronous learning networks* (pp. 239–260). Mahwah: Erlbaum.

Szabo, Z., & Schwartz, J. (2011). Learning methods for teacher education: The use of online discussions to improve critical thinking. *Technology, Pedagogy and Education, 20*(1), 79–94.

Underwood, J., & Dillon, G. (2011). Chasing dreams and recognising realities: Teacher responses to ICT. *Technology, Pedagogy and Education, 20*(3), 317–330.

Underwood, J., Baguley, T., Banyard, P., Dillon, G., Farrington-Flint, L., Hayes, M., et al. (2010). *Understanding the impact of technology: Learner and school-level factors.* Coventry: Becta.

Wallace, S. (2002). *Managing behaviour and motivating students in further education.* Exeter: Learning Matters.

Wood, P. (2012). Blogs as liminal space: Student teachers at the threshold. *Technology, Pedagogy and Education, 21*(1), 85–99. Routledge.

Yang, Y. C. (2008). A catalyst for teaching critical thinking in a large university class in Taiwan: Asynchronous online discussions with the facilitation of teaching assistants. *Education Technology and Research Development, 56,* 241–264.

CHAPTER 10

How Do Teacher Educators Prepare Trainees for Disruptive Classes?

THE BELIEF IN EMBEDDING

This chapter examines how teacher educators approach training teachers to prepare them for working within the post-school sector in terms of dealing with disruptive students. The focus is again on empirical research to explore what teacher educators say about the training they offer. Do they teach specific theorists or particular strategies? Is there a module devoted to behaviour management on their training courses? In fact, some courses do offer single modules on this topic, but every institution researched here (bar my own) embedded behaviour management into other areas of their teaching course.

There is an underlying question as to which approach is the most effective.

This research questioned managers of training courses at different training organisations, colleges and universities. There is a central section of this chapter based around interviews with teacher educators, asking them about the advice and strategies they offer trainees. Data for this chapter was gathered through focus groups, interviews and surveys. It was collected through systematic and randomised approaches, exploring and questioning attitudes on this area of concern. I wanted to know how teacher educators said they prepared their trainees for behaviour management issues faced in the classroom. I wanted to listen to teacher educators' voices in a number of contexts and in the next chapter compare this with what trainees said about their training.

© The Author(s) 2017
M. Lebor, *Classroom Behaviour Management in the Post-School Sector*, DOI 10.1007/978-3-319-57051-8_10

Teacher educators from over two dozen teacher education departments and four different universities were sent questionnaires at different points about their views on behaviour management. A group of 35 teacher educators was approached at a meeting to fill in questionnaire forms and then questioned in an open discussion. There were focus groups where they were asked about their approaches towards classroom management, but then 15 teacher educators were subsequently interviewed on their individual perspectives on teaching class management to trainee teachers.

Was It Ethical?

Again, there were concerns about research ethics that particularly applied to collecting data on this sensitive topic. Would teacher educators want to admit that there were problems in teaching this subject or that their trainees had problems in classrooms? There could be difficulties of stigma associated with their teaching institution or where observations were taking place for their trainees. As we have said, if an institution is characterised as being associated with violent behaviour, this might well have implications for marketing courses. It could also raise concerns that this area of training might involve trainees in dealing with aggressive behaviours that might alienate them from their course or career. As soon as this topic is explored, it raises negative assumptions about anyone admitting that there are problems with their ability as a classroom teacher. The concern can also apply to teacher educators as they are responsible for preparing trainees for these scenarios.

We have already heard teachers say that they had been ill-prepared for the realities of the teaching experience.

Researching this area can show differences between what teacher educators say they teach and then exposing those statements to triangulation, by asking trainees what they believe they have been taught. A gap between these two sources of information might and did open up. The data had to be gathered showing considerable sensitivity for issues of anonymity, both for individuals and institutions. Nevertheless, all participants were asked to sign a consent form, allowing me as data collector to use their opinions and views in research and all were given the option to withdraw from the research. All remained anonymous (BERA 2011).

There was also a concern with validity with respect to how I was going to make a selection of trainers in order to give a representative account of how teacher educators said they prepared their trainees for teaching in this sector. The problem was that individuals were speaking for both themselves and their institution. Were teacher educators being selected on the basis of being more outspoken or concerned about these issues and therefore the sample would be unbalanced or unrepresentative? Issues of validity could be further investigated.

AND WHAT METHODOLOGY?

Again, qualitative research was used as a methodology, whilst mixed methods were tools for triangulating data from a range of teacher educators. Ultimately, more in-depth interviews were sampled on the basis of educators' interest and willingness to be interviewed either on line or by telephone (Cohen et al., ibid., pp. 409–443). A survey was used (Cohen et al., pp. 256–288) in order to find out what a range of teacher educators said about delivering behaviour management on the teacher education curriculum. The problem was how many responses was I going to receive? Triangulation occurred through these responses from different universities and colleges and extra depth of understanding was gained by asking semi-structured questions in interviews in order to enrich the data available (Newton 2010).

After the initial consent form and individual details about the context where they were teaching, teacher educators were asked about the percentage of time spent on this topic compared to other areas of study. The next question asked about the aspects of behaviour management and theorists covered. Tutors were asked to describe effective practice, issues trainees faced and how support was offered. There was a blank space for extra comments.

Time Spent

All colleges and universities approached claimed to teach class management as an integrated topic that was implicit in all modules they delivered. Some taught it in a minimal way directly, but offered a more embedded model through teacher observation. Another method was through 'sharing of practice' in group tutorials. Cawdor College claimed this amounted to 50% of course time in group discussions. In this research, this was unusually high. For some colleges it was not seen as needing a specific slot, but support was offered where needed. Where there were difficulties in trainee practice, discussions would revisit problems as they emerged. There was sometimes reliance on a specialist conference or key note speakers who addressed all trainees, giving an expert view. The problematic aspect of this is that 'the experts' often refer to generalised strategies that may not work in specific contexts. Once alone with a class, challenging behaviour can be deeply isolating.

In terms of time devoted to this topic, this varied greatly between institutions and to some extent could not be quantified because it changed with the needs of trainees and specific tutors, but also perceptions were diverse and sometimes highly individualised. These ranged from departments such as the Athens Institute, Rom, Veron, Manta and Glam colleges who all said it was 'difficult to quantify' as 'embedded throughout the programme' and therefore could not be distinguished as a separate topic. Several other departments specified percentages, such as 15%. The Ness Centre said 10%. The Donall Centre said they devoted 2 × 3 hour sessions to behaviour management per year, whilst Palace College said they used 1/30th of the course for this topic. Firth College said 1/31st which represented one class per year. The Forrest Institute said 1/60th (= half a session). Duff College said three hours for the whole course. For one department it varied, but remained 'relatively small, but more had to be offered as a response to the request for more practical teaching skills.' The Castle Centre said it devoted 'equal amount of time to this as other topics.' Representatives from the Dunsinane Institute said, 'Probably two sessions – and then the issue is addressed for individual cases where required.'

All colleges and universities approached said that they 'embedded' behaviour management into other modules or parts of the course. No college or university viewed this issue as of sufficient importance to devote a whole module to its exploration for trainees. The problem was whether the so-called embedding meant that:

(a) The issue was actually never dealt with.
(b) Was there enough time to focus on this issue since there seemed to be so many other pressing concerns?
(c) It did not have to be tackled because it was not formally part of the qualification.
(d) Disruptive behaviour was not happening in all Education and Training environments and therefore did not seem to apply to all trainees.

(e) Trainees felt that they were not being supported with a highly challenging area of the work they were entering.

(f) Maybe teacher educators did not feel sufficiently experienced, trained or qualified themselves to engage with these issues in an authentic way.

Nevertheless, colleges and universities said they offered a range of approaches to behaviour management. There was, in fact, a vast amount of data on this topic and here I am giving only the barest summary of what a small sample of Teacher Educators said.

The Content of What Was Taught

Alex College, for example, said they taught ground rules, motivation, rewards, respect and reflection. The Elsinore Institute claimed that they put forward 'teaching and learning strategies to promote positive behaviour and meet the needs of groups of learners.' The Palace said that they looked at the causes of disruption, strategies for dealing with situations, such as seating plans, choices, disciplinary procedures, case studies, importance of planning and communications skills. Meanwhile The Castle believed in 'Restorative Practice' techniques for resolving conflicts and thinking about the classroom environment and how it could be improved. The Donall Centre said they explored a range of behaviours experienced in the classroom and their causes. They also said they examined trainees' abilities to create a sense of responsibility and strategies for encouraging and developing a culture of positive behaviour in the classroom.

Cypher College said they focussed on learner needs and group profiles, classroom management, rules, behaviour and contracts, boundaries, roles, professional values, wider participation, Humanism and Behaviourism. Duff College said they examined practical skills, and causes of poor behaviour, whilst The Efeus Centre's approach was effective teaching and learning, classroom management in terms of class layout, communication skills and strategies for dealing with disruption. The Tarsis Institute gave importance to 'working a room, facial gesture, proximity, use of space, line of sight, space management and use of a tutorial system, involving meetings and disciplinary actions.' The Cloten School advocated strategies to engage learners and 'manage disruptive behaviour.' But this merely begged more questions.

Finally, Athens offered a range of approaches that included: making links to learning difficulties, case studies from previous trainees, real life situations, videos from schools, whilst others at Athens suggested communication skills, emotional intelligence, examples of teacher language, verbal and non-verbal responses to difficult situations, whilst looking at reasons why students 'misbehaved' and practical strategies for dealing with disruptive behaviour.

There were vast amounts of data on this topic from dozens of other teacher educators and centres. This sample offers a flavour of what was generally said.

Effective Practice Witnessed

When asked about examples of effective practice, much positive advice emerged.

Athens said 'three strikes and you're out,' 'phones in a box at the start of a lesson,' 'use of questioning to deal with disruption, re-calling students to get their attention.' Other representatives of Athens said, 'Group rules, clear sanctions, music used in the classroom either for the whole class or individuals to listen to their head-phones.' A key note session outlining what all trainees should do was seen as good practice.

But if tutors were not allowed to implement the ultimate sanction of removing students from the class, then what was really available? It might be as simple as the sanction of students not passing the course.

The Rom Centre suggested seating plans through profiling so as to understand group dynamics, thus avoiding issues in the first place, but also involving students who arrived late as soon as they entered the room. Veron College suggested putting theory into practice. This meant addressing the problem by standing next to the student and diplomatically guided them back on track, all in a low-key manner.

Tarsis teacher educators used their tutorial programme and newly-implemented 'tracking system' to target behaviour on a long-term basis. Duff teachers suggested de-escalating techniques. Cypher College described a range of effective practice including trainees visiting institutions with diverse practice, such as PRUs, prison education, Humanist schools and outstanding academies. They also had workshops on behaviour management including negotiating class rules, ownership, autonomy, plus observations where feedback was offered to trainees whilst on teaching practice. The Perry Institute also said their trainees set ground rules which were re-enforced each session in order to work with a mentor to gain consistency. Trainees carried out research in developing personal skills to be applied in practice.

Finally, Alex College suggested prevention by keeping students busy; the teacher asserting authority with respect, whilst the classroom was set out strategically with differentiation embedded. The Oswald Centre offered Transactional Analysis, but also de-escalation techniques, however, the teacher educator felt that this was problematic as sometimes de-escalating one individual meant that others began to assert themselves and this person could possibly dominate the session.

It seemed that there were a wide variety of approaches and not one uniform answer to the question advising trainees what they should do when confronted with challenging or problematic classes.

What Issues Were Faced by Trainees?

Through this survey I asked the teacher educators about the sorts of disruptive behaviours they *thought* their trainees faced in the classroom. Unsurprisingly, many different sorts of behaviour were reported.

Alex College listed many examples of low level disruption, including the use of mobile phones, talking, punctuality problems, lack of respect, inappropriate language, verbal abuse, refusal to engage, rudeness, bullying and verbal abuse of peers. The Forrest College educators mentioned disengaged students on English programmes. External issues were impacting on students' concentration which meant that students wanted to talk about issues not connected with the session and wanting others in the class to become disengaged. This was said to be normative in at least 5 classes. The Palace reported on swearing, disrespectful, challenging behaviour, not doing the work, off task behaviour and students trying to disrupt others. The Castle suggested that raising the compulsory school leaving age meant that FE teachers had to manage reluctant, demotivated students in new ways. There was much confusion for teaching staff as there was inconsistency in imposing rules and boundaries across the whole college.

The Temple Centre said there was low-level disruption which included talking in class, lateness, avoiding set tasks, but also many equality issues, such as underlying sexism and homophobia. Initially trainees took time to adapt to the problems they had to face in classes which they saw as 'big issues' when they first started. Cypher College reported that Functional Skills sessions were particularly problematic because students were often not engaged. Learners became disruptive because of changes in staff or dealing with students' difficulties in their personal lives, such as homelessness. There were also problems of attendance. Those trainees involved with SEN students faced some difficult issues of attention, engagement and support for individuals.

Duff College trainees faced low level disruption, inappropriate language and a general lack of motivation due to teaching reluctant learners. Trainees feared presenting material at any length because they knew learners wouldn't listen. One trainee had spoken of an incident where a student had verbally assaulted her in class, asking 'who are you to be teaching us??!'

The Glam Centre primarily viewed class behaviour issues as resulting from the tutor's lack of confidence. The key issues for trainees, according to Glam were related to a lack of student motivation, no matter the age. Even amongst adults low-level disruption was reported as being 'quite common.' Manta College reported that the worst aspects were demotivated learners who were disengaged because there was a requirement to re-sit certain subjects or a curriculum with which they did not want to engage. Trainees were often being talked over or students just were not listening or were using their mobile phones in class. Athens reported examples of spitting, swearing, lack of attendance, refusal to participate, physical assaults and students' refusal to do homework. Dealing with diversity related issues was also quoted as a source of problematic behaviour in the classroom. Finally, it was mentioned that trainees had to deal with drug and alcohol-related problems, lateness, talking out of turn, lack of co-operation, disrespect and, possibly counter-intuitively, classes that remained silent and would not talk when they were asked to.

But What Did All This Data Mean?

It could be argued that:

1. These teacher educators were reporting on exceptional circumstances.
2. The sample was too small to interpret wider problems.
3. These trainees needed more systematic training to prepare them for working in colleges where some very negative behaviour was rife.

The evidence seemed to suggest that disruptive behaviour was a key feature of trainee teachers' lives in a wide range of colleges.

The sample covered departments from at least 10 different urban plus three rural areas. The sample referred to seven different counties. Each department was referring to activities that happened at several colleges and training departments within their remit. The meaning, in my view, was that these were not isolated incidents confined to particularly 'rough' or deprived geographical locations, but were rather a theme that permeated much trainee teacher experience as perceived by teacher educators.

The Focus Group

As a result of what I considered to be worrying findings, I held a focus group meeting to explore these problems in greater depth and then followed this up with more detailed interviews with 15 individual teacher educators over a number of months. The focus group discussion took place as the prelude to a meeting. There were 35 managers of teacher education and/or teacher educators present for this discussion. The issues were explored in more depth in an open public format facilitated by myself, whilst two scribes took down detailed notes of what was said.

The first question in the facilitated discussion was whether behaviour management was an issue for trainees. The reason for asking this question was supposed to air publicly the concern for this issue and allow for different views to be expressed in the same room.

Diana said that Sport level 1 tutors frequently asked for strategies to engage with students. Georgie affirmed that her trainees had problems working with lower level students who were often de-motivated. Emilia said that students felt demoralised having to take GCSEs in year 1 of a course. Students needed motivation for having to re-take exams. Problems tended to surface in Functional Skills classes. Asad said that FE student groups could be diverse in terms of ethnicity, class and gender. This could be challenging for trainees to know how to handle a variety of students. Lucia confirmed that Foundation learners were particularly problematic. Noel said that although the problem was mainly level 1 and 2 students, it was not confined to lower levels and could affect even level 5 classes.

Jan explained that A-level students in social sciences often turned away and ignored the trainee teacher or just refused to participate in discussions. Jonathan said that pre-service trainee groups had deep concerns over behaviour management? They were reported to be terrified of going into challenging classes. Len said that pre-service shadowing took place, so that trainees could be aware of the ground rules that had been relayed to students. Gertrude claimed that 'low level disruption' was a problem for all trainees. Angus said that trainees were complaining that students were constantly on their mobile phones, but the problem was that trainees used mobile phones themselves and disrupted training classes. 'They need to model good behaviour themselves.'

Teacher educators said that they had seen some dramatic situations whilst observing trainees in classes. Thus Cassia said she witnessed a trainee being verbally abused by a student. The student had used the fact that the trainee was not yet a teacher in order to attack her. Emilia said that young female trainees had to deal with sexual innuendos from students. Inappropriate comments were continually said within hearing distance of the trainee. There was sexual harassment and sometimes female trainees had to modify how they looked (in terms of their clothing) in order to deal with these situations when they had male students in their classes. William said there needed to be much more support from vocational tutors in the communication or numeracy sessions to help avoid these situations.

How Did the Teacher Educators Help Trainees Resolve These Issues?

Lucia offered sessions called 'Headache and aspirins/shared strategies' as a way of exploring the problems trainees faced, whilst supporting them in their contexts. During these sessions she heard about extreme behaviour from students, involving physical and verbal attacks in their classes. Esther said that trainees were asked what happened each week in the training session. Trainees received support from peers through the process of discussing what occurred in their classes.

The question that then arose was how teacher educators taught behaviour management in their classes. Emilia said she used films, but mainly based in schools, stopped the film and asked trainees how they would resolve problem situations. Lucia said that she relied on conferences, but also connected behaviour management and confidence to practical sessions which she said trainees found useful. She also used role play in class, but did not say how that worked.

Queenie offered practical sessions in assertiveness techniques, particularly focussing on the language used by trainees. Esther explained that she identified problem students with coming from 'poor backgrounds.' However, this was an assumption and, as we have seen, is not always the case. Clio said she used a range of techniques in class to help trainees look at why someone would react in a certain way, for example, there had to be reasons behind an action, such as throwing a chair and then discussing the responses with the trainees. However, this assumed that there were reasons for this behaviour that could be elicited from discussions without questioning the students involved themselves. Questions on how to react to these situations did not surface in this part of the research.

SHOULD THERE BE A SEPARATE MODULE?

The final question was whether it was better to have a stand-alone specialist module devoted to behaviour management or whether this should be taught discretely embedded through a range of other modules, key note lectures, reflection and via the observation system. Generally, the sense of the meeting was that behaviour management should be embedded into other activities and teaching. Thus, Cassia said if a separate module was introduced some trainees would feel it was not appropriate or relevant to their needs or practice. According to her the issue needed to be built into trainees' needs or that it should be embedded into reflective practice sessions. Diana suggested that we should consider the possibility of trainees choosing behaviour management as an option to develop this skill where appropriate, but it should not be a compulsory element within a teachers' training course. Duncan said that the sector was too diverse to have one module on the subject. Jan disagreed and said the strategies, techniques and theories were relevant for all. Jonathan argued that there were particular problems and many issues associated with teaching Maths and English. The issue was how relevant was behaviour management for all trainees in their different contexts? Noel said he was not sure if a whole module was desired, however some trainees would benefit from more information on the subject. Trainees at most departments had said they wanted a module. Queenie made the crucial point that teachers were not therapists, whilst Emilia suggested that practical experience was far more effective than theory sessions on this topic.

The overall feeling in the room was that there should not be a separate module on behaviour management in teachers' training courses. However, this view was not deeply challenged in the session. The next stage of the research was to ask teacher educators for their views individually and then outline some of the counter-arguments to embedding behaviour management and put forward a case for a separate module on this topic.

INTERVIEWING TEACHER EDUCATORS

Fifteen teacher educators were later interviewed and asked about the sorts of problems their trainees faced, what advice they gave, their own personal experience of disruptive behaviour, but also whether they thought that there should be a separate module devoted to behaviour management on teachers' training courses.

When asked about the problems their trainees faced, all teacher educators in the sample reported on a wide range of behaviours. Angie said that trainees commented on low-level chatting, phones, socialising, but that there were also attendance problems, punctuality, attention seeking. One trainee reported teenage autistic students spitting, biting and scratching other students as part of the norms of the culture where they studied. This was very difficult for the trainee to handle.

Bennie claimed that there were numerous problems reported by trainees, such as punctuality, low-level disruption, mobile phones, disrespectful behaviour, talking in an inappropriate way, banter, and sexist language. There was no respect for teachers. One student lay down on three chairs; the teacher left him and then woke him to carry out tasks. Obscene language was continually spoken to female members of staff. According to Bennie the problems had got much worse during his 30-year career.

Margaret said that some trainees had problems with this issue, whilst some did not; according to her it was about half and half. Typically, trainees encountered the use of mobile phones, low-level disruption, students not being on task, but sometimes it was abusive behaviour where a teacher was verbally attacked in front of the whole class. She felt that the problems were worse because 16–19 year-olds were in college on a mandatory basis. There were particularly problems with students from other countries, whereby new students did not fit in very well and there could be ethnic tensions of alienation from the 'the other.'

Luciana reported on general low-level disruption; use of mobile phones and social media, lateness and chatting during sessions. Trainees also said that they had noticed many more students rocking back with feet on other people's chairs as if they did not respect their environment.

Mariana said it was crucial to understand that her trainees were on placement; the classes were **not** their own. There was sometimes a difference between how the trainee and main teacher perceived problems. Mariana and her trainees designated disruptive behaviour as 'tomfoolery,' i.e. silly behaviour. This tended to be inappropriate behaviour for employment or further study, for example lateness, not listening, talking, lack of respect for others, swearing, calling across the room, not doing the work required, and so on. If not controlled, 'tomfoolery' had the potential to turn into much more serious 'shenanigans,' as Mariana termed it. This kind of humorous terminology had helped, according to her, for trainees to distinguish whether 'something was a serious issue.' It could be a matter of dispute where the boundaries were between these two concepts. The infantilisation of language might give the feeling that these negative activities were being trivialised or arguably this was a way of seeking relief by joking about the situation.

Adriana confirmed that incidents tended to be much worse at entry level, special needs students, ADHD or 'on the spectrum.' Eighty percent of students from these categories, she claimed were disaffected in her trainees' classes. In significant parts of sessions, students were reluctant to learn. It was almost as if students were fighting a battle against being educated. She had witnessed swearing, setting fire to work sheets, 'messing around' or students just getting up and leaving the classroom.

Peter said issues for his trainees ranged from talking over the tutor when he or she was trying to speak to critical incidents, such as shouting, students refusing to work, fighting or again just leaving the room all of which he had witnessed on many occasions. Oliver said that his sense was that trainees faced an extra level of problem beyond regular teachers. This was because students sensed that they were not qualified teachers and therefore they didn't have to be respected. On the other hand, Jack said that it purely depended on the specific vocational area and this determined students' attitudes. Thus, subjects like agriculture and equine studies taught at a rural college meant there were very few difficulties. Students were polite, interested and rarely broke the disciplinary codes. However, when he worked in a more urban environment, there was often 'seriously challenging' behaviour.

WHAT ADVICE?

The next question asked teacher educators about the advice they gave trainees to counter challenging behaviour. Bennie suggested praise for achievement which he believed worked well. Christopher advised trainees to separate the behaviour from the individual. He said that students were often rebelling against authority. They had had bad experiences at school or been involved in violence there. Sometimes really badly behaved classes behaved well when they were observed. This he interpreted as respect for the teacher. Luciana thought it all depended on influence, but really 'serious cases of abuse ought to be addressed at managerial level.' Mariana advised talking to students after the lesson or taking them to one side so as to avoid confrontations in front of the whole class.

Adriana had several strategies, such as planning varied lessons with practical activities to avoid students getting bored. Communications, body language, Emotional Intelligence, managing lesson transitions, assertiveness were all key features. She suggested that her trainees be pleasant, polite and efficient. They should set ground rules – revisit them regularly so they could not be forgotten. She advised that trainees be consistent – challenge rule-breaking on every occasion and treat all students equally and fairly at all times; 'do not play favourites.' 'Make sure instructions are clear and repeated.' For major disruption, she said there was a safety issue. Depending on the context, she said she would try to isolate the individual behaving disruptively and request assistance.

The problem is that help is not always available. As we saw earlier security officers can be made redundant. Financial values rule.

Bianca ran a session on learning difficulties where she looked at the sociological and psychological causes of disruptive behaviour, showing trainees how to separate the behaviour from the person. She explored case studies. She said trainees must build up techniques for managing incidents in the future. Trainees had to be able to determine whether this was a genuine problem and what they should do about it. But how could one define 'genuine?' She taught reframing language, developing group rules, watching videos of disruptive behaviour and analysed why it occurred and work out ways of dealing with it.

Peter acknowledged that being a trainee could feel like an isolating experience, especially if trainees encountered difficult issues in their classrooms. The main message he wanted to share with trainees was that this should not be dealt with alone; trainees had support from other teachers, their mentor or head of department. He also talked about critical incidents and appropriate strategies as part of ongoing reflective practice and reflection in action in the classroom.

Jack gave trainees advice on setting the ground rules/behaviour agreements or contracts, consistency and strategies for non-confrontational behaviour management, experimenting with different strategies and reflecting on their effectiveness. He felt that getting 'to know your student was the most powerful tool of all' for behaviour management.

LEARNING FROM EXPERIENCE

When asked about their own experience, there were a variety of responses. Bennie said that he had worked with 'entry level kids.' There were often fights. In a welding workshop, students set fire to the bench. But there was also a lack of engagement. Jason commented that there were always violent situations, but in his experience, they seemed to have got worse.

Margaret and Luciana admitted that they had very little experience of highly disruptive students because both had worked with more mature students. Their students had chatted, been late and used mobile phones in class. However, they had never encountered anything more dramatic. Mariana trained in secondary schools with specific behaviour management strategies and worked on Youth Training Schemes in community workshops in a multi-ethnic area with high unemployment at a time of riots, so there was great disaffection in classrooms, working with students with 'learning, emotional and behavioural disabilities.' As a teacher educator, she maintained practice with the local high school where there was currently much disruptive behaviour.

Adriana had taught in an FE college, entry level, in a referral unit, but also worked with students who had severe needs. There were often difficult or challenging adults or emotionally disturbed students jumping out of windows and running outside the classroom. Peter said he started his career teaching Key Skills to construction students, so he had to deal with disruptive classes on a daily basis. It was very daunting at first, but he felt able to share these experiences with new trainees. Jack had a broad experience of teaching students with behaviour management and other issues before he came into teacher training. For example, he taught groups that had been removed from mainstream schools and were taught separately due to behavioural issues, working with social services and other external agencies, supervising community service for students who had poor behaviour.

BUT WHAT WERE THE SOLUTIONS?

Bennie said that it was 'about creating the right conditions.' He had three strategies. One was building relationships. He said 'when there's violence, stamp on it immediately.' Presumably this did not mean physically. He said that 'thinking and feeling equalled behaviour.' As a result of this view, he tended to show students how he felt first in order to build the relationship and show openness. He said 'once they know and trust you, then they can build up their relationship.' His final stage was 'positive re-enforcement. If you ignore negative behaviour and emphasise good, this can work well. Some authorities and colleges don't like this, but I think it works.'

Peter said he used to explore 'root problems with male students. One student swore aggressively 27 times in 90 seconds. I took notes and confronted him about it. In the end we had to work on the basis of three strikes and you are out.'

Margaret tried to clarify the problems students faced. She wanted to model good behaviour and particularly worked on communication issues with students. Luciana said she tried to stop negative behaviour 'straight away and depending on the nature of it, might speak to individuals involved after class.' However, the problem not mentioned is that teachers have to deal with difficult behaviours of particular individuals, whilst maintaining the class momentum for the majority.

Luciana believed in Kounin's 'with-it-ness' (1997), showing awareness of what was happening in all areas of the classroom and to respond quickly to possible disruptions; thus stopping inappropriate behaviour from spreading. Adriana said the key was getting to know the people in your class and building up the relationship which could take a long time. It was important, according to Adriana, to ask students what they had enjoyed in the past. The bad behaviour, she said, was 'a manifestation of learning in the transition to becoming an adult.' This was definitely a positive interpretation, but did this help with immature students who were adults?

Peter promoted Schon's reflection in and on action; thus, taking the time to sit with the line manager and discuss the issues, then coming up with strategies to deal with them, but also following the college's behaviour and disciplinary process carefully and involving parents and carers where necessary. This assumed that students were not parents themselves.

A Separate Module?

The vast majority, over 85% of teacher educators sampled from over 35 different institutions, when asked whether a separate module should be devoted to behaviour management believed that this should be embedded. In some universities it was a question of having full 30 credit modules and therefore there would not be enough material to justify this emphasis. Other reasons were that it was not relevant to all trainees, thus some trainees worked, for example, in the NHS or at universities where it was claimed there was little direct disruption. Another teacher educator said that there were 'more important issues' to cover, whilst others stated that they would be worried if too much prominence was given to this issue and that the focus needed to be on good practice of which disruptive behaviour was merely a part. If it became an option, then other elements of the curriculum would be missed and in any case it was implicit in everything trainees learnt about in teaching and learning. A further difficulty was that the range of issues and contexts were so varied that it would be difficult to separate out into one module.

THE OTHER SIDE OF THE ARGUMENT

However, there were arguments on the other side of this question. It was a key focus for many trainees on teachers' training programmes, and it was important to equip them with the appropriate skills required. It was also said to be the area about which trainees were most anxious. Every year they stated this in evaluation forms. Even in areas where disruption did not take place, it was useful to receive the training because the trainee had to be prepared for every circumstance not only where they happened to be on placement. Was the PGCE/Cert Ed. qualification to prepare trainees for all scenarios or only where they currently worked? Others argued that there was a need for a separate module because events and issues were happening at a much worse level than certain trainers could remember. Students were said to be becoming more insulting, more aggressive, acting sometimes in 'disgusting ways.' Trainees needed to have a module devoted to these problems. A small minority of teacher educators were saying that it was now 'vital' to give this topic far more prominence in the teacher education curriculum. If it was not a whole module in itself, how could we guarantee that it was definitely going to be taught?

In our penultimate chapter we will start to ask trainees about their experiences and what they feel they need in order to prepare them for dealing with these unpredictable and challenging situations.

Some Suggestions

1. Try to identify causes of the problem by questioning students on what is happening in their lives.
2. Some tutors showed their own feelings as a way of connecting with the feelings of difficult students.

3. Negotiate ground rules and regularly revisit as required.
4. Be consistent and challenge rule-breaking on every occasion.
5. Separate the behaviour from the individual.
6. Avoid confrontations in front of the whole class. Try to see the individual disruptive students either during the break, outside or after the class.

BIBLIOGRAPHY

British Educational Research Association. (2011). *Ethical guidelines for educational research.* London: BERA.

Kounin, J. (1997). *Discipline and group management in classrooms.* New York: Holt, Rhinehart and Winston.

Newton, N. (2010). The use of semi-structured interviews in a qualitative research: Strengths and weaknesses. Online. Available at http://www.academia.edu/1561689/Theuseofsemistructuredinterviewsinqualitativeresearchstrengthsand weaknesses

CHAPTER 11

And What Did the Trainees Say?

It's Our Problem

This chapter covers what trainee teachers said they experienced and what they wanted from their training. This research involved questioning trainees on PGCE, Cert Ed. pre-service and in-service courses as to what they found the most successful or effective aspects of the training they received with respect to disruptive behaviour.

The motivation for this research came from an interview I carried out with a newly qualified teacher at a training unit in the East of the country. She told me that on her PGCE placement there was what she called 'appalling student behaviour; fighting, kicking and screaming in the classroom…' When she asked her teachers' training tutor at her university what she should do about it, he said, 'This is not my problem, it's your problem.' My positionality is quite explicitly that I think this is *our* problem. As teacher educators, trainers, managers and teachers, I think we have to be constantly working out flexible strategies on how our trainees and teachers might find a supportive framework for understanding and dealing with challenging behaviour, encouraging reflection and reflexive practice that can affect classroom behaviours.

The Research Methods

In order to ascertain their views on being taught about these issues, questionnaires were sent out to over 1000 trainees. Two focus groups were later run with other sets of trainees in order to triangulate views and

© The Author(s) 2017   187
M. Lebor, *Classroom Behaviour Management in the Post-School Sector*, DOI 10.1007/978-3-319-57051-8_11

explore these issues in more depth and check whether the points made on paper or digital surveys were backed in verbal conversations.

Again this topic is extremely sensitive. If trainees admit that they are having problems in the classroom with disruptive students, it might mean that they fail their teaching practice and therefore might not qualify as teachers. This is perhaps the most sensitive area of this book because the implication of admitting that one cannot cope with disruptive students as a trainee is a possible admission of early failure. It might lead to failing the PGCE or Cert Ed. course. The trainee is in the most vulnerable position with least power. Thus, when asking research questions, there had to be particular vigilance with respect to anonymity, ethical concerns and protection for the views, outlook and attitudes of those questioned.

Questionnaires were sent to trainees in over 30 teacher education departments through administrators. There was a problem of approaching trainees directly because of issues of confidentiality and data protection. Hard copies of the questionnaire were given out to in-service and pre-service trainees in a range of venues and this seemed to produce a larger number of responses. My initial question was how had behaviour management been taught on their teachers' training courses. I wanted to hear the perceptions of trainees, thus offering some triangulation on what teacher educators had *said they* offered.

WHAT WERE TRAINEES TAUGHT?

Thus, for example, Ros said that behaviour management had been confined to the teacher's role in setting up a safe environment, ground rules and learning theories. She claimed that it was not as relevant for her as she was based in a 'higher level' environment, but still the content and time spent on this issue had been limited. Celia said there was one planned session at her department and she had had to resort to reading up the literature herself in order to understand the issues that might come up for her. Frederick said he had not received 'much information on this issue.' He said 'we studied few aspects of behaviour management' during the first year on the PGCE course, but not at all in the second year. Rose could not remember 'it being part of the Cert Ed. at all.' Bertram commented that he was unsure whether this had ever been raised on his course even once. Haley said it just had not been covered at her centre.

Sylvia and Audrey said that they had not covered this topic. Izzy said 'we have only covered a small amount of behaviour management.' Charles said 'strategies, coping mechanisms, reasons for bad behaviour, teaching styles and different ways students learn' were topics that came up, but were not taught in a systematic way. Phebe said 'discussions of different learners' behaviour and managing students in the classroom' were topics, but this was 'not taught from the point of view as to when things went wrong.' In other words as long as the students conformed to what was required, teaching and learning could take place as planned. According to these trainees, no one seemed bothered about the real conflicts that took place in classrooms.

Minnie merely suggested 'Behaviourism,' whilst Katie said 'psychological theories,' but this turned out to be more theoretical discussion of learning models, rather than the practical problems of engaging with challenging students in classrooms. Viola said, 'I haven't received any sessions on behaviour management, but there have been some informal discussions in class.' She also said, 'I learn more about it through conversations with my peers. I was taught at another department where it was not covered either.' In other words again this topic was not formally on the syllabus or curriculum, but was introduced only in a random way when it came up in class conversation.

Not the Main Focus

The vast majority of the 200 trainees who answered this survey from over 20 centres repeatedly said that this topic was not covered on their course. Clara explained, 'I don't feel a lot of time is spent on behaviour management.' Uri said that there was only one session in year 1, but again this 'mostly focussed on classroom management in secondary schools.' It was, he said, 'very limited.' Much of the material and films were based within the school sector, so school models and understandings were inappropriately brought into training teachers to work in the post-school sector where the issues, atmosphere and dynamic are entirely different.

Again, Antonia said, 'I haven't had much input on this topic. We only had one very basic lesson related to behaviour management within a school setting.' It was only 'tangential to our course.' Merci said 'Equality and diversity' was a key theme, but this never focussed on problematic students. Candy answered that 'It has not been delivered yet.' Val said 'only through one workshop at a conference,' not systematically as part of the PGCE course.

Seating Plans

Marti explained that the solution he had been taught was to encourage students 'to sit with students of a similar ability.' This seemed quite a weak piece of advice from this trainee's point of view. How would he know which students had the same ability, if coming into a class for the first time? Would putting all the 'weaker' students together compound problems? Was class management merely a problem of seating plans? Sometimes students just refused to move or change seats. One plumbing trainee was accused of racism by students for wanting to break up a group of non-English -speakers. Another trainee was accused of racism because she had allowed groups to sit according to their ethnic identity, thus emphasising Black/White difference. One trainee was advised to give out seat-numbers for seating plans as students filed into the room. This assumed that students were initially outside the classroom. Seating plans can be highly loaded tools of social engineering, but also an effective strategy for controlling difficult classes.

The Experiential Approach

Barbara and Lucie said 'ground rules' as the main advice they had been given. But this seemed quite limited, since they had been on their course for two years. What happened if students did not agree with the rules or refused to obey? How did the ground rules impact on classroom experience? Kirsty said, 'Throughout the PGCE behaviour management is discussed frequently when trainees encounter difficult situations.' It was said that in practice, most students did follow the ground rules in her context.

The experiential approach seemed quite typical for many trainees to whom I spoke. Thus, Judith said, 'During the course of the PGCE programme, behaviour is covered when issues are raised sporadically when we as trainees encounter issues.' The trainees either had had minimal or no input on this topic or it had been taught in a piecemeal way on the basis of what happened to emerge in each student group or cohort as a response to particular incidents while trainees were on placement or if in-service as part of their jobs. Receiving support from the rest of the class for each incident that takes place is obviously an extremely useful methodology, for many reasons. Firstly, it is acknowledging what is happening to trainees in their own contexts. Secondly, it is using the teacher education training room as a laboratory for working out possible strategies. Thirdly, it possibly argues that because problems are so diverse and unpredictable, this is possibly the only way to think about the issue. Any prescriptive advice will always be wrong because it will not work in dynamically developing or different contexts.

The weakness of this position is that one might be reliant on the possibility that at least one trainee in the class will be suffering from having been timetabled with disruptive students. This might or might not be the case. If there are no disruptive classes for that particular cohort, it might mean that this issue is never discussed. The problem then becomes that this group has not been prepared for the possibility that they might be faced with difficult classes in the future as they would have never discussed this in training. There must be some balance between input and the experiential happenings of what is going on currently in trainees' classrooms.

More Reply

It was true that I did receive many replies that were more positive. However, none said that they had been on a course that devoted a specific module to this topic, that it was taught in a systematic way or that it was mandated into the PGCE course they attended.

The most positive approach was that it was embedded; Ron, Sophie, Tim, Kaur, Matt, Hetty, Elaine, Ross, Lee, Ali and Pete, all from different teachers' training departments, said 5% of their course had been spent discussing this issue. Whether this could be calculated in this way was a moot point. Again, many individuals complained that 1% or less time was spent discussing class room management, for example, Izzy said 'minimal,' Roger said 'little' and Reece said 'not a lot.' Nevertheless, one or two individuals perceived that they had in fact spent more time focussed on behaviour management. It was admittedly problematic to legislate on how to deal with this topic or how it should be approached, but certainly some trainees said that much less time had been spent discussing disruptive students than they had expected and they felt quite dissatisfied with teacher educators' attitudes and approaches. Trainees from most departments said that it really involved dealing with problems as they arose. But was there a systematic mechanism for doing this? Would some trainees suffer in silence? Were practical sessions built into every programme? It had to be said that in most cases the answer was negative.

What Did Observers See?

However, as a result of this practical focus, I began to ask whether lesson observers had commented on this aspect of practice, since it is such a key element of Ofsted's requirements. If lesson observers commented on behaviour management, what did they say and was it helpful to the trainees?

Ros, Phebe, Audrey, Celia and Phil amongst two dozen others said that nothing had been mentioned about class-management in their observations. Frederick said that he had been told that he had 'handled behaviour issues very well during observations,' for a previous qualification, but when it came to his PGCE, he received no comment. Charles said that he had been told that there was 'too much "teacher talk".' He 'should trust students to get on with group work and deal with behaviour issues as and when they arrive.' However, he was not told how to deal with these issues.

Nevertheless, some trainees were well supported on this issue. Thus, Sylvia said, 'Yes, some positives, such as [my] ability to move [the] class along at a good pace which doesn't give learners the time to disrupt.' However, observers have commented on 'pulling learners up' on their negative behaviour and attitudes more often.' Implicit here is more evidence of trainees faced with problematic classes. Candy claimed that her observation tutor said that 'I kept my learners engaged and there were only minimal disruptions.' Perry said that lesson observations had highlighted the need to separate certain students and change the classroom dynamic of the students being taught. This was an example of engaged, useful feedback for the trainee within a specific environment.

Rose said 'I have been told my behaviour management is good, but the students behave when an observer is present.' Again this raises an important issue that when classes are watched, the behaviour of the class changes, so the level of information presented to observers might actually be quite limited. Observations are also dependent on the particular regime of observation under which the observer has been trained, the individual's ways of interpreting the observation criteria and the observer's own experience of teaching, all of which must affect the objectivity of observing trainees.

Which Theorists Did Trainees Use?

When asked which theorists or writers they had been taught, Ros, Sani, Sylvia, Viola, Izzy, David and Ian, all from different departments, said 'None.' Celia said 'sorry not able to name any.' Dussy and Gretel both said 'none that come to mind.' Anthony said 'can't recall any specific names.' Charmian said 'None specific to behaviour.' Merci said 'None that I can remember.' Alexis said 'I cannot remember.' Were these trainees particularly forgetful? Were there few relevant books to the sector or was this area not thought worthy of attention?

When trainees did mention specific names, they tended to talk about general theories of teaching and learning, such as, 'C. Rogers, Maslow, Humanists and Constructivists,' or 'Milgram, Skinner and Watson.' 'We touched on Skinner and Maslow for motivation, but it was not a requirement'; 'Behaviourism, Cognitive and Humanist;' 'Behaviourism, Gagne' and 'Skinner and Gagne.' Many said 'Pavlov and Skinner.' 'Behaviourism, Cognitivism, Gestalt and Constructivism' were constantly re-iterated by trainees from different colleges and universities.

Behaviourism was systematically referred to in dozens of answers. It was as if, any discussion of behaviour management or disruptive behaviour in classrooms evoked the theory of Behaviourism. The implication was that trainees assumed that either Behaviourism was the solution to behaviour management problems or that as soon as behaviour was mentioned Behaviourist theories came to mind. Many left this section on the questionnaire blank. Very few respondents suggested any writers, such as Cowley, Wallace and Vizard who specifically dealt with this issue; most spoke of generalised books on teaching, such as Petty or Avis or broad theories of learning. When they did refer to a particular book on behaviour management, it was significant that, as in the case of Bel, it referred to the compulsory school sector.

So What's Good Practice?

In order to counter the impression that discussion of this issue merely involved negative experiences, I asked trainees for examples of good practice they had witnessed during their time as student teachers. There was a wealth of positive examples. Although again, many trainees answered 'none,' it seemed as if solutions came out of practical situations.

Ros said 'Calm acceptance till behaviour modifies itself.' But this seemed to suggest that the teacher had no agency in the situation. Paul said 'Using a token reward scheme to encourage positive behaviour. Students are given a token if they arrive on time, then each time a student contributes positively to a lesson, they receive another token. At the end all tokens are collected, and then a winner is selected at random.' This seemed to be a system based on Behaviourism and a belief in extrinsic motivation; it could also be argued that this method might have an infantilising effect on students. The 'random' aspect seemed to turn the reward into an undeserved process and might be counter-productive in creating resentment in 'well-behaved' or productive students who were not given a prize.

Celia said 'containing pupils.' But is containment a sufficient justification for education? Doesn't this mean that the educational process is really social control? Charles said 'not giving students options for bad behaviour, giving a command and thanking them for carrying it out.' This seemed a useful strategy appropriate for those teachers who can develop this quality of voice to gain presence and attention. Izzy said 'carrot and reward,' whilst Phebe suggested 'reward systems, positive disciplines, sanctions.' Leo said 'behaviourism theory,' because he said 'it works all the time.' This was more confirmation that many trainees believed in the Behaviourist model of reward and punishment. The problematic aspect of this view was that students sometimes felt this was demeaning, did not respond to this interaction or just did not want or believe in the rewards on offer. It also did not acknowledge the benefits of students' potential or intrinsic interest in the subjects they were studying.

There were some more subtle examples of good practice, such as when Bess said, 'It is important to recognise that most behaviours can be managed if we explore reasons for challenging behaviour, such as anxiety, mental health, learning difficulties [and]boredom.' This view offered an analysis based on an understanding of the feelings, inner reactions and attitudes of the students. This inner world could only be accessed through discussion.

Grace gave an example of good practice, describing how 'students were disrupting the lesson as usual. After a few warnings, I decided to leave it and have a word at the end of the session.' It was a policy of non-interference or withdrawal. Terry posed 'questions at students who were talking.' Edmund said, 'As a teacher, it's important to explore students' feelings.' Trainees were beginning to discuss the importance of the affective domain, developing the emotional literacy of their students. Reggie said 'don't get into an argument,' whilst Jeanie said 'walking near talkers/phone users, staying calm, following up incidents, taking learners to one side.' Ali said 'circulating the room, eye contact and staying calm.' As mentioned earlier proximity can have its own problems in terms of gender difference, sexuality and the multiple meanings of being physically close to someone. Nevertheless, it was a common tactic that trainees said they used. Sitting next to a student can be a key method of building a learning relationship.

Chester said 'positive language; remain calm and confident authority shown.' Gemma said, 'I feel the important thing is not to shout, but to speak calmly and give clear instructions of what you want and expect. A tip I have taken from my mentor which I have been doing myself has been to just remain silent until the students stop talking themselves. It usually ends in a student asking everyone to be quiet.' The problem with this approach is that the teacher can be silenced, whilst the students merely continue talking.

These all seemed rational, effective and successful strategies. The problem is trying to apply all these ideas in different circumstances. The emotional and psychological changes in individual teachers over different days and parts of days, areas in the college, the different climates, moods and range of behaviours in classrooms can lead to unpredictable events and attitudes.

Sandi said 'Not to worry if I make mistakes. It's part of the learning process.' He also claimed not to have been supported at all on this issue in either his teachers' training course or on his placement. Demi said 'I was taught to find my own way to learn how to deal with classroom behaviour. I did not receive particular guidance.' Laurie said 'Using positive language, highlighting the good rather than the negative.' This was effective because it had 'practical use in my classroom.' Many others also had this outlook, such as Sophie who also said, 'Using positive instead of negative language.' Tom said 'effective communication with students, mutual respect, eye contact,' and yet again the ambiguous benefit of 'proximity.'

There were a vast number of other responses and pieces of advice from dozens of trainees based in over 30 different institutions. Many were focussed on building up positive relationships with individual students, but most adopted behavioural procedures centred on Behaviourist philosophies and approaches that they had learnt at university or college under the category of learning theories. However, when finally asked in this survey what changes trainees would make to their course nearly 90% said that they would prefer to have a separate module where these issues could be discussed openly, systematically and supportively. However, some raised the question of whether classroom management could ever be taught in training as situations were always evolving and context was so critical.

Did Focus Groups Confirm or Undermine the Evidence?

Two focus groups were administered in different contexts with groups of trainees from different vocational and academic backgrounds from a variety of institutional settings. The first recorded here was with a group of second year trainees from Manta College. It was a session before their lesson began where an open discussion explored some issues of behaviour management facilitated by myself.

When questioned about how many sessions had been devoted to behaviour management, Sarah said there had been one lesson on this topic. Ruth disagreed and said that there were no formal sessions on behaviour management. It had been covered outside class through discussion between trainees. Corinne said that she used to go to another college where it was never covered either.

Benjamin explained that the problem was that they were never taught what to do if a really difficult situation came up. He described how there was 'absolutely no training in this on the PGCE course.' Sarah said that training tended to be all about learning theories. She said 'We get taught about Behaviourism and Humanism which we have to cover, but the problem is we don't know how to apply these theories to classroom management. They are not made directly relevant. Just because I know about Pavlov doesn't help with interactions in class...' Corinne said that class management was once mentioned as an after-thought, yet it was something that affected their daily lives as teachers. Ruth confirmed that 'this is a massive issue for us, but it is never covered in any depth on this PGCE course.' Benjamin said the problem was with boundaries. It was 'really difficult to know what you can and can't say in any given situation...' Jo said, 'We are not taught how to deal with difficult classes. What to say and what to do...' Claudia wondered what could be done about 'conversations that are happening all around in class? Do we clamp down on them if they are not totally relevant?'

The next question was asking these in-service trainees whether they were experiencing problems of disruption in the various colleges where they currently worked.

Corinne said that she had to cope with much negative behaviour in an academy setting. 'I am finding it really difficult to manage a mixed class of girls and boys and their reactions to each other.'

Jo said: 'We set ground rules, but no one takes any notice. Students are swinging on their chairs. We ask them to come forward and they don't.

One student flung all the [window] blinds on to the floor. I was completely unnerved. I went up to the student and asked her if she would have acted like that at home and she said she wouldn't. I asked her why she felt she could act like this at college. This seemed to embarrass her. She [the student] was definitely being attention-seeking. But I felt I had never been told how to deal with these sorts of problems in my teachers' training class.'

The significant aspect of this description is that teacher educators and books on teaching theory keep telling trainees to set ground rules. The point here is that the students in some situations are not interested in or refuse to conform with the rules that have been set. The formal rules are outside their sphere of interest. It is then important for trainees to develop confidence, negotiation and communication skills in order to either order or persuade the student into compliance or relationship.

Louise said: 'I think it's getting worse. One student sprayed deodorant all over the class. Another was so angry he picked up the table and was going to throw it.' Sarah said that there was 'a real issue around mobile phones whether they are something that should be suppressed or whether we should be using them in class as a resource.' Benjamin said: 'Even mature students can be really difficult...' Michael said that they had been videotaping students to show how their negative behaviour affected the class. Claudia described how one student 'was really arguing and shouting in class. It is really difficult to deal with and no one has gone through this with us.' Sarah explained how there was 'a big man threatening me. He had a real problem with anger management. How do we deal with that?'

The trainees' frustration with their teacher educators and trainers was coming out so strongly, they were almost desperate to hear about solutions from myself as researcher. However, I started to ask whether these challenging situations were typical in all the colleges where they were placed. The answers were, unfortunately, almost 100% affirmative. Sarah said, 'No, I wouldn't say so, but there are incidents nearly every day.' Jo said: 'We have to deal with a lot of rudeness. What should I say in these situations? The boundaries are not clear...' Claudia commented that her students 'shout in class or they just don't want to engage.' Mari said that the problem was 'just trying to get students to concentrate in class. Lateness is another big issue. Whatever we say doesn't make a difference... 'Jo ended this section by just saying that a student in an art lesson 'picked up a wax pot and threw it at another student.'

Then the question emerged as to what trainees did when confronted with these challenging situations. Sarah tended 'to walk to the front and stand in silence and then the levels of noise tend to stop. Or sometimes walk towards the people who are talking or messing around...' Ruth said that 'setting the boundaries is really important...' but she did not explain how this could be done where these were not accepted by the students. Michael said that treating 'students as colleagues is really helpful. It means the students try and act more like adults and therefore tend to behave at a better level with more maturity. The problem is sometimes getting them to speak or keep quiet.' Corinne said 'This student knew he'd done something wrong. I just stood there staring at him until he stopped.'

Had this group been taught about any theories or recommended any books on this topic? The answer came back 100% as none. Sarah said: 'It's more that we have been taught a lot about learning theories and motivation. In the assignments we have covered all the major learning theories and particularly about learning styles so that we can be inclusive in our approach. It's more a problem of how these apply...'

Should there be a separate module on this topic? There was 100% agreement that there should be. Ruth said 'it must be more relevant than learning about professionalism or theories of the curriculum...'

But were these trainees being just badly taught by their teacher educator? Or were these trainees placed in unusually difficult or particularly challenging work situations? In other words was this a specific case that was unusual or were other groups from different teachers' training colleges or universities saying the same thing?

Unfortunately, More Confirmation

The second focus group took place at the Athens Centre and was a discussion with trainees from a range of departments. There was just one basic question which asked trainees about their experiences of behaviour management in their own contexts at different institutions and colleges.

Elizabeth said that the main problem was that the senior management at the college where she worked turned a 'blind eye' to student misbehaviour. 'If you complain to the management, they say that you are not managing the classroom effectively enough. Even if the student misbehaves quite badly, there is pressure on the member of staff to pass the student. There are financial implications to not passing students.' When asked about the type of behaviour she had experienced, she referred to swearing and much bullying that 'goes on in lessons all the time.'

Anne explained that it was sometimes problems of young people on the autistic spectrum and their aggressive behaviour in class. However, they also had problems with 'members of staff riling the students so that they would be wound up for the next class. They have a grudge or are jealous about the next teacher. This is actually quite common...'

Elizabeth said that one of the key problems was not having control over the environment. Students often wanted to sit in their ethnic groups and refused to move. Even if the teacher used 'different methods for setting up people to work with students from a different ethnicity to themselves, they often refused to co-operate.' If the teacher tried 'seating plans or used different methods of arranging the class, the students refused to sit where you want them and then will complain to the management if you try and force them.'

CRIME AND PUNISHMENT

Anne described how the internet added a different dimension. 'If a student is punished, then they can hit back via the internet with pictures of the teacher in compromising poses.' The sort of problems they encountered were students 'throwing chairs or tables around, punching other students in the face, holding another student by the throat and smashing their glasses.' The consequences of these actions were perceived as being inappropriately mild, considering the violent activities to which teachers and students were subject. Thus, those who disrupted the session were asked to miss a break. There was a 'swear box' where students would have to put money for 'bad language' and this seemed effective. But there were often arguments in class. This was a regular occurrence. The other problem was that teachers went off absent and there was inconsistency between staff in their approaches to behaviour management. Consistent training across colleges seemed to be crucial, maybe as part of the induction into employment.

Charlotte recalled that at her work they were exposed to many different types of negative behaviours. There was often an attitude of students not wanting to sit next to each other. She said 'seating plans just don't work... you try to move them and they refuse to move.'

Emily said they had covered enormous amount of material on their teacher education course. They had 'tons of hand-outs on every subject of teaching and learning, inclusion and behaviour management.' But there seemed to be no direct discussion on how 'we actually can deal with difficult or challenging situations. We know all about lesson planning and Schemes of Work, but I don't really feel we have been prepared for dealing with these problems.'

Charlotte said there were major problems with groups of 18 year olds who were on vocational courses. 'Basically they hate English. They have failed English GCSE maybe up to five times. There is negativity about Functional Skills. They will not co-operate. They come in late, are loud and want attention.' She explained how it was very difficult to engage these students and as trainees they had not been given any support, help or advice on how to overcome these problems.

This focus group which was drawn from several different departments seemed to show great frustration with the work they were being asked to carry out in their teacher education classes and again the lack of training, support, help or advice they received from teacher educators.

Some Analysis

I ran four other focus groups of 11, 12, 14 and 27 in-service and pre-service trainees in different environments at later stages where a range of similar views and experiences were re-iterated. It has to be said that the research did focus on trainees mostly working within northern, urban environments. It is possible that if the focus had been in rural colleges in less deprived areas, the results might have been different. The other issue was that I as data –collector might have triggered more of a 'safe-space' for trainees to speak truthfully about their experiences either through a sense of relief that someone was at last listening or that there were going to be no punitive consequences for admitting to negative situations taking place in the classes for which they had responsibility. I am known to speak at conferences on this topic and trainees might have either heard me, read my articles or known that I was interested in the problematic nature of what is happening in many learning situations.

This is a contentious and difficult area of research dealing with highly charged emotional and physical situations of great complexity.

Firstly, it should be said that much good practice was reported by trainees, both in terms of their theory lessons and on placement where over 50% of trainees said they were given sound advice on how to deal with challenging or difficult situations. Whilst not specifically addressed in a whole module by any of the universities or colleges approached, behaviour management issues were said to be embedded into a range of other modules. At many departments many techniques and strategies were again said to be in place for ensuring that trainees were prepared for entering classrooms with confidence. A majority of trainees in, admittedly, a small sample confirmed this to be the case. Particularly useful with respect to this training, were trainees' experiences which were discussed in training sessions. Other very helpful features of training sessions were teaching trainees about communications, emotional intelligence and techniques for making interventions into students' negative behaviour.

Secondly, much theory and practice of teaching and learning did take place in all departments questioned as part of normative training sessions and this meant that trainees were prepared for teaching students from a wide spectrum of backgrounds. Typically, trainees in practical terms were told to put in place and reiterate ground rules, produce well-planned and interesting sessions with pace and a variety of activities, so that students remained engaged. This seemed to work for a certain number of trainees.

However, many trainees in the sample felt there had been little focus on the issue of what to do when things went wrong. Many dozens said this topic had not been covered at all in the two years on their PGCE or Cert Ed. course. Others said they felt ill-prepared for the extreme situations they said they had to face regularly in class. Many said that no books or authors on class management had been recommended to them. Trainees recounted many extreme violent and challenging situations that they had either dealt with in the past or were facing on a regular basis in their current classes.

Conclusion

Although most teacher educators had argued that there shouldn't be a separate module devoted to this subject on grounds that there wasn't sufficient time and that the focus should be on normative good practice in teaching and learning. It wasn't an issue for some trainees and it wasn't a substantial enough area for a full module, yet it seemed there were many poignant reasons for instituting a specific module on behaviour management into training courses or to put this topic in place as a mandatory part of a current module.

The reasons for introducing a module are:

1. Many trainees sampled said behaviour management had not been covered on their course at all. It is theoretically 'embedded,' but this embedded teaching often does not happen.

2. This was the aspect of teaching that trainees said they feared the most.
3. Most trainees and teacher educators reported on many extreme and challenging situations they had or currently faced.
4. Nearly all trainees questioned during focus groups said they wanted a separate module devoted to this topic.
5. Many trainees said that classroom situations seemed to be getting worse particularly with the mandated students associated with the raising of the education leaving age and growing ethnic tensions in classrooms.

But the problem remains. How can an ever-changing, dynamic series of situations that is always different in every teaching and learning context be taught? What strategies could be implemented that could be generic for all teachers? How could this issue be approached by teacher education? Our last chapter offers some ideas about how this might be done.

CHAPTER 12

A Possible Module for Teaching About Disruptive Behaviour

WHICH APPROACH?

So what is the answer to these multifarious problems identified in the simple words 'disruptive behaviour'? Which theorists should trainees or practitioners follow? Should they believe in Kohn or Kounin, use intrinsic motivation procedures, be managerial facilitators or become more draconian? Be more like Fred Jones or Harry Wong? With the growing complexity, problematic and stressful nature of many issues concerning vulnerable or even aggressive learners, should teachers be using therapy models or behavioural rewards and punishments? As we have seen, causes of 'bad behaviour' may not be easily determined. There might be socio-economic, biological or gender issues or differences in ethnicity that might impact on group or cultural atmospheres or identities in classrooms. There might be an oppositional culture between the teacher and students, assumptions about class difference. Wars in other parts of the world could be replicated in the classrooms of England. On the other hand, the teacher and student can come from the same culture or background, but this can also be a source of dislike, resentment, self-hate or even contempt. As has been reiterated throughout, it is not easy to legislate or pre-determine why difficulties happen. Although practical solutions have been discussed, the underlying attitude has been to examine the complex nature of these challenging situations, view different sets of recommendations and try to unravel the key elements that have emerged in each area of research undertaken.

© The Author(s) 2017   203
M. Lebor, *Classroom Behaviour Management in the Post-School Sector*, DOI 10.1007/978-3-319-57051-8_12

So how should we prepare trainees and teachers for disruptive classes?

In my view all trainees need to undergo a mandatory module or course in behaviour management, focussing on disruptive or difficult student behaviours in classrooms that they may encounter during their careers. A version of this should be made available for those newly qualified or already teaching. There are many reasons why I believe this should be the case. We have instigated this in our own very successful teachers' training programmes at our University Centre and trainees have very much appreciated this programme in terms of preparing them in a realistic way for the challenges in their chosen profession.

The arguments against introducing such a module are that:

1. There is not enough time.
2. These problems are not relevant to all trainees in their current placements.
3. We should focus on the norms of good teaching practice, not on aberrations.
4. The problems are so diverse, it is impossible to legislate or prepare trainees for every eventuality.
5. If trainees are taught how to teach effectively, then problems will not arise.

The reasons for constructing and teaching a mandatory module on this topic are that many trainees fear this aspect of teaching more than any other as has been shown in research mentioned earlier. Many teachers are leaving the profession because of the stresses connected with the sometimes overwhelming nature of problem classes. Many have said they feel the national situation of classroom management is getting worse. Certainly, the Behaviour Czar brought out a report that corroborates much of what is said here, but in the school sector (Bennett 2017). It is difficult to confirm this view that there has been deterioration of behaviour, but from the sheer number of cases outlined in this book, it should become apparent that this is a major problem for many tutors in the post-school sector as well. Just because teachers teach does not mean that learners learn.

It feels as if not teaching trainees about this issue in a systematic way is almost avoiding what teacher educators themselves find difficult to name or even admit to. By going through worse case scenarios, this prepares teachers for a range of situations that might occur in their careers. Even if the exact situation never actually happens to the tutor, having gone through a role play or explored the possible responses to difficult or confrontational classes means that tutors can develop some verbal tools, weapons, strategies or actions for dealing with these existential moments of being in conflict with classes or individuals. It is a way of working through the processes of what one might, could or should do in a range of different situations. It should be a way of developing teachers' inner resources and outward behaviour.

It is true that many of these problems may not be relevant or never emerge for many tutors. However, being prepared for adversity, helps to fine-tune tutors' reactions to all classes. If the tutor can deal with the most aggressively un-co-operative groups, then more pliable or conformist classes will feel so much more comfortable to teach.

So what should the content of such a module be? Aims might be to:

Demonstrate knowledge of ways to manage challenging behaviour across a wide range of contexts in the Education and Training sector.

Critically explore some of the contextual and causal factors for challenging behaviour.

Critically analyse two models or theories of behaviour management and show how these might or might not be applicable in a challenging classroom context.

Objectives could be to:

Critically evaluate empirically grounded and theoretically informed knowledge in the field of behaviour management to enact solutions to a practice problem.

Justify at least two current practices and/or procedures for coping with challenging behaviour.

Recommend at least one course of action for overcoming disruptive behaviour in a particular context.

The tasks could be a presentation, professional discussion, role play or case study looking at a particular event or classroom situation. Each trainee could give a brief lecture outlining the views of Jones, Wong, Glasser, Gibbs, and so on. More content could involve exploring a series of case studies either from pre-written material, as for example, outlined in this book, or alternatively, it could be based on situations faced by trainees in their classroom placements or past experiences. However, one cannot be too prescriptive as trainees might be on a pre-service course without immediate access to current classroom experience. The course could explore recommendations made by Bennett, Cowley, Dix, B. Rogers, Vizard and Wallace, subjecting their ideas to discussions of how each suggestion would work when applied to actual classroom situations or their own context. Trainees would use classroom realities to critique theory, and theory to critique the classroom.

Content might also involve teaching the main theories of learning in terms of what happens when learning is disrupted when using this model. Teaching Behaviourism, Humanism, Cognitivism and Constructivism not merely as abstracted descriptions or prescriptions of what learning means, but applying these theories to case studies and asking the question as to which understanding is most effective as an explanatory system of what happens when 'things go wrong.' Trainees might wish to draw on these theories to offer potential solutions.

One oral task could be to ask trainees or tutors about the range of disruptive behaviours they (have) encounter/ed in classes. Which behaviours trainees find personally most challenging and explore reasons for their occurrence. How do these experiences affect the individual trainee? What is it that triggers their emotional reaction? A session in small groups might explore why these behaviours are happening in different contexts. Trainees could debate different behaviours, such as, abusive language, refusal to carry out tasks, defiance or disrespectful/ dominant patterns in students. What approaches are available?

Another key task could be to keep a reflective log where, as advised by Sue Wallace (2017), trainees try out different strategies, write down what works in each context. The problem sometimes is that what worked perfectly with one group on one particular day does not work with the same group on a different day. Keeping a reflective log builds up evidence and information.

Throughout this book we have mentioned 'ground rules.' But which ground rules? There are many sets. Maybe spending a section of a training lesson debating which ground rules would be the most successful for operating in a range of challenging climates. We often hear the word 'respect' mentioned in this context, but it can be a street-language word of comic derision. Again 'listening to others' is often in the mix of worthy sentiments, but one person's intense attention is another person's dozing off to sleep. The key might be engaging with the language, consciousness and understanding of boundaries within each group. This needs to be thoroughly debated within training.

It is important to get trainees to present their understanding of a case study. This means that: firstly, they move from sitting behind their desks as passive recipients of teacher-led knowledge into the teaching position at the front of the class. This should be empowering for all trainees. Secondly, they become the experts in the position of authority, explaining and unravelling the complexities and behaviour of students in possibly their own classrooms from a position of strength at the front of their training class. The point about this is that by becoming expert speakers on their own situation or the cases they have faced in class-rooms, they begin to contradict the powerlessness and isolation of being by themselves with very difficult groups. They get credit and support for their analysis of how they dealt with or offer practical solutions to complex and difficult environments. Thirdly, this style of assessment has the advantage over attending a lecture on behaviour management in that it turns the trainees into teachers. Teaching is quintessentially the best way of learning.

As has probably become apparent, I feel it is much better to question, debate and discuss all these issues as openly and thoroughly as possible. Thus instead of facing disruptive classes being something shameful or even disgraceful, it is credited with marks for how these situations can and might be resolved in a range of classrooms.

Engaging trainees in discussions of how they could respond to many negative challenges from students, helps them to build up or maybe reject a series of strategies, tools, verbal defences and weaponry. It allows the debate on what might happen in classrooms to take place as a realistic encounter with different options at their disposal. Trainees should be encouraged to build networks with other trainees, operating as support for sharing how each tutor would deal with problems faced by others, offering suggestions and ideas for each other as explained in Chap. 8. This perspective should be central to every teacher's training course and should continue into the workplace. Institutions need to develop their own training to help tutors respond within the specific culture of that context.

The fact that the trainee is at the front of the classroom explaining their views to the rest of the class helps to create confidence in the trainee. They are in the commanding situation, but discussing their own vulnerability or the problems they face and how to overcome them, using a wide range of different theories, previous case studies plus many hints, strategies and tactics that have been used in a plethora of previous encounters.

The point about this is that the trainees are learning from the past, but also from other trainees in the class. They have prepared the presentation. They are leading the discussions as to what works and what does not work for them. They are in the position of expertise, talking about difficulties they do or might face without feeling ashamed or somehow worsted by unpleasant behaviours. They are developing and modelling a self-reflective methodology for how they and their colleagues can or might deal with difficult situations in the future. The other important point is that they are generating solutions themselves which is crucial because in the final analysis the energy, direction and approaches are existentially to do with their own presence in the classroom. The solutions have to come from within themselves and their own personal self-development, self-understanding and self-regulation. The strategies that work for one teacher might be deeply uncomfortable for someone else.

It could be argued that delivering or leading a discussion with other teacher trainees is nothing like the challenge or experience of facing a difficult class. Mostly polite or engaged debate and even academic criticism is not the same as encountering angry, disgruntled or disaffected students who show waves of hatred for the teacher as shown earlier in this book. This is true. However, it must be better than the brief or even non-existent lectures from teacher educators who mostly have not been near a difficult or challenging class for many years.

It is also true that trainees at different levels of becoming a teacher are often asked to carry out micro-teach sessions on their specialist subject or even deliver short sessions on behaviour management theories. The demands of this module would focus on using theory to critique practice or particularly a case study that the trainee has experienced themselves or one from a book or situation they have encountered, exploring why it might have happened and some practical solutions for dealing with these situations in the future.

Sessions need to be in place where trainees role play facing difficult students, for example:

1. An angry student is frustrated with the content of the lesson and says: 'This subject is rubbish!!'
2. The student says to the teacher: 'It's unfair you're always picking on me!!'
3. The student is disrespectful, sneers and says: 'You can't teach; you're only in training!!'

4. The student says: 'I hate your lessons, why do I have to come?'
5. The male student is completely disengaged and says: 'Why are these lessons always about women? I'm just not interested in this stuff...!'

These are all existential attacks on the teacher's presence in the class. Trainees and teachers need to find comebacks, humour, repartee or blocking devices for protecting themselves and progressing the session. Embedded role plays would be a way of increasing flexibility, confidence and social skills without which it is becoming impossible to teach in contemporary classrooms. Arguably, some training in how to restrain violent students should be made available where approapriate.

Another element in the module that might be useful where trainees are facing particularly difficult classes is to adopt in-the-moment training that we use at our University Centre. This happens where a trainee is teaching a class and is being observed by their tutor for the Applied Behaviour Management Module. Normally, observations are supposed to be more objective events where trainees are judged on whether they have met the standards of being a teacher. The trainee receives formative assessment on how they can improve their ability to teach and how their students can improve their learning in these sessions. It could be very useful for teacher educators to become actors in these scenarios especially where trainees are struggling to control a class or find it difficult to react to particularly challenging student behaviour.

There would obviously have to be consent by the institution and the trainee involved, but sometimes observer interventions would be highly desirable. The problem might be that the teacher educator themselves might feel out of their depth and be unable to wield the respect that would be required to bring the class under control. However, the point here is that teacher educators are often comfortable with a theoretical perspective of being in the position of authority in the training class, but here the demand is that they would have to model or show the trainee how to have that difficult relationship with students in a 'real teaching environment.'

This is deeply challenging for teacher educators, but would have a significant impact on the credibility of their professional standing, would develop their understanding of current classroom practice and offer an opportunity for them to present themselves as more supportive in a committed way to the training relationship. Are teacher educators capable of teaching difficult classes or only geared towards *talking about* teaching difficult classes? This will, no doubt, remain an interesting conundrum.

A major part of the teaching could examine case studies generated by the trainees themselves and/or situations outlined in this book. For example, another group of teachers I interviewed said:

Malcolm: 'My class are no longer responding to me, they have become alienated, what should I do?'
Polly: 'A student keeps singing rude songs about me in the lesson...'
Arnie: 'One student is always unpleasant in my class, but not in my colleague's...'
Patricia: 'Two students keep doing star jumps at the back of my classroom....'
Andrew: 'My students are running feral through the college corridors during sessions....'

And so it goes...

Concluding Remarks

Conclusions might be multifarious. Yet, the unions blame management; management blame teachers; teachers blame students; students blame their parents; parents blame the government; the government blames teacher educators; teacher educators blame Ofsted and Ofsted blames everyone!!

That **was** a joke, but the serious points are: sometimes the negative situations are so relentlessly grim, that it is important to retain a sense of humour. More important I do believe that we all need to collaborate, working together with students, teachers and managers to solve these sorts of problems. In my view Ofsted should be supporting and advising. Their observations should help teachers with what needs to be done in each case. But then inspectors would have to have a thorough understanding of all aspects of education. Ofsted merely commenting on disruptive behaviour as suggested by Bennett (2017) is, in my view, insufficient. As we have heard disruptive classes are often well-behaved for observers. One lead Ofsted inspector to whom I spoke said his team never witnessed much 'bad behaviour' in colleges. Management can just ask difficult classes to be off site when inspectors call or students realise that they have to behave for the awesome Ofsted (Thompson, 2016).

The solution could be draconian, no-notice inspections. Yet all the incidents I have described in this book have happened under Ofsted's watch. The problem is that the word Ofsted fills teachers with fear. If Ofsted started to have a policy of supporting teachers with strategies on how learning could be improved, rather than attacking teachers for not having these strategies already in place, giant strides could be made (Coffield 2008). If Ofsted became the friend of the teacher, then we might start to see genuine improvements of relationships in the classroom.

More support in classrooms, less isolation of teachers; less of the business model of education, smaller groups, more attempts to listen and understand what students are saying to us are all possible directions. We need to recognise, understand, prevent and deal with situations (Clarke and Murray 1996). Ofsted should be underpinning this process.

This book shows that it is difficult to argue a simple case of causality on issues of why disruptive behaviour happens. Nor is it able to offer a one-size-fits-all solution, because, as has been stated, the dynamics and contexts of each situation are different and aspects of class, gender, ethnicity, gang cultures, area of the country, media influences, outside political and economic factors can all be elements impacting on classrooms. This is not a moral panic. It is the beginning of an attempt to listen to students and their concerns as well as other stakeholders. What happens in education both influences and is influenced by wider societal pressures and processes.

There are, nevertheless, some generic pieces of advice that have emerged during this research. The advice of being thoroughly prepared, setting tasks that are intrinsically interesting for the specific group of students being taught, setting ground rules, building good relationships with individual students, engaging with the whole group of learners must be generic. These are the principles of all good teaching and learning. However, the converse is not true that, if teachers carry out all these processes, then disruption will not happen. As we have seen in particular cases, these tactics or approaches did not work, or there were conditions beyond the teacher's control that did not allow these strategies to be put in place. Sometimes it is a question of case study after case study as to how individual classes or specific students can be brought within a productive learning culture. It may need meetings, discussions, negotiation, further training or analysis of each circumstance which could be about individuals or whole classes.

If there are any 'shoulds' to emerge from all this, it is that teachers *should* feel completely secure to be able to talk about challenging classes in an open and constructive way in staff rooms, in front of managers and colleagues with impunity. There should be no sense that there is something shameful or wrong with the tutor if they are finding classes difficult or impossible to teach. In these situations they need support. In these cases, managers must be able to put in place a series of strategies, personnel, supportive discussions of tactics or meetings in order to counter the problem.

Again, training has to prepare new teachers in a highly directive way for dealing with a wide spectrum of difficult situations. Not doing this, in my view, is a dereliction of duty by teacher education institutions and universities. The fact that trainees have heard about a wide range of negative experiences that have happened in the past in other classrooms, and how these situations were approached or overcome, prepares trainees psychologically and emotionally for dealing with situations further up the scale of distress, aggression and confrontation. It puts low-level disruption that many teachers complain about into proportion as a phenomenon that can be understood in the context of even worse problems. Sometimes it might involve working with smaller groups, putting in place support workers for individual difficult students. It might need teachers to sit to the side of students and listen to what is happening for them in their lives. Why are they acting like this? What has happened to them? What attention do they want? What would be helpful? Few people feel listened to...

These questions need to be skilfully deployed.

Hopefully, engaging with these issues in a more realistic and emotionally and psychologically supportive way will lead to more dynamic, effective ways of embedding a productive learning culture into all Education and Training classrooms in the future.

However, if everything I have said in this book fails to support you at all, I would advise you to just 'keep calm and pretend it's on the lesson plan.'

BIBLIOGRAPHY

Bennett, T. (2017). *Creating a culture: How school leaders can optimise behaviour.* DfE. https://www.gov.uk/government/uploads/system/uploads/attachment_data/file/602487/Tom_Bennett_Independent_Review_of_Behaviour_in_Schools.pdf

Clarke, D., & Murray, A. (1996). *Developing and implementing a whole-school behaviour policy.* London: David Fulton Publishers.

Coffield, F. (2008). *Just suppose teaching and learning became the first priority.* London: Learning and Skills Network.

Thompson, C. (2016). Ofsted is responsible for a culture of fear in schools that too often results in job losses. *TES.* https://www.tes.com/news/school-news/breaking-views/ofsted-responsible-a-culture-fear-schools-too-often-resultsjob

Wallace, S. (2017). *Behaviour management: Getting it right in a week.* St. Albans: Critical Publishing.

BIBLIOGRAPHY

Agatston, P. W., Kowalski, R., & Limber, S. (2007). Students' perspectives on cyber bullying. *Journal of Adolescent Health, 41*, 59–60.

Anderson, C. (2001). Online cheating: A new twist to an old problem. *Student Affairs Online*, Winter. http://www.studentaffairs.com/ejournal/Winter_2001/plagiarism.htm

Anon. (2014, October 1). I know students who buy essays online are being ripped off – I used to write them. *The Guardian*. http://www.theguardian.com/education/shortcuts/2014/oct/01/i-know-students-buy-essays-online-being-ripped-off-i-used-to-write-them

Armitage, A., Bryant, R., Dunhill, R., Flanagan, K., Hayes, D., Hudson, A., Kent, J., Lawes, S., & Renwick, M. (2007). *Teaching and training in post-compulsory education* (3rd ed.). Maidenhead: Open University Press, McGraw-Hill Education.

Association of Teachers and Lecturers (ATL). (2013). Disruptive behaviour in schools and colleges rises alongside increase in children with behavioural and mental health problems. *Annual Conference Press Release*, 24 March.

Atkins, L. (2013). Researching 'with', not 'on': Engaging marginalised learners in the research process. *Research in Post-Compulsory Education, 18*(1–2), 143–158.

ATL. (2016). Education staff facing physical violence from pupils. https://www.atl.org.uk/media-office/2016/education-staff-facing-physical-violence-from-pupils.asp

Aviram, A., & Talmi, D. (2004). The impact of ICT on Education: The three opposed paradigms, the lacking discourse. Retrieved from *Elearning Europa* Website http://www.elearningeuropa.info/extras/pdf/ict_impact.pdf

© The Author(s) 2017

M. Lebor, *Classroom Behaviour Management in the Post-School Sector*, DOI 10.1007/978-3-319-57051-8

Avis, J. (2002). Policing the subject: Learning outcomes, manageralism and research in PCET. *British Journal of Educational Studies, 48*(1), 38–57.

Avis, J., Fisher, R., & Thompson, R. (2015). *Teaching in lifelong learning: A guide to theory and practice.* Maidenhead: Open University Press.

Bailey, S. (2011). *Academic writing: A handbook for international students* (3rd ed.). London: Taylor & Francis.

Ball, S. (2003). The teacher's soul and the terrors of performativity. *Journal of Education Policy, 18*(2), 215–228.

Bandura, A. (1977). *Social learning theory.* Englewood Cliffs: Prentice- Hall.

Barnes, D. (2001). Research methods for the empirical investigation of the process of formation of operations strategy. *International Journal of Operations and Production Management, 21*(8), 1076–1095.

Bates, I., & Riseborough, G. (1993). *Youth and inequality.* Buckingham: Open University Press.

Bathmaker, A. (1999). Managing messes and coping with uncertainty: Reviewing training for teachers in post-compulsory education and training. *Journal of Further and Higher Education, 23*(2), 185–195. doi:10.1080/0309877990230203.

Bathmaker, A. (2013). Defining 'knowledge' in vocational education qualifications in England: An analysis of key stakeholders and their constructions of knowledge, purposes and content. *Journal of Vocational Education & Training, 65*(1), 87–107. doi:10.1080/13636820.2012.755210.

BBC. (1998). Corporal punishment banned for all. http://news.bbc.co.uk/2/hi/uk/politics/69478.stm

Beere, J. (2012). *The perfect Ofsted lesson.* Carmarthen: Crown House Publishing.

Belsey, B. (2008). Cyberbullying. Retrieved August 03, 2008, from http://www.cyberbullying.org

Bennett, T. (2015). New behaviour tsar Tom Bennett's top ten tips for maintaining classroom discipline. *TES.* https://www.tes.com/news/school-news/breaking-views/new-behaviour-tsar-tom-bennetts-top-ten-tips-maintaining-classroom

Bennett, T. (2017). *Creating a culture: How school leaders can optimise behaviour.* DfE. https://www.gov.uk/government/uploads/system/uploads/attachment_data/file/602487/Tom_Bennett_Independent_Review_of_Behaviour_in_Schools.pdf

Beran, T., & Li, Q. (2005). Cyber-harassment: A study of a new method for an old behaviour. *Journal of Educational Computing Research, 32*(3), 265–277.

Boud, D., & Walker, D. (1998). Promoting reflection in professional courses: The challenge of context. *Studies in Higher Education, 23*(2), 191–206.

British Educational Research Association. (2011). *Ethical guidelines for educational research.* London: BERA.

Brookfield, S. (1993). Through the lens of learning: How the visceral experience of learning reframes teaching. In D. Boud et al. (Eds.), *Using experience for learning.* Buckingham: Open University Press.

Brophy, J. (2010). *Motivating students to learn* (2nd ed.). New York: Routledge.

Carr, W. (2000). Partisanship in educational research. *Oxford Review of Education,* *26*(3), 437–449. doi:10.1080/713688539.

Child, D. (2004). *Psychology and the teacher* (7th ed.). London: Continuum.

Chowcatt, I., Phillips, B., Popham, J., & Jones, I. (2008). *Harnessing technology: Preliminary identification of trends affecting the use of technology for learning.* Coventry: Becta.

Clarke, D., & Murray, A. (1996). *Developing and implementing a whole-school behaviour policy.* London: David Fulton Publishers.

Clutterbuck, D., & Megginson, D. (2004). *Techniques for coaching and mentoring.* Oxford: Elsevier, Butterworth-Heinmann.

Coffield, F. (2008). *Just suppose teaching and learning became the first priority.* London: Learning and Skills Network.

Coffield, F. (2009). *All you ever wanted to know about learning and teaching, but were too cool to ask.* London: Learning and Skills Network.

Coffield, F., Moseley, D., Hall, E., & Ecclestone, K. (2004). *Learning styles and pedagogy in post-16 learning: A systematic and critical review.* London: Learning & Skills Research Centre.

Cohen, L., Manion, L., & Morrison, K. (2011). *Research methods in education.* London/New York: RoutledgeFalmer.

Colley, H. (2003). *Mentoring for social inclusion: A critical approach to nurturing mentor relationships.* London: RoutledgeFalmer.

Cooper, P. (2002). *Effective schools for disaffected students: Integration and segregation.* London: Routledge.

Cornford, I. (2002). Reflective teaching: Empirical research findings and some implications for teacher education. *Journal of Vocational Education and Training, 54*(2), 219–234.

Costa, A., & Kallick, B. (1993). Through the lens of a critical friend. *Educational Leadership: Journal of the Department of Supervision and Curriculum Development, N.E.A, 51*(2), 49–51.

Cowley, S. (2007). *Guerilla guide to teaching.* London: Continuum.

Cowley, S. (2014). *Getting the buggers to behave* (5th ed.). London: Bloomsbury Education.

Cowley, S. (2015). In M. Gregson, L. Nixon, A. Pollard, & P. Spedding (Eds.), *Readings for reflective teaching.* London: Bloomsbury.

Crace, J., & Lebor, M. (2000). One strike and you're out. *The Guardian.* https://www.theguardian.com/education/2000/feb/08/furthereducation.theguardian1

Creswell, J. (2013). *Qualitative inquiry and research design: Choosing among five traditions.* Thousand Oaks: Sage Publications.

Cuddy, A. (2012). Your body language shapes who you are. *TED Global.* https://www.ted.com/talks/amy_cuddy_your_body_language_shapes_who_you_are

Cunliffe, A. (2004). On becoming a critically reflexive practitioner. *Journal of Management Education, 28*(4), 407–426.

Curzon, L., & Tummons, J. (2013). *Teaching in further education: An outline of principles and practice* (7th ed.). London: Bloomsbury.

Darlene, C. (2014). *The successful virtual classroom: How to design and facilitate interactive and engaging live online learning*. New York: Amacom.

Denscombe, M. (2010). *The good research guide for small social research projects*. Maidenhead: OUP, McGraw-Hill Education.

Derrick, J. (2011). The messiness of real teaching and learning. In J. Derrick, U. Howard, J. Field, P. Lavender, S. Meyer, E. von Rein, & T. Schuller (Eds.), *Remaking adult learning: Essays in honour of Alan Tuckett*. London: Institute of Education.

Dewey, J. (1938). *Experience and education Kappa Delta PI*. New York: Free Press.

DFE. (2012). Pupil behaviour in schools in England. *DFE-RR218*. https://www. education.gov.uk/publications/

Dix, P. (2015). Three secrets to a successful FE behaviour policy. *TES*. https:// www.tes.com/news/further-education/breaking-views/three-secrets-a-successful-fe-behaviour-policy

Dixon, L., Harvey, J., Thompson, R., & Williamson, S. (2010). Practical teaching. In J. Avis, R. Fisher, & R. Thompson (Eds.), *Teaching in lifelong learning: A guide to theory and practice*. Berkshire: OUP.

Doyle, T. (2008). *Helping students learn in a learner-centered environment: A guide to facilitating learning in higher education*. Sterling: Stylus.

Dreikurs, R., Cassel, P., & Dreikurs, E. (2005). *Discipline without tears: How to reduce conflict and establish co-operation in the classroom*. Hoboken: Wiley.

Dreyfus, H., Dreyfus, S., & Athanasiou, T. (1986). *Mind over machine: The power of human intuition and expertise in the era of the computer*. New York: Free Press.

Dweck, C. (2000). *Self-theories: Their role in motivation, personality and development*. Philadelphia: Taylor & Francis.

Ecclestone, K. (2012). From emotional and psychological well-being to character education: Challenging policy discourses of behavioural science and 'vulnerability'. *Research Papers in Education, 27*(4), 463–480.

Education and Training Foundation. (2014). *Professional standards for teachers and trainers in education and training – England*. London: ETF.

Ellis, S., & Tod, J. (2014). *Promoting behaviour for learning in the classroom: Effective strategies, personal style and professionalism*. London: Routledge.

Eraut, M. (1994). *Developing professional knowledge and competence*. London: Falmer Press.

Evans, L. (2008). Professionalism, professionality and the development of education professionals. *British Journal of Educational Studies, 56*(1), 20–38.

FELTAG. (2013). Paths forward to a digital future for further education and skills. http://feltag.org.uk/wp-content/uploads/2012/01/FELTAG-REPORT-FINAL.pdf

Fisher, T., Higgins, C., & Loveless, A. (2006). Teachers learning with digital technologies: A review and of research and projects. Futurelab Report No 14. Retrieved from http://www.futurelab.org.uk/research/lit_reviews.htm#lr4

Flick, U. (2006). *An introduction to qualitative research*. Thousand Oaks: Sage.

Foucault, M. (1991). *Discipline and punish*. Harmondsworth: Penguin.

Freire, P. (1972). *The pedagogy of the oppressed*. Harmondsworth: Penguin.

Gallagher, B., Creighton, S., & Gibbons, J. (1995). Ethical dilemmas in social research: No easy solutions. *British Journal of Social Work, 25,* 295–311.

Gardner, H. (2011). *Frames of mind: The theory of multiple intelligences*. New York: Basic Books.

Gatongi, F. (2007). Person-centred approach in schools: Is it the answer to disruptive behaviour in our classrooms? *Counselling Psychology Quarterly, 20*(2), 205–211. Routledge, Taylor & Francis.

Gibbs, J. (2001). *A new way of learning and being together*. Windsor: Centresource Systems.

Glasser, W. (1986). *Control theory in the classroom*. New York: Perennial Library.

Gold, J., Thorpe, R., & Mumford. (2010). *Leadership and management development* (5th ed.). London: Chartered Institute of Personnel and Development.

Goleman, D. (1999). *Working with emotional intelligence*. London: Bloomsbury.

Goyder, C. (2012). How to voice projection. You Tube. https://www.youtube.com/watch?v=ynmemxQicQk

Granberg, C. (2010). Social software for reflective dialogue: Questions about reflection and dialogue in student teachers' blogs. *Technology, Pedagogy and Education, 19*(3), 345–360. Routledge.

Gravells, A., & Simpson, S. (2014). *The certificate in education and training*. London: Sage.

Greenberger, D., & Padesky, C. (1995). *Mind over mood*. New York/London: Guilford Press.

Gregson, M., Nixon, L., Pollard, A., & Spedding, T. (Eds.). (2015). *Readings for reflective teaching*. London: Bloomsbury.

Gregson, M., Spedding, P., & Nixon, L. (2016). Helping good ideas to become good practice. Enhancing your professional practice through joint professional development. *Intuition*, Research Issue 1 (pp. 7–8). Society for Education and Training. https://set.et-foundation.co.uk

Gunaratnam, Y. (2003). *Researching 'race' and ethnicity: Methods, knowledge and power*. London: SAGE Publications.

Hannah, V. (2012). How to teach behaviour management. http://www.guardian.co.uk/education/2012/aug/27/pupil-behaviour-management-teaching-resources

Hattie, J. (1999, August 2). *Influences on student learning*. Inaugural Lecture: Professor of Education, University of Aukland. Available from http://library. hud.ac.uk/summon

Haydn, T. (2012). *Managing pupil behaviour: Improving the classroom atmosphere* (2nd ed.). London/New York: Routledge, Taylor & Francis.

Heywood, J. (2000). *Assessment in higher education; student learning, teaching, programmes and institutions*. London/Philadelphia: Jessica Kingsley Publishers.

Hobson, A. J., Malderez, A., Tracey, L., Ashby, P., Mitchell, N., McIntyre, J., et al. (2009). *Becoming a teacher: Teachers' experiences of initial teacher training, induction and early professional development*. Final Report DCSF Research Report DCSF- RR115. https://www.education.gov.uk/publications/eOrderingDownload/DCSF

Honey, P., & Mumford, A. (2000). *The learning styles helpers guide*. Maidenhead: Peter Honey Publications.

Howard, S. J., Ehrich, J. F., & Walton, R. (2014). Measuring students' perceptions of plagiarism: Modification and Rasch validation of a plagiarism attitude scale. *Journal of Applied Measurement, 15*(4), 372–393.

Hyland, T. (2006). Vocational education and training and the therapeutic turn. *Education: Journal Articles, 299–306*. Paper 1. http://digitalcommons. bolton.ac.uk/ed_journals/1

Illeris, K. (2007). *How we learn: Learning and non-learning in school and beyond*. Oxon: Routledge.

Iveson, C., George, E., & Ratner, H. (2012). *Brief coaching: A solution focused approach*. East Sussex: Routledge.

Jones, F., Jones, P., & Jones, J. (2007). *Tools for teaching; discipline, instruction, motivation*. Santa Cruz: F.H. Jones & Associates.

Jurdi, R., Hage, H., & Henry, P. (2011). Academic dishonesty in the Canadian classroom: Behaviours of a sample of university students. *The Canadian Journal of Higher Education, 41*(3), 1–35.

Kaplan, A., Gheen, M., & Midgley, C. (2002). Classroom goal structure and student disruptive behaviour. *British Journal of Educational Psychology, 72*, 191–211.

Kennet, K. (2010). Professionalism and reflective practice. In S. Wallace (Ed.), *The lifelong learning sector reflective reader* (pp. 66–79). Exeter: Learning Matters.

Knippen, J. T., & Green, T. B. (1997). Asking for positive reinforcement. *Journal of Workplace Learning, 9*(5), 163–168.

Knowles, M. (1975). *Self-directed learning. A guide for learners and teachers*. Cambridge/Englewood Cliffs: Prentice Hall.

Kohn, A. (1983, 1992). *No contest: The case against competition*. Boston/New York: Houghton Mifflin.

Kohn, A. (1993). *Punished by rewards*. Boston/New York: Houghton Mifflin.

Kohn, A. (2006). *Beyond discipline: From compliance to community* (2nd ed.). Alexandria: ASCD Books.

Kounin, J. (1997). *Discipline and group management in classrooms.* New York: Holt, Rhinehart and Winston.

Kress, G., & Pachlere, N. (2007). Thinking about the 'm' in m-learning. In N. Pachlere (Ed.), *Mobile learning: Towards a research agenda* (pp. 7–32). London: WLE Centre, Institute of Education.

Kyriacou, C. (1998). *Essential teaching skills* (2nd ed.). Cheltenham: Stanley Thomas.

Ladd, G. W., & Burgess, K. B. (1999). Charting the relationship trajectories of aggressive, withdrawn, and aggressive/withdrawn children during early grade school. *Child Development, 70,* 910–929.

Lambert-Heggs, W. (2011). The 'F' word: Conflicts and tensions in a community of practice when mentors confront the possibility of failing a trainee in teaching observations. *Teaching in Lifelong Learning, 3*(1), 29–39.

Lankshear, C., & Knobel, M. (2004). *Teacher research: From design to implementation.* Maidenhead: Open University Press.

Lebor, M. (2011). Licence to teach. *Every Child Matters,* Vol. 2.4.

Lebor, M. (2013a). Class wars: Initial steps into the fray. *Teaching in Lifelong Learning, 4*(2), 14–23.

Lebor, M. (2013b). War and peace in the classroom: Moments of reprieve; a strategy for reflecting on and improving students' classroom behaviour. *Teaching in Lifelong Learning, 5*(1), 21–31.

Lebor, M. (2013c). So what can possibly be wrong with blended learning? *E-learning Update.* www.teachingtimes.com. News Reports.

Lebor, M. (2014a). How to overcome chaos in the classroom. *School Leadership Today,* Vol. 5.5.

Lebor, M. (2014b). War stories how experienced teachers said they responded to disruptive students in the lifelong learning sector. *Teaching in Lifelong Learning, 5*(2), 12–21.

Lebor, M. (2015a). The fear of being assessed. *Teaching in Lifelong Learning.* University of Huddersfield, 6(2). pp. 5–15.

Lebor, M. (2015b). What did disruptive students say they wanted from their classes? *Teaching in Lifelong Learning.* University of Huddersfield, 6(2). pp. 16–24.

Lebor, M. (2016). So what do managers say about disruptive students? *Journal of Further and Higher Education, 40*(4), 568–583. Taylor & Francis.

Liu, D. (2005). Plagiarism in ESOL students: Is cultural conditioning truly the major culprit? *ELT Journal, 59*(3), 234–241.

Livingstone, S. (2011). Critical reflections on the benefits of ICT in education. *Oxford Review of Education, August,* 1–16.

Lynch, M. (2004). *Learning online: A guide to success in the virtual classroom.* London: Routledge.

Marzano, R. J., Marzano, S., & Pickering, D. J. (2003). *Classroom management that work: Research-based strategy for every teacher.* Alexandria: Association for Supervision and Curriculum Development.

Maslow, A. (1987). *Motivation and personality.* New York: Harper and Row.

Massey, A. (2011). *Best behaviour school discipline, intervention and exclusion.* London: Policy Exchange.

Mendler, A., & Curwin, R. (2008). *Discipline with dignity.* Virginia: ASCD.

Mezirow, J. (2000). *Learning as transformation: Critical perspectives on a theory in progress* (pp. 3–34). San Francisco: Jossey-Bass.

Milne, F. (2010). Top tips for trainee teachers: Get work experience in more than one school. http://careers.guardian.co.uk/top-tips-for-trainee-teachers-get-work-experience-in-more-than-one-school

Mitchell, C., Pride, D., Howard, L., & Pride, B. (1998). *Ain't misbehavin'. Managing disruptive behavior.* London: Further Education Development Agency.

Mitra, S. (2010). The hole in the wall. http://www.ted.com/talks/sugata_mitra_the_child_driven_education.html

Mulholland, H. (2012). Millions paid out to teachers for classroom assaults and accidents. http://www.guardian.co.uk/education/2012/apr/05/teachers-classroom-assaults-accidents

NASUWT. (2016). *Behaviour management.* https://www.nasuwt.org.uk/advice/in-the-classroom/behaviour-management.html

National Institute of Adult Continuing Education. (2012). *Managing challenging behaviour within skills provision for unemployed adults.* Leicester: NIACE.

Newton, N. (2010). The use of semi-structured interviews in a qualitative research: Strengths and weaknesses. Online. Available at http://www.academia.edu/1561689/Theuseofsemistructuredinterviewsinqualitativeresearchstrengthsandweaknesses

Nisbet, J. (2013). What is educational research? Changing perspectives through the 20th century. *Research Papers in Education, 20*(1), 25–44. doi:10.1080/0267152052000341327. Routledge.

O' Leary, M. (2006). Can inspectors really improve the quality of teaching in the PCE sector? Classroom observations under the microscope. *Research in Post-Compulsory Education, 11*(2), 191–198. Routledge.

Ofsted. (2006). *Improving behaviour, HMI 2377.* London: Crown Copyright.

Ofsted. (2012). *The framework for school inspection from September 2012.doc.* http://www.ofsted.gov.uk

Ofsted. (2014). Below the radar: Low level disruption in classrooms. https://www.gov.uk/government/publications/below-the-radar-low-level-disruption-in-the-countrys-classrooms. Accessed 31 Mar 2016.

Oppenheimer, T. (2003). *The flickering mind: The false promise of technology in the classroom and how education can be saved.* New York: Random House.

Organisation for Economic Co-operation and Development. (2011). *Has discipline in school deteriorated?* PISA in Focus 2011/4 May. Paris: OECD Publishing. http://wwwoecd/dataoecd/18/63/47944912

Palloff, R., & Pratt, K. (2007). *Building online learning communities: Effective strategies for the virtual classroom* (2nd ed.). San Francisco: Jossey-Bass.

Palmer, P. (1998). *The courage to teach: Exploring the inner landscape of a teacher's life.* San Francisco: Jossey-Bass.

Parry, D., & Taubman, D. (2013). *UCU whole college behaviour management: Final report.* https://www.ucu.org.uk/media/5693/UCU-whole-college-behaviour-policy-projectreport/pdf/UCU_Whole_College_Behaviour_Management_Final_Report_June_2013.pdf UCU = publisher

Paton, G. (2012). Bad behaviour in schools 'fuelled by over-indulgent parents'. http://www.telegraph.co.uk/education/educationnews/9173533/Bad-behaviour-in-schools-fuelled-by-over-indulgent-parents.html

Patterson, C. H. (1980). Theories of counselling and psychotherapy cited in P. T. Clarke (1994) A person-centred approach to stress-management. *British Journal of guidance and Counselling, 22,* 27–37.

Petty, G. (2014). *Teaching today: A practical guide* (5th ed.). London: Oxford.

Polio, C., & Shi, L. (2012). Perceptions and beliefs about textual appropriation and source use in second language writing. *Journal of Second Language Writing, 21*(2), 95–101.

Porter, L. (1997). *Creating the virtual classroom: Distance learning with the internet.* New York: Wiley.

Powell, D. (2012). *Teacher educators from the lifelong learning sector working together to develop the use of modelling in their practice: An action research project.* Consortium for PCET annual conference 2012 in association with Higher Education Academy Seminar Series 2011–12, Friday, 29th June 2012, University of Huddersfield.

Powell, S., & Tod, J. (2004). A systematic review of how theories explain learning behaviour in school contexts. In *Research evidence in education library.* London: EPPI-Centre, Social Science Research Unit.

Prasad, P., & Caproni, P. (1997). Critical theory in the management classroom: Engaging power, ideology and praxis. *Journal of Management Education, 21*(5), 284–291.

Pritchard, A. (2009). *Ways of learning: Learning theories and learning styles in the classroom.* Abingdon: Routledge.

Randall, M., & Thornton, B. (2001). Supervision and the three-stage model of helping. In *Advising and supporting teachers* (pp. 61–76). Cambridge: CUP.

Reece, I., & Walker, S. (2003). *Teaching, training and learning: A practical guide incorporating FENTO standards* (5th ed.). Sunderland: Business Education Publishers.

Reinis, N. (2013). FE sector fights back over Ofsted. *InTuition, 2*(Spring), 12–14.

Reinke, W., Lewis-Palmer, T., & Merrell, K. (2008). The classroom check-up: A classwide consultation model for increasing praise and decreasing disruptive behaviour. *School Psychology Review, 37*, 315–332.

Rennie, S. (2015). Underneath the observational snapshot: Looking for sense and meaning behind the first impressions of a learning interaction. *Teaching in Lifelong Learning: A Journal to Inform and Improve Practice, 6*(2), 25–32. ISSN 2040-0993.

Rogers, C. (1961). *On becoming a person: A therapist's view of psychotherapy.* London: Constable.

Rogers, B. (2015). *Classroom behaviour* (2nd ed.). London: Sage.

Rushton, I. (2010). Managing Meat One: Perceptions and anxieties of trainee teachers as they enter the learning and skills sector for the first time. *Teaching in Lifelong Learning, 2*(1), 15–22.

Ruthven, K., Hennessey, S., & Brindley, S. (2005). Teacher perspectives on integrating subject teaching: Commitment, constraints, caution and change. *Journal of Curriculum Studies, 37*, 155–192. Routledge.

Sellgren, K. (2013). Disruptive behaviour rising, teachers say. http://www.bbc.co.uk/news/education-21895705

Sellgren, K. (2014). Cyberbullying 'on rise'- Childline. *BBC News.* http://www.bbc.co.uk/news/education-25639839

Shacklock, G., & Thorp, L. (2005). Life history and narrative approaches. In B. Somekh & C. Lewin (Eds.), *Research methods in the social sciences* (pp. 156–163). London: Sage.

Simmons, R. (2009). An overview of the lifelong learning sector and its 'condition. In J. Avis, R. Fisher, & R. Simmons (Eds.), *Issues in post-compulsory education and training: Critical perspectives.* Huddersfield: University of Huddersfield Press.

Simmons, R., & Thompson, R. (2011). *Education and training for young people at risk of becoming NEET: Findings from an ethnographic study of work-based learning programmes.* London: Routledge.

Skrbic, N., & Burrows, J. (2014). Specifying learning objectives. In L. Ashmore & D. Robinson (Eds.), *Learning, teaching and development strategies for action* (pp. 39–69). London: Sage.

Spiers, E. (2011). Bad behaviour in the classroom is not the problem. http://www.guardian.co.uk/teacher-network/2011/nov/03/bad-behaviour-classroom

Stover, D. (2006). Treating cyberbullying as a school violence issue. *Education Digest, 72*(4), 40–42.

Sutherland, R., Armstrong, V., Barnes, S., Brawn, R., Breeze, N., Gall, M., et al. (2004). Transforming teaching and learning: Embedding ICT into everyday classroom practices. *Journal of Computer Assisted Learning, 20*, 413–425.

Swan, K., & Shea, P. (2005). The development of virtual communities. In S. R. Hiltz & R. Goldman (Eds.), *Learning together online: Research on asynchronous learning networks* (pp. 239–260). Mahwah: Erlbaum.

Szabo, Z., & Schwartz, J. (2011). Learning methods for teacher education: The use of online discussions to improve critical thinking. *Technology, Pedagogy and Education, 20*(1), 79–94.

Tauber, R. (2007). *Classroom management: Sound theory and effective practice* (4th ed.). Westport/London: Praeger.

Townend, M. (2013). Massive rise in disruptive behaviour, warn teachers. http://www.guardian.co.uk/education/2013/mar/24/schools-disruptive-behaviour

UCU. (2013). *Classroom management: UCU continuing professional development.* http://cpd.web.ucu.org.uk/files/2013/07/CPD-factsheet-6.pdf

Underwood, J., & Dillon, G. (2011). Chasing dreams and recognising realities: Teacher responses to ICT. *Technology, Pedagogy and Education, 20*(3), 317–330.

Underwood, J., Baguley, T., Banyard, P., Dillon, G., Farrington-Flint, L., Hayes, M., et al. (2010). *Understanding the impact of technology: Learner and school-level factors.* Coventry: Becta.

UNISON. (2016). School support staff facing high levels of violence and abuse, says UNISON. https://www.unison.org.uk/news/press-release/2016/06/school-support-staff-facing-high-levels-of-violence-and-abuse-says-unison/

VanWynsberghe, R., & Khan, S. (2007). Redefining case study. *International Journal of Quality Methods, 6*(2), 1–10.

Vizard, D. (2007). *How to manage behaviour in further education.* London: Sage.

Vizard, D. (2009). *Meeting the needs of disaffected students.* London: Network Continuum.

Vizard, D. (2012). *How to manage behaviour in further education.* London: Sage.

Vygotsky, L. S. (1978). *Mind in society: The development of higher psychological processes.* Cambridge, MA: Harvard University Press.

Wachob, P. (2011). Critical friendship circles: The cultural challenge of cool feedback. *Professional Development in Education, 37*(3), 353–372.

Wallace, S. (2002). *Managing behaviour and motivating students in further education.* Exeter: Learning Matters.

Wallace, S. (2007). *Managing behaviour in the lifelong learning sector.* Exeter: Learning Matters.

Wallace, S. (2013a). *Doing research in further education and training.* London: Learning Matters.

Wallace, S. (2013b). *Managing behaviour in further and adult education.* Exeter: Learning Matters.

Wallace, S. (2017). *Behaviour management: Getting it right in a week.* St. Albans: Critical Publishing.

Weale, S. (2016). Almost a third of teachers quit state sector within five years of qualifying. https://www.theguardian.com/education/2016/oct/24/almost-third-of-teachers-quit-within-five-years-of-qualifying-figures

Wellington, J., & Cole, P. (2004). Conducting evaluation and research with and for 'disaffected' students: Practical and methodological issues. *British Journal of Special Education, 31*(2), 100–104.

Wenger, E. (1998). *Communities of practice: Learning, meaning and identity.* Cambridge: Cambridge University Press.

Willis, P. (1977). *Learning to labour: How working class kids get working class jobs.* Aldershot: Ashgate.

Wilson, L. (2014). *Practical teaching: A guide to teaching in the education and training sector* (2nd ed.). Andover: Cengage.

Winter, R. (1982). Dilemma analysis: A contribution to methodology for action research. *Cambridge Journal of Education, 12*(2), 161–174. Taylor & Francis Online.

Wolf, A. (2011, March). *Wolf review of 14–19 vocational education.* London: DfE.

Wong, H. (2009). *The first day of school: How to be an effective teacher.* Mountain View: Harry Wong.

Wood, P. (2012). Blogs as liminal space: Student teachers at the threshold. *Technology, Pedagogy and Education, 21*(1), 85–99. Routledge.

Yang, Y. C. (2008). A catalyst for teaching critical thinking in a large university class in Taiwan: Asynchronous online discussions with the facilitation of teaching assistants. *Education Technology and Research Development, 56,* 241–264.

Index

A

acting/drama, 9, 18, 53, 62, 64, 66–8, 140, 185, 212
adult learning, 60
aims and objectives, 50, 55, 82
A level, 3, 62, 84, 152, 160, 161, 177
andragogy, 39, 144, 146, 147
art, 3, 36, 140
assessment, 2, 6, 21, 32, 89–103, 113, 151, 155, 157, 162–4, 207, 209
Attention Deficit Hyperactivity Disorder (ADHD), 17, 44, 78, 181
Avis, J., 57, 60, 108, 133, 138, 193

B

Ball, S., 37, 86, 138
Behaviour Czar, 204
Behaviour Tsar, 20
behaviourism, 66, 173, 189, 193, 194, 196
body language, 28, 49, 182
boundaries, 58, 92, 113, 175, 181, 198, 206

British Educational Research Association (BERA), 79, 91, 99, 109, 125, 127, 128, 155, 160, 170
Brophy, J., 32, 33, 59
buddying, 22, 117
bullying, 13, 41, 51, 101, 133, 159, 175, 198

C

case studies, 1, 14, 17, 21, 43, 49, 52, 71, 73, 89, 91, 98, 99, 102, 108, 133, 137, 139, 147, 173, 182, 205–8, 210, 211
Certificate in Education (Cert Ed.), 2, 23, 40, 51, 52, 131, 137–9, 185, 187, 188, 201
challenging behaviour, 2, 3, 6, 23, 78, 90, 116, 137, 138, 172, 175, 181, 187, 194, 205
Cinderella syndrome, 44
Coffield, F., 4–6, 33, 120, 211
Cognitive Behavioural Therapy (CBT), 92, 94, 99

© The Author(s) 2017
M. Lebor, *Classroom Behaviour Management in the Post-School Sector*, DOI 10.1007/978-3-319-57051-8

cognitivism, 193, 206
Colley, H., 19, 93
communication, 3, 9, 36, 52–4, 57, 67, 101, 115, 119, 120, 132, 133, 145, 160, 162, 173, 174, 178, 182, 184, 195, 197, 201
corporal punishment, 2, 3, 8
counselling, 22, 24, 62, 68, 92, 124
Cowley, S., 20, 43, 86, 193, 206
Critical Friendship Groups (CFG), 140
curriculum vitae (CVs), 54–6, 60, 61, 70
Curzon, L., 5, 119

D
data collection, 78–80, 152, 164
Department for Education (DfE), 123, 138
Derrick, J., 119
Dewey, 4, 5
differentiation, 32, 69, 175
digital learning, 148, 151–66
disaffected students, 99, 102, 109, 115, 127, 128, 163, 208
discipline, 4, 30, 33, 42, 45
disruptive behaviour, 15–17, 23, 33, 37, 41, 44, 51–3, 66, 71, 77–81, 84–6, 92, 114, 116, 118–20, 129, 130, 151, 159, 160, 165, 172–6, 180–3, 185, 193, 203–12
Dix, P., 18, 206
Dreyfus, H., 34
Dweck, C., 43

E
Education and Training (sector), 1, 4, 6, 20, 21, 23, 27, 28, 30, 37, 40, 42, 44, 79, 107, 118, 127, 158, 205
Emotional intelligence, 174, 182, 201

English for Speakers of Other Languages (ESOL), 3, 62, 91, 92, 108
entering the classroom, 49–73
equality, 11, 145, 157, 175, 189
ethics, 80, 90, 99, 127, 165, 170
extrinsic motivation, 34, 36, 37, 142, 193

F
fighting, 2, 18, 65, 80, 116, 130, 132, 181, 187
focus groups, 7, 97, 107, 109, 110, 113–15, 119, 131, 169, 170, 187, 196, 198–200, 202
functional skills, 3, 19, 100, 101, 139, 140, 147, 175, 200
further education, 3, 9, 19, 20, 43, 44, 118, 142, 154, 158, 164
Further Education Development Agency (FEDA), 14

G
games, 37, 65, 102, 117, 141
GCSEs, 3, 13, 18, 72, 91, 101, 102, 151, 177, 200
Glasser, 34, 205
Gregson, M., 43
ground rules, 2, 10, 24, 49, 58, 61, 63, 64, 81, 82, 86, 111, 116, 119, 173, 174, 177, 182, 188, 190, 196, 197, 201, 206, 211

H
Hannah, V., 58, 59
hatred, 9–11, 32, 208
Haydn, T., 90
Higher Education, 2, 3, 13
Humanism, 173, 196, 206

I

ICT, 22, 23, 63, 72, 73, 145, 151–65
Illeris, 5
interviews, 1, 7, 20, 21, 39, 50, 65,
  69, 77, 85, 89, 90, 97, 98, 107,
  110, 115, 116, 127, 132, 138,
  152, 155, 159, 165, 166, 169,
  171, 177, 187
intrinsic motivation, 32, 35, 43, 44,
  59, 203

K

key skills, 31, 66, 183
Kounin, J., 20, 34–7, 59, 184, 203

L

learning contracts, 111
learning styles, 32, 33, 198
literacy, 3, 11, 18, 62, 64, 115, 129,
  194

M

management, 7, 11–15, 17, 20, 21,
  23, 24, 27, 30, 34–8, 40, 41, 43,
  49, 59, 60, 64, 70, 73, 77, 83,
  86, 90, 96, 107–20, 129, 131,
  138, 143, 144, 152, 153, 163,
  165, 169–74, 177–80, 182–4,
  188–93, 196–201, 204, 205,
  207, 208, 210
Maslow, A., 3, 29, 30, 34, 92, 193
methodologies, 7, 8, 20, 22, 30, 31,
  40, 109, 110, 112, 137–48, 154,
  162, 171, 190
mobile phones, 12, 41, 80, 108, 110,
  151, 175, 176, 178, 180, 183,
  197
motivations, 29, 32, 33, 60, 63, 72,
  85, 138, 173, 176, 187, 193,
  198

N

narratives, 1, 7, 8, 11, 20, 21, 60, 79,
  80, 83, 84, 89, 93–8, 127, 141
needs, 29–30
numeracy, 5, 100, 101, 129, 139, 145,
  178

O

observations, 1, 6, 7, 13, 20, 21, 23,
  51, 61, 72, 89, 114, 126, 147,
  170, 171, 179, 192, 209
Ofsted, 2, 4, 11, 51, 86, 112, 138,
  139, 146, 192, 210, 211
only connect, 66–71

P

Panopticon model, 38
pathological demand syndrome, 44
pedagogy, 8, 11, 23, 37, 39, 43, 58,
  90, 152–4
Petty, G., 27, 41–3, 53, 54, 58, 59,
  64, 119, 133, 144, 145, 193
Post-graduate Certificate in Education
  (PGCE), 2, 23, 40, 52, 187–92,
  196, 201
plagiarism, 151, 152, 154, 157–9,
  161, 162, 164, 165
punishments, 8, 33, 34, 66, 94, 143,
  144, 199, 203
Pupil Referral Unit (PRU), 13, 79, 81,
  83, 174

Q

qualitative research, 77–9, 109, 152,
  153, 171

R

racism, 9–12, 190
reflective lens, 97, 139

reflective/reflexive practice, 44, 103, 139, 146, 179, 182, 187, 206
restorative practice, 114, 173
rewards, 29, 32, 34, 36, 37, 82, 144, 145, 173, 193, 194, 203
Rogers, B., 49, 50, 61, 112, 113, 206
Rogers, C., 3, 82, 92, 144, 193
role play, 10–12, 62, 67, 178, 205, 208, 209
Rushton, I., 51

S
scenarios, 52–6, 62–6, 72, 73, 123, 125, 185, 204, 209
schools versus colleges, 16, 17, 30, 31, 37–40, 43, 111
seating plans, 111, 173, 174, 190, 199
Sellgren, K., 15
sexism, 11, 12, 95, 175
Simmons, R., 19, 57
solution-focus, 89, 92, 124
strategies, 10–14, 20–2, 28, 31–3, 35, 41, 43, 45, 49, 52, 59, 61, 62, 64, 71, 73, 74, 77, 79, 81–3, 86, 89, 95, 98, 99, 103, 107, 109–14, 116–20, 125, 126, 129, 131, 133, 169, 172, 173, 177, 182–4, 187, 189, 195, 201, 202, 205–7, 211, 212

T
Taubman, D., 13, 15, 17, 27, 38, 51, 109, 113
teacher educators, 1, 23, 34–6, 139, 141, 148, 152, 169–85, 187, 188, 191, 197, 201, 202, 204, 208–10
teachers attacked, 13

teachers' training, 23, 52, 148, 179, 180, 185, 187, 188, 191, 195, 197, 198, 204
teaching practice, 23, 52, 188, 204
theory/theorists, 1, 20, 23, 27–45, 49, 60, 69, 111, 131, 152, 169, 171, 174, 179, 192, 200, 201, 203, 206, 208
therapy, 21, 84, 92, 99, 124, 126, 203
trainees, 22, 23, 28, 43, 44, 49–52, 54, 57, 59, 61, 86, 137, 139–45, 147, 148, 169–202, 204–10, 212
Turnitin, 151, 157

U
unions, 7, 15, 210
University and College Union (UCU), 15–17, 41

V
validity, 21, 77, 84–6, 108, 132, 170, 171
violence, 8–15, 19–21, 40, 51, 80, 81, 89, 90, 92, 108, 123–6, 129, 144, 151, 181, 183
Vizard, D., 45, 53, 58, 59, 86, 90–2, 144, 193, 206

W
Wallace, S., 14, 17, 18, 20, 43–5, 70, 86, 119, 125, 128, 129, 132, 154, 193, 206
Wenger, E., 5, 120, 139
whole college, 17, 18, 38, 175
with-it-ness, 35
Wong, H., 30, 31, 59, 203, 205

The manufacturer's authorised representative in the EU is Springer
Nature Customer Service Centre GmbH, Europaplatz 3, 69115 Heidelberg,
Germany. If you have any concerns regarding our products, please
contact ProductSafety@springernature.com

Printed and bound by CPI Group (UK) Ltd, Croydon, CR0 4YY
27/04/2026
02097625-0001